MASTERING C++

MASTERING C++

Second Edition

An Introduction to C++ and Object-Oriented Programming for C and Pascal Programmers

CAY S. HORSTMANN
San Jose State University

JOHN WILEY & SONS
New York • Chichester • Brisbane • Toronto • Singapore

ACQUISITIONS EDITOR   Steven M. Elliot
MARKETING MANAGER   Debra Riegert
PRODUCTION EDITOR   Tony VenGraitis
DESIGNER   Kevin Murphy
MANUFACTURING MANAGER   Dorothy Sinclair
ILLUSTRATION   Sandra Rigby
OUTSIDE PRODUCTION   Publication Services, Inc.

This book was set in 10/12 Palatino by Publication Services, Inc., and printed and bound by
Courier/Stoughton. The cover was printed by Lehigh Press.

Recognizing the importance of preserving what has been written, it is a
policy of John Wiley & Sons, Inc. to have books of enduring value published
in the United States printed on acid-free paper, and we exert our best
efforts to that end.

The paper in this book was manufactured by a mill whose forest management programs
include sustained yield harvesting of its timberlands. Sustained yield harvesting principles
ensure that the number of trees cut each year does not exceed the amount of new growth.

ISBN 0-471-10427-2

Printed in the United States of America

10 9 8 7 6 5 4 3 2 1

PREFACE

C++ is a superset of the hugely successful C programming language. (The ++ in its name originates from the C increment operator ++.) C++ offers enhancements of C in five directions:

- Operator and function overloading
- Information hiding
- Inheritance
- Polymorphism (virtual functions)
- Library building (templates, exceptions)

This book contains a thorough introduction to C++, with particular emphasis on techniques used in real-life programs.

This book does not require knowledge of the C programming language. The reader familiar with Pascal or Modula-2 will find numerous "Pascal Notes" to aid in the transition to the C/C++ syntax. The reader who already knows C can skim through Chapters 2, 3, 4, and 6 and watch for "C Notes", which point out differences between C and C++.

In this book, I attempt to show C++ in the context of realistic programming situations. I purposely stay away from contrived examples. There are no data types for small appliances, furry animals, or edible objects. No objects are called my_stack, no data types derived_1 when examples involving useful data structures can be easily given.

It is easy for students (as well as for some authors) to think they know a programming language when all they actually know is its syntax. I place little emphasis on syntax and mechanics; instead, I try to develop the ideas underlying the language concepts and show them in the context of realistic examples.

The policy of supplying realistic examples starts with Chapter 1, which gives a quick tour of two exciting capabilities of C++: operator overloading and virtual functions. (The introduction of classes is deferred until Chapter 5 because of the required syntactical overhead.) I didn't want to disappoint the reader with pointless toy examples; therefore some of the programs in Chapter 1 are quite long and, I hope, interesting. The reader should not be discouraged by their complexity. It is not necessary to grasp all details in Chapter 1. Later chapters provide in-depth coverage of all concepts.

I try to put the methodology of object-oriented programming in its proper perspective. Not all of C++ is concerned with object-oriented programming, and object orientation, while extremely useful for many applications, is not the appropriate paradigm for all programming tasks. The book shows the use of C++ in the context of both traditional and object-oriented programming.

Most differences between Pascal and C++ are cosmetic and easily mastered. However, C++ has a few irksome syntactical quirks that tend to confuse newcomers. I point this out when this is the case, so students can then place the blame for the confusion squarely where it belongs—on the language syntax, rather than themselves. C++ is an excellent language, but it is a human creation and as such not perfect or above criticism. I hope the reader does not construe such occasional comments as an indication that some other language is "better" just because it happens to employ a clearer syntax for some of its constructs.

There are many exercises. The exercises are part of the text, rather than at the end of the chapter. The reader is encouraged to skim through them as they appear. Some develop an interesting sideline; others simply give feedback on how much knowledge should have been acquired at that point. Many exercises render simple graphics on a terminal screen, using the time-honored strategy of joining * characters to form lines, boxes, and so forth. This has two advantages: Students do not have to learn a graphics subsystem at the same time they learn C++, and the code is kept highly portable.

The code for all programs in the book can be obtained from my web page (http://www.mathcs.sjsu.edu/faculty/horstman/cay.html). Instructors can obtain the solutions to all exercises through their Wiley sales representative.

Many chapters contain sections on "pitfalls", illustrating common programming problems. These sections serve two purposes: (1) They can be read as textual material to illustrate complicated aspects of the language; and (2) they can be used as a reference to find a way out of problems arising during programming. The idea for these sections is stolen[1] from [Koenig].

The reader should be familiar with standard data structures: arrays, stacks, queues, sets, linked lists, binary trees, and their implementations. Some mild understanding of college mathematics is also assumed, but certainly no more than necessary for a computer graphics course. Lines, vectors, matrices, polynomials, and complex numbers are used in some of the examples.

In this second edition I updated the presentation to reflect the current state of C++. In particular, templates and exception handling are now covered, replacing the section on generic containers based on a cosmic root class. Quite a few of the code examples have been streamlined and made more consistent. I added a number of new pitfalls that I discovered in the last three years. Apart from those changes, the flavor of the book is unchanged. It is still a short

---

[1]"Lesser artists borrow, great artists steal" (*Igor Stravinsky*)

book, suitable for self-study or a one-semester course. The book is still accessible to anyone with a basic understanding of C, Pascal, or a similar language. I purposefully kept the detailed treatment of array/pointer duality and memory management. These topics are not object-oriented and not fashionable, but they are essential for successful C++programming.

My thanks go to Earl Tondreau of John Wiley & Sons for prodding me to write this book. I also thank my reviewers, John Vlissides of Stanford University and another reviewer who wishes to remain anonymous, whose critical and insightful comments prodded me to rewrite the book. Many thanks to Graham Mark of Los Alamos National Laboratories, and Jesse Heines of the University of Massachusetts at Lowell, for their errata lists, and to Michael Barnett of the University of Idaho and Konstantin Laufer of Loyola Universtiy for their help with the second edition. I am most grateful to Hamilton Richards of the University of Texas at Austin, who has given many suggestions of improvement for both editions of this book.

Cay S. Horstmann

CONTENTS

C H A P T E R 1

A QUICK TOUR
THROUGH C++

Let us start with some examples to illustrate the main features of C++. These examples are simple but complete—you can try them out on your computer. This is not a rigorous introduction to the language. Most details, rules, and exceptions are left for later chapters. No knowledge of C is assumed (although it would be helpful). You merely should know some modern programming language, such as Pascal or Modula 2. C programmers will notice that many program fragments could be improved by standard C tricks.

The **Pascal Note**s and **C Note**s compare C++ with those languages. If you know both Pascal and C, read them all. It is always helpful to see a new feature put into perspective by comparing it with something known. And you may well learn something about the "old" languages in the process.

I am consciously omitting several C++ features from this introduction, in particular the data-hiding and encapsulation mechanisms. Those mechanisms are extremely important for sound programming practice, so their relegation to later chapters should not prompt you to think otherwise. C++ makes it easy to perform data hiding, but it does require a certain amount of syntactic overhead that I believe obscures the discussion of more crucial language issues.

1.1. "HELLO, WORLD"

Here is our first C++ program:

```
#include <iostream.h>

int main()
{   cout << "Hello, World\n";   // print a string
    return 0;
}
```

Let us look at its structure. main is a *function*. Every C++program is a collection of functions, at least one of which must be called main. int means that main returns an integer (namely 0). The operating system may look at the value returned by main. Conventionally, 0 denotes success—any nonzero value indicates some error condition encountered during program execution. The braces {} denote the beginning and the end of the main function. Strings such as "Hello, World\n" are enclosed in double quotes. The \n denotes a *newline character*, which is a part of the string and causes a new line to be started after the string. The << (put to) operator can take objects (such as strings or numbers) and send representations of them to an *output stream*. cout is the standard output stream; by default, anything sent to it will appear on the screen. The two slashes // start a *comment*, which extends until the end of the line. Finally, the #include is a directive to the *preprocessor* to include all lines from the file iostream.h for inspection by the compiler. That file contains declarations of cout and the << operator, as well as many others.

Pascal Note

In Pascal a program is a single unit, called **program**, which contains variables, functions, and procedures nested within. In C++, no such nesting occurs, and the main function is the equivalent of the **program**. The type of the value returned by a function is written before the function name, and there is no special **function** keyword. The parentheses () signify a function declaration to the compiler. They are present even if the function has no arguments (as in main()). C++ does not distinguish between functions and procedures. A procedure is simply a function returning void. The braces {} are the equivalent of **begin** and **end**. In C++ all statements are terminated with a semicolon, even the last statement of a block, but there is no semicolon following the closing brace. The operation cout << is like the Pascal **write;** there is no special **writeln** analog. To obtain a blank line, simply send a string containing a newline '\n'.

Many Pascal compilers have an analog to the #include directive that opens another file and includes its contents for compilation. Sometimes this is implemented as a pseudocomment directive **(*$I** *filename***)**.

C Note

The void indicator has been present in C implementations for quite a while and is part of the ANSI standard. In C++ a function with an empty argument list (such as main()) has *no arguments*. In the rare case in which you must specify a function with some unknown number of arguments, use an ellipsis (...). There are two valid styles of comment, C style /* ... */ and the new C++ style //, which extends to the end of the current line. We will use the second style in this book. cout is the stream equivalent of stdout. The << operator with a stream variable on the left side has nothing to do with left shift. It is like a super-printf that can tell the format from the type of the operand to be printed. We will see later how this is implemented by overloading the << operator.

How do you get this program to run? First, use any file editor to create a text file containing the program lines. Depending on your compiler, you may have to choose the file name to end in .c, .cpp, or .cxx. (Some systems have header file names ending in .hpp or .hxx. Then change the names in the `#include` statements before compiling.) The command to invoke the compiler also depends on your system. Typical commands for compilation are

```
CC  hello.c
```

and

```
bcc  hello.cpp
```

The name of the executable file also varies. Depending on your system, you might need to type

```
a.out
```

or

```
hello
```

to run your program. Of course, you should then expect to see the line

```
Hello, World
```

on your screen.

● **Exercise 1.1.1.** Get the hello program to run on your system. What happens when you omit the \n? The n only? The line `#include <iostream.h>`? Explain.

● **Exercise 1.1.2.** Find the file iostream.h on your system and look at it. Where is cout defined?

1.2. A CHEAP CALCULATOR

To illustrate the basic control structures in C++, let us write a program that can read in integers and operations from the keyboard, such as

```
2 * 5 + 7 - 4 =
```

print the answer, and exit. Just as on a cheap pocket calculator, addition and multiplication have the same precedence, and evaluation is strictly left to right. For example,

```
1 + 2 * 3 =
```

prints 9 because $1 + 2 = 3$ is computed before the multiplication.
Here is the program:

```
#include <iostream.h>

int main()
{ int first, second;
  char ch;
```

```
cin >> first >> ch;
while( ch != '=' )
{ cin >> second;
  switch( ch )
  { case '+':
      first = first + second; break;
    case '-':
      first = first - second; break;
    case '*':
      first = first * second; break;
    case '/':
      if( second != 0 )
        first = first / second;
      else
        cout << "Division by zero.\n";
      break;
    default:
      cout << "Input error.\n"; return 1;
  }
  cin >> ch;
}
cout << "Result: " << first << "\n";
return 0;
}
```

The program consists of a single main function. The first two lines declare *variables*. first and second are declared to be of type int, and ch is declared to be of type char. int is a data type denoting integers of the size most conveniently handled by the processor. char is an integer type just large enough to hold a single character. That is almost universally the range $-128 \ldots 127$ or $0 \ldots 255$. All characters are represented by their integer code under the encoding scheme used by the system, such as ASCII or EBCDIC. Character constants are enclosed in single quotes and denote the *numerical* code of the character. For example, under the ASCII encoding scheme, 'a' == 95. (To be precise, 'a' is of type char and 95 of type int, but they represent the same number.) The codes of nonprinting characters are denoted by characters preceded by a backslash \. For example, '\n' is a newline, '\t' is a tab. Note the difference between the *character code* '\n' (the number 10 if ASCII code is used) and the *string* "\n" containing the character '\n'.

The >> (get from) operator is used for reading from a stream. cin is the standard input stream—that is, the keyboard. Here we are reading an integer and a character from the keyboard and placing them into the variables first and ch. White space (the space character, tabs, and newline) is automatically discarded by >>. The != (not equal) operator tests for inequality. The while loop is executed while the condition inside the (...) remains true. The body of the while loop is enclosed in {...} because it consists of more than one statement. The `switch` branches to one of the `case` labels, depending on the value of ch, or to the `default` label if none of the case labels match. Execution then resumes until a `break` or the end of the switch is reached.

In C++, assignment is denoted by =, as in first = first + second. To test for equality, == is used. The `if` statement tests the condition inside the (...). If it is true, the statement following it is executed. An `else` clause is optional.

The last line shows that the << operator can be chained to send more than one item to an output stream, just like the >> operator in the beginning of the program.

Pascal Note

Here we see variable declarations for the first time. Unlike Pascal, all declarations in C++ first list the type and then the variable name. This is consistent with the declaration of functions, which also has the return type before the function name, and it makes it easy to *initialize* variables when they are declared: int i = 0, n = 1;.

The differences between Pascal and C++ control structures are cosmetic. **while ... do begin ... end** becomes while(...) {...}, and **if ... then ...** becomes if(...) {...}. The `switch` statement is like **case**, except for the curious `break` terminating each branch. The chained >> operator is just like **read**. Some operators are different, with :=, =, and **<>** becoming =, ==, and !=, respectively. That is unpleasant and can lead to nasty surprises. x = 0 does not test whether x is zero but stores a 0 into x!

C Note

The only unexpected constructs are >> and << and their chaining ability. The >> operator is a super-scanf that supplies both the format string and the &. For example, cin >> first >> ch is equivalent to scanf("%d %c", &first, &ch). We will see later that the amazing capabilities of these stream input/output operators—the chaining, automatic format recognition, and automatic address taking by >>—are natural consequences of C++ features. No special knowledge of << and >> is hardwired into the C++ compiler.

In C (as well as old versions of C++) character constants (such as 'a') are *not* of type char but of type int.

● **Exercise 1.2.1.** Enter the calculator program and run it.

● **Exercise 1.2.2.** Extend the calculator to compute the remainder function. The C++ instruction x % y computes the remainder of the division x/y. In Pascal, this operator is called **mod**. Use the same % symbol for the remainder command. For example, the input 4 * 2 % 3 = should print 2.

1.3. A STACK-BASED CALCULATOR

In this example, arrays and the syntax of function definitions are introduced. We will program a reverse-Polish calculator that places numbers on a stack. Operators act on the numbers most recently pushed. Some scientific calculators use reverse Polish notation, as does the PostScript® printer control language. For example, when the user enters

```
1 2 3 * + =
```

the calculator goes through the following sequence of events:

1	Push 1
2	Push 2
3	Push 3
*	Pop 2 and 3, multiply them and push the product 6
+	Pop 1 and 6, add them and push the sum 7
=	Pop 7 and print it

Parentheses are never required. To compute $(1 + 2 * 4)/(1 + 2)$, the user enters

```
1 2 4 * + 1 2 + / =
```

Here is the implementation of the stack.

```
const int STACKSIZE = 20;

int stack[ STACKSIZE ];
int stackPointer = 0; // points to the next free stack entry

void push( int n )
{ if( stackPointer <= STACKSIZE - 1 )
  { stack[ stackPointer ] = n;
      stackPointer++;
  }
}

int pop()
{ if( stackPointer > 0 )
    stackPointer--;
  return stack[ stackPointer ];
}
```

The `const` declaration gives a symbolic name for the size of the stack. It is always a bad idea to use "magic numbers" such as 20 in a program. If the stack size changes, you would not want to search the program for 20s and 19s and modify them all except for all the 20s and 19s that have nothing to do with stack size. Compilers are smart enough to perform constant arithmetic such as `STACKSIZE - 1` at compile time.

The next declarations allocate an array of 20 `ints` and a single `int` initialized with 0. The first array index is 0; that is, the array consists of `stack [ 0 ]`, `stack[ 1 ],...` , `stack[ 19 ]`.

Two function declarations follow. The first function takes an integer argument and returns nothing. It enters a number on the stack and increases the stack pointer. The second function has no argument and returns an `int`, namely the top of the stack. The `++` and `--` operators increment or decrement the variable. `stackPointer++` is a convenient shortcut for `stackPointer = stackPointer + 1`. Error handling is poor. If the stack is full, further calls to `push` will simply do nothing. If it is empty, `pop` will return `stack[ 0 ]`.

Pascal Note

Array declarations require one number only, because all C++ arrays start at 0. An array with n elements has subscripts in the range $0...n - 1$. There are no keywords **function, var**, or **array**. The compiler deduces this information from the presence or absence of ( ) or [ ].

The mechanisms for determining the return value of a function are very different in Pascal and C++. Rather than assigning a value to a variable with the same name as the function, the `return` statement is used. `return` sets the return value *and leaves the function immediately.*

C Note

The `const` declaration is new in C++. It is preferred over the use of `#define` to set manifest constants because it gives the compiler a chance to perform type checking. All C++ functions are in ANSI C format, with the function arguments inside the ( ). Old-style declarations

```
push( n )
int n;
```

are not acceptable. Return types should be specified. Do not rely on `int` being the default. Use `void` if the function returns nothing. Contrary to ANSI C, the preferred syntax for functions with no arguments is an empty argument list (), not (`void`).

Here is the code for the main program.

```
int main()
{ char ch;
  int first, second, num;

  cin >> ch;
  while( ch != '=' )
  { if( '0' <= ch && ch <= '9' )
    { cin.putback( ch );
      cin >> num;
      push( num );
    }
```

```
    else
      switch( ch )
      { case '+':
          push( pop() + pop() ); break;
        case '*':
          push( pop() * pop() ); break;
        case '-':
          second = pop();
          push( pop() - second );
          break;
        case '/':
          second = pop(); first = pop();
          if( second == 0 )
          { cout << "Divide by 0.\n";
            return 1; // error—return non-0 value
          }
          else
            push( first / second );
          break;
        default:
          cout << "Input error.\n"; return 1;
      }
      cin >> ch;
    }
    cout << pop() << "\n";
    return 0;
}
```

When the program reads a character, it may be an operator such as + or =, or it may be the first digit of a number. If it is a digit, we should not have used cin >> ch but cin >> num. Fortunately, we can push one character back onto the input stream, pretending that we had not read it, with the cin.putback function. (The appearance of the dot . in the function call will make sense later.) This effectively gives a one-character lookahead.

By the way, our calculator has a curious limitation. You cannot enter negative numbers. For example, -10 would be interpreted as the - operator followed by the integer 10. (For that reason, reverse Polish calculators have a special *change sign* key.) We will simply assume the user will not object to entering 0 10 - instead.

With noncommutative operators we must be careful with the order of the popping. In an expression pop() - pop(), the compiler is free to evaluate subexpressions in any order, not necessarily left-to-right. The code above ensures correct results.

If a division by zero is attempted, a return statement is executed. This means an immediate exit from main and, as main is the top-level function, return to the operating system.

Pascal Note

In Pascal, the value of **input^** provides one-character lookahead while keeping the character available for a subsequent **get**.

C Note

`cin.putback( ch )` is the stream equivalent of `ungetc( ch, stdin )`.

● **Exercise 1.3.1.** Enter the reverse Polish calculator and test it.

● **Exercise 1.3.2.** Improve the `push` and `pop` routines to give error messages at overflow and underflow.

● **Exercise 1.3.3.** Implement a unary minus key _. For example, 3 _ 3 - = should print -6.

● **Exercise 1.3.4.** Implement a debug feature. The input L (or 1) should list the contents of the entire stack. Find out how to use the standard function `toupper` (which converts lowercase letters to uppercase) and write a separate function `stack Show`.

● **Exercise 1.3.5.** C++ does not have a built-in power function. Implement a power function by writing a function `int power( int, int )`. Enhance the calculator to call this function when a ^ command is entered. What is the correct power value for negative exponents?

1.4. A FRACTION CALCULATOR

Right now the calculator handles integers only. Computing 4 3 / = will print 1 because division in C++ is integer division if both arguments are integers. One could easily modify the calculator to handle floating-point numbers, but we want to implement exact fractions instead. For example, we want to store 1/3 exactly rather than as 0.333333333 ... in such a way that

    1 3 / 3 * =

computes 1 and not 0.99999999 ... We will simply store numerator and denominator separately:

```
struct Fraction
{ int num;
   int den;
};
```

We can now declare fractions

```
Fraction f;
```

and set values

```
f.num = 1;
f.den = 3;
```

Pascal Note

In Pascal these aggregates are called **record**s, not structs. To be able to declare variables of a record type, one has to make a **type** declaration.

C Note

In C we would have to declare f as a struct Fraction or have a typedef. In C++, the structure name becomes a type name.

Naturally, we now want to add, subtract, multiply, and divide fractions. We could supply functions addFrac, subtractFrac, and so forth; although this would be entirely sufficient for our calculator, it would be very unpleasant in other situations. Expressions such as

```
divideFracByInt( addFrac( multiplyFrac( a, b ), c ), 2 )
```

look terrible.

Pascal Note

In Pascal we could not even do that. A Pascal function cannot return a record, so one would have to make do with

procedure addFrac(a: Fraction, b: Fraction, var result: Fraction)

    . . .

and break up the computation into individual steps, saving intermediate results in temporary variables. The alternative would be to define a fraction as a pointer to a record, because Pascal functions can return pointers. This, too, is a hassle, because the memory for the fractions must then be allocated on the heap.

Fortunately, it is possible in C++ to define the standard arithmetic operators + - * / for fractions and write (a * b + c) / 2 where a, b, and c are of the type Fraction. To do this, we define functions

```
Fraction operator+( Fraction a, Fraction b );
Fraction operator-( Fraction a, Fraction b );
Fraction operator*( Fraction a, Fraction b );
Fraction operator/( Fraction a, Fraction b );
```

This process is called *operator overloading*. When the compiler sees an expression

```
x + y
```

where x and y are Fractions, it will translate this into a call to operator+ (x, y). Of course, if x and y are of type int, they will just be added. This means extra work for the compiler. Whenever it sees a +, it has to consider the types of the operands and check whether to compile it into an addition or a call to operator+. In fact, operators may be overloaded more than once. It is possible to define another operator+ for strings (to concatenate them). Of course, that function has nothing in common with the fraction version of operator+, and the compiler has to make the correct choice depending on the types of the operands of +.

To program the operator functions for fractions, we observe that

$$\frac{r}{s} \pm \frac{t}{u} = \frac{ru \pm ts}{s \cdot u}, \qquad \frac{r}{s} \cdot \frac{t}{u} = \frac{r \cdot t}{s \cdot u}, \quad \text{and} \quad \frac{r}{s} \bigg/ \frac{t}{u} = \frac{r \cdot u}{s \cdot t}$$

and that it will be necessary to reduce to lowest terms afterward. For example, $\frac{2}{3} \cdot \frac{1}{2} = \frac{2 \cdot 1}{3 \cdot 2} = \frac{2}{6} = \frac{1}{3}$. Let us therefore first define

```
int gcd( int a, int b ) // compute the greatest common divisor
{   if( a < 0 ) return gcd( -a, b );
    if( a == 0 ) return b;
    if( b < a ) return gcd( b, a );
    // now 0 < a <= b
    return gcd( b % a, a );
        // b % a is the remainder of the division b / a
}


Fraction reduce( Fraction f ) // reduce to lowest terms
{   Fraction r;
    int g = gcd( f.num, f.den );

    if( g != 0 )
    {   r.num = f.num / g;
        r.den = f.den / g;
    }
    return r;
}
```

The gcd function recursively calls itself, with ever smaller values of a and b. It works for the following reason: Suppose $0 < a \le b$. Let q be the quotient of the division b/a, r the remainder. Then

$$b = a \cdot q + r \quad \text{and} \quad \gcd(a, b) = \gcd(a, a \cdot q + r) = \gcd(a, r)$$

because every number dividing a must also divide $a \cdot q$. The first and third line in the gcd function just arrange a and b to obtain the condition $0 < a \le b$, and the second line returns the final answer. ($\gcd(0, b) = b$ because every number divides 0.) Here is an example:

$$\gcd(40, -15) = \gcd(-15, 40) = \gcd(15, 40) = \gcd(10, 15)$$
$$= \gcd(5, 10) = \gcd(0, 5) = 5$$

● **Exercise 1.4.1.** Rewrite the gcd function to be nonrecursive.

● **Exercise 1.4.2** The probability that two randomly selected integers have gcd to 1 is approximately $6/\pi^2$. Write a program to verify this fact experimentally. Use the rand() function in stdlib.h to generate the random numbers. Each call to rand() generates a new random number between 0 and RAND_MAX.

Pascal Note

The % operator is called **mod** in Pascal. It is important to realize that the return statement not only sets the return value but exits the function immediately. For example, in computing gcd(0, 5), the second if is true, and the return statement returns the value 5 immediately. The third line is not executed. It is quite common to take care of exceptions or trivial cases at the beginning of a C++ function, with an immediate return exit. This is quite pleasant because it avoids confusing if ... else if ... else if ... else ... constructions and multiple indentations that crowd the really important code to the right margin of the screen.

C Note

In some pre-ANSI versions of C, functions could not receive or return struct values; only pointers to structures were permitted. In ANSI C, as well as in C++, struct values are permitted both as function arguments and as return types. Of course, this involves copying the members of the structure onto the stack.

We are ready to write the operator functions.

```
Fraction operator+( Fraction a, Fraction b )
{ Fraction r;

    r.num = a.num * b.den + b.num * a.den;
    r.den = a.den * b.den;
    return reduce( r );
}

Fraction operator-( Fraction a, Fraction b )
{ Fraction r;

    r.num = a.num * b.den - b.num * a.den;
    r.den = a.den * b.den;
    return reduce( r );
}

Fraction operator*( Fraction a, Fraction b )
{ Fraction r;
```

```
    r.num = a.num * b.num;
    r.den = a.den * b.den;
    return reduce( r );
}

Fraction operator/( Fraction a, Fraction b )
{ Fraction r;

    r.num = a.num * b.den;
    r.den = a.den * b.num;
    return reduce( r );
}
```

We would like to be able to perform computations such as $2 + 1/3$ without having to define

```
Fraction operator+( int n, Fraction b );
```

and the other seven corresponding operators (with + - * / and the int in the front or the back). This is achieved by supplying a type conversion int $\rightarrow$ Fraction, with a so-called *constructor*. The constructor must be placed in the struct declaration.

```
struct Fraction
{ int num;
  int den;

    Fraction( int n = 0, int d = 1 ) { num = n; den = d;}
        // for type conversion int → Fraction
} ;
```

We can now declare and initialize fractions with

```
Fraction f( 1, 3 );    // initialized as 1/3
Fraction t( 2 );       // initialized as 2/1
Fraction 2;            // initialized as 0/1
```

The = 0 and = 1 in the constructor are default arguments, to be chosen if none are explicitly given. When the compiler sees 2 * f, it will use this constructor to make a new fraction 2/1, then call operator*.

Now we have all the tools together needed to enhance our calculator to handle fractions. The stack must be changed to an array of fractions: Fraction stack[STACKSIZE]. Care must be taken when declaring an array of any type that has one or more constructors. C++ wants to initialize such an array and requires that one of the constructors can be called with *no* arguments. Both default arguments are used to initialize all array entries with 0/1. The push and pop functions are unchanged except for the argument and return type. The main function is almost unchanged, except that variables are now declared as fractions, integers are converted to fractions before being pushed onto the stack, and both numerator and denominator must be printed. It is quite remarkable that so much of the code can be reused without change.

```
const int STACKSIZE = 20;

Fraction stack[ STACKSIZE ];
int stackPointer = 0;

void push( Fraction n )
{ if( stackPointer < STACKSIZE )
  { stack[ stackPointer ] = n;
    stackPointer++;
  }
}

Fraction pop()
{ if( stackPointer > 0 )
    stackPointer--;
  return stack[ stackPointer ];
}

int main()
{ char ch;

  Fraction second, result;
  int num;

  cin >> ch;
  while( ch != '=' )
  {
    if( '0' <= ch && ch <= '9' )
    { cin.putback( ch );
      cin >> num;
      push( Fraction( num )); // convert to fraction
    }
    else
      switch( ch )
      { case '+':
          push( pop() + pop() ); break;
        case '*':
          push( pop() * pop() ); break;
        case '-':
          second = pop();
          push( pop() - second );
          break;
        case '/':
          second = pop();
          push( pop() / second );
          break;
```

```
        default:
          cout << "Input error.";
          return 1;
      }
    cin >> ch;
  }
  result = pop(); // print as fraction
  cout << result.num << " / " << result.den << "\n";
  return 0;
}
```

Entering fractions into the calculator is not as pretty as it might be. One cannot enter 1/2 directly. This would be interpreted as pushing the 1, dividing the previous element on the stack by 1, and pushing the 2. But entering 1 2 / will cause 1/2 to be deposited on the stack. This is similar to the problem of entering negative numbers discussed in the previous section.

● **Exercise 1.4.3.** Implement and test the fraction calculator.

● **Exercise 1.4.4.** Implement a power function operator^ for fractions. For example, Fraction(3,4)^3 should be 27/64. Add the ^ operation to the calculator. If the exponent is not an integer, you can generate an error message. But negative integers are okay: $(a/b) {\wedge} (-n) = (b/a) {\wedge} n$.

● **Exercise 1.4.5.** Add a command ? that shows the top of the stack without popping it off. Do this by modifying the push function to return the value it pushed. Then use push(pop()) to nondestructively obtain the top of the stack.

It is interesting to note that there is no "divide by 0" error in our fraction calculator. Why not? Use operator/ to divide 1/2 by 0/1. The result is a struct with num containing 1 and den containing 0. There is nothing illegal about this. One might even call this value "infinity":

```
Fraction infinity( 1, 0 );
```

It behaves quite nicely like the mathematical ∞. Adding it to any number results in ∞. For example, $1/2 + \infty$ yields r.num = $1 {\cdot} 0 + 2 {\cdot} 1$, r.den = $2 {\cdot} 0$ in operator+, and after the call to reduce, the result is again num = 1, den = 0 (because gcd $(2, 0) = 2$).

However, the multiplication $0/1 \cdot \infty$ produces an even stranger number, with num and den both 0. Adding, subtracting, multiplying, or dividing this quantity with anything else replicates itself. There is no mathematical analog to this strange object. That is not a problem. Our pairs of integers are not fractions. They are merely a *model* of fractions, imitating them quite well under certain conditions and acting strangely under other, we hope less frequent circumstances. Providing reasonable *models* of objects and actions is an essential aspect of programming.

1.5. A FLOWCHART PLOTTER

In this section we will investigate a program that is a little off the beaten track: a *flowchart plotter*. This example, which is much longer than the previous programs, will illustrate the concept of *object-oriented programming*. I want to present a nontrivial application that demonstrates the benefits, not just the mechanics, of object-oriented programming and hope that you will be patient and bear with me. Object-oriented techniques are particularly helpful for organizing large projects, typically far more complex than even the sample of this section.

Our objects are flowchart blocks, such as

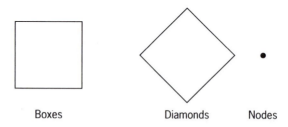

Boxes   Diamonds   Nodes

The program will read in boxes, specified by their type and the coordinates of their center; plot them; and place them on a stack. There will be a stack operation *join* that joins the top two objects on the stack:

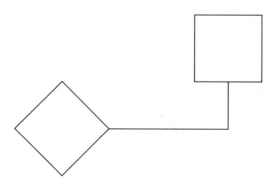

Together with two stack operations, *pop* and *exchange* (which exchanges the top two items on the stack), it will be possible to draw complex flowcharts.

1.5.1. Screen Display Routines

The flowcharts will be displayed on a terminal screen. We therefore will use a coordinate system with 24 rows and 80 columns and represent lines by sequences of *'s in a 24 × 80 array of characters. (Because some terminal software adds a new line when adding a character into column 80, we will use the first 79 columns only.) Here is the code to manage the plotting of lines and the display of the accumulated drawing.

```
const int GRID_XSIZE = 79;
const int GRID_YSIZE = 24;


char grid[ GRID_YSIZE ][ GRID_XSIZE + 1 ];
  // + 1 to hold a '\0' at the end of each line

void gridClear()
// initialize the array with spaces
{ for ( int y = 0; y < GRID_YSIZE; y++ )
  { for ( int x = 0; x < GRID_XSIZE; x++ )
    grid[ y ][ x ] = ' ';
    grid[ y ][ GRID_XSIZE ] = '\0';
  }
}


void gridLine( int xstart, int ystart, int xend, int yend )
// Foley, Van Dam, Feiner, Hughes,
// Computer Graphics, 2nd ed., 1990, p. 75
{ int dx = xend - xstart;
  int dy = yend - ystart;
  if ( abs( dy ) < abs( dx ) ) // |slope| < 1
  { if ( dx < 0 )
    { gridLine( xend, yend, xstart, ystart );
      return;
    }
    double y = ystart + 0.5;
    for ( int x = xstart; x != xend; x++ )
    { grid[ int( y ) ][ x ] = '*';
      double m = double( dy ) / double( dx );
      y += m;
    }
  }
  else
  { if ( dy < 0 )
    { gridLine( xend, yend, xstart, ystart );
      return;
    }
    double x = xstart + 0.5;
    for ( int y = ystart; y != yend; y++ )
    { grid[ y ][ int( x ) ] = '*';
      double m = double( dx ) / double( dy )
      x += m;
    }
  }
  grid[ yend ][ xend ] = '*';
}
```

```
void gridShow( )
// show the result on the standard output device
{ for ( int y = 0; y < GRID_YSIZE; y++ )
    cout << grid[ y ] << "\n";
}
```

The local variables x and y are declared in the for loop, just when they are needed.

Pascal Note

Two-dimensional arrays are declared with the bounds in separate brackets: char grid[24][80]. Both bounds start at 0. Then of course the (i, j)th element is referred to as grid[i][j]. Omitting one of the brackets denotes a one-dimensional subarray; for example grid[i] is the ith row of the two-dimensional array. This is used in the gridShow function, which simply considers grid as an array of strings, strings themselves being one-dimensional arrays of characters. To print a string, its end must be known. It is a C++ convention that all strings end in a *zero byte*, that is, a byte with the numerical value 0 (*not* '0'). The zero character is often denoted by '\0', although it really is no different from 0.

The += operator in gridLine stands for "increment by". y + = m is the same as y = y + m.

● **Exercise 1.5.1.** Using the foregoing data structures, write a program that draws a stop-sign shape

and prints it.

1.5.2. Flowchart Shapes

All flowchart shapes (boxes, diamonds, nodes) have a center, and we will define

```
struct Shape
{ int xcenter;
  int ycenter;

  Shape( int x, int y ) { xcenter = x; ycenter = y; }
    // a constructor
```

```
    virtual int xleft( ) { return xcenter; }
    virtual int xright( ) { return xcenter; }
    virtual int ytop( ) { return ycenter; }
    virtual int ybottom( ) { return ycenter; }
    virtual void plot( ) { }
    virtual void print( )
    { cout << xcenter << " " << ycenter << "\n";
    }
};
```

There are two notable aspects of this structure declaration. The structure contains functions, so-called *member functions,* and these functions are declared virtual. As we will see presently, this means that they can be replaced by other functions for certain Shapes. It is a coincidence that all member functions of Shape are virtual and that all of them take no arguments. Member functions need not be virtual, and they can have arguments.

The syntax for a member function call is similar to selection of data members. For example, if s is a Shape, then s.print() prints its center coordinates. The particular s is an *implicit argument* [as if the call was print(s)], and its xcenter and ycenter values are printed. The member names used in member functions always refer to the implicit first argument that precedes the . in the call.

Here is the declaration of a box.

```
struct Box : Shape
{ int xsize;
  int ysize;

  Box( int x, int y, int xs, int ys )
  : Shape( x, y )
  { xsize = xs;
    ysize = ys;
  }
  // a constructor, calling the base class constructor
  int xleft( ) { return xcenter - ( xsize + 1 ) / 2 + 1; }
  int xright( ) { return xcenter + xsize / 2; }
  int ytop( ) { return ycenter - ( ysize + 1 ) / 2 + 1; }
  int ybottom( ) { return ycenter + ysize / 2; }
  void print( ) { cout << "Box "; Shape::print( ); }
  void plot( )
  { gridLine( xleft( ), ytop( ), xright( ), ytop( ) );
    gridLine( xright( ), ytop( ), xright( ), ybottom( ) );
    gridLine( xright( ), ybottom( ), xleft( ), ybottom( ) );
    gridLine( xleft( ), ybottom( ), xleft( ), ytop( ) );
  }
};
```

The : Shape denotes that a Box is *derived* from the *base class* Shape. That is, a box has all members of a Shape; in addition, it has other characteristics. For example, if b is a Box, b.xcenter is defined, although the xcenter field is not explicitly mentioned in the structure definition but *inherited* from the Shape type. A box has special data fields, namely horizontal and vertical dimensions, and special ways of plotting and producing the left, right, top, and bottom margins.

The Box type refers to its base class in two instances: the Box constructor causes the base class constructor to be executed through the : Shape(r, c) clause, and in listing box data the data-listing function of the base class is invoked through the Shape::print( ) call. The Shape:: operator is called a *scope resolution operator*. It is often used in C++ to indicate to what structure a function or variable name belongs.

The next type, Node, relies much more heavily on the base class, because the default actions for finding the extent of a Shape with the left(), right(), top(), bottom() functions can be inherited. Only the plot and list actions need to be specified.

```
struct Node : Shape
{ Node( int x, int y ) :  Shape( x, y  ) {}
    // a constructor, calling the base class constructor
    // and doing nothing else
    void plot() { grid[ ycenter ][ xcenter ] = '*'; }
    void print() { cout << "Point "; Shape::print(); }
};
```

Finally, we need to describe diamonds. One data element, radius, is required. It denotes the distance from the center to one of the four corners.

```
struct Diamond : Shape
{ int radius;

    Diamond( int x, int y, int r )
    : Shape(x, y)
    { radius = r;
    }

    int xleft() { return xcenter - radius + 1; }
    int xright() { return xcenter + radius - 1; }
    int ytop() { return ycenter - radius + 1; }
    int ybottom() { return ycenter + radius - 1; }
    void print() { cout << "Diamond "; Shape::print(); }
    void plot()
    { gridLine( xcenter, ytop(), xright(), ycenter );
      gridLine( xright(), ycenter, xcenter, ybottom() );
      gridLine( xcenter, ybottom(), xleft(), ycenter );
      gridLine( xleft(), ycenter, xcenter, ytop() );
    }
};
```

● **Exercise 1.5.2.** Write a program that prints a box and a diamond, both centered on the grid, and places a node at the center:

1.5.3. Joining Flowchart Shapes

How are two shapes joined? First draw a horizontal line from the left or right end of the first shape to the center column of the second shape, then draw a vertical line from the end point of the first line to the top or bottom of the next shape. However, if the shapes are centered in the same row or column, only one line is drawn. The details depend on how the first and second shapes are located relative to each other. The following diagram shows various possibilities. The outlines of the shapes are deliberately left vague because the same method should work for all shapes.

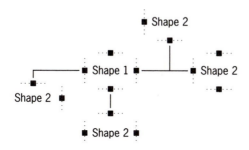

Joining is an asymmetric operation. The following diagram shows the difference between joining shape 1 with shape 2 (————) versus joining shape 2 with shape 1 (————)

Here is the code for the join function. The function receives two pointers to Shapes. It does not matter whether they are boxes, diamonds, or nodes.

Why pass the pointers rather than the real things? The various actual objects have different sizes! A box takes more storage than a node. Therefore, they cannot be simply passed to a function. At compile time, the size of each function argument must be known to generate the correct code to pass it to the function and locate it inside the function. On the other hand, pointers (addresses) have uniform size no matter what object type they point to.

```
void join( Shape* from, Shape* to )
{ int x, y; // row, col of intermediate point

    if ( from->ycenter == to->ycenter )
    { if ( from->xcenter < to->xcenter )
        x = to->xright();
      else
        x = to->xleft();
    }
    else x = to->xcenter;

    if ( from->xcenter == to->xcenter )
    { if ( from->ycenter < to->ycenter )
        y = from->ybottom();
      else
        y = from->ytop();
    }
    else y = from->ycenter;

    if ( from->xcenter < to->xcenter )
        gridLine( from->xright(), y, x, y );
    else if ( from->xcenter > to->xcenter )
        gridLine( x, y, from->xleft(), y );

    if ( from->ycenter < to->ycenter )
        gridLine( x, y, x, to->ytop() );
    else if( from->ycenter > to->ycenter )
        gridLine( x, to->ybottom(), x, y );
}
```

Pascal Notes

At this time we need to master two syntactical quirks of C++. Pointer dereferencing is denoted by a *, not a ∧, and the * is a prefix operator. Instead of p∧, one writes *p. A pointer p to a type T is declared as T* p; for example, Shape* from declares from as a pointer to a Shape. If one wants to find the xcenter field of the structure that from points to, one can write (*from).xcenter. The parentheses are necessary because . has a higher precedence than *. This is cumbersome, and as it appears so often, an operator ->, *dereference and access member*, exists that allows accessing the xcenter field as from->xcenter. In general, p->m is identical to (*p).m.

In Pascal no such syntactic problem exists, because the dereferencing operator ∧ is postfix, and one simply writes **p∧.m**.

The Pascal style **p∧** is a better choice than the C style **∗p**. This is not simply a matter of taste. Because the . [] () operators are traditionally postfix, a postfix pointer-dereferencing operator saves parentheses and makes complex expressions easier to read. The C style sometimes requires parentheses. It also forces the reader to scan complex expressions bidirectionally.

To get a pointer that points to an existing object x, C has an *address* operator. &x is the address of x. (This will typically be the memory location of the first byte of x, although the language does not prescribe the relationship between pointer values and memory locations.) It can be assigned to a pointer variable (p = &x) or passed to a function with a pointer argument (join(&x, &y)). There is no analog to this operation in Pascal. All pointers in Pascal point to objects on the heap and are obtained through **new**.

The center coordinates of the shapes are stored in the base class and hence are accessible as from->center, etc. The margins can be obtained through calls to from->bottom(), and so on. (Recall that the syntax for calling a member function is identical to selection of member data: through the . or -> operator.)

However, there is one fundamental difference between the data member access from->center and the function call from->bottom(). Locating the data members is independent of the actual type of the shape. On the other hand, computing the bottom margin, for example, is very different for a Node and a Box. The correct bottom function must be selected, and furthermore it must be selected at *run time*, because the join function may be called many times with pointers to different shapes. This is precisely what is accomplished by the virtual attribute of the functions in the base class. A call to a virtual function is translated into code that selects the proper actual function at run time, depending on which derived class the current shape belongs to or the pointer points to.

● **Exercise 1.5.3.** Write a program to test the join function. It should join a box and a diamond in two ways:

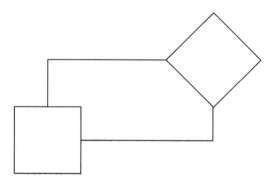

Construct the box and the diamond:

```
Box b(...);
Diamond d(...);
```

Join them:

```
join( &b, &d );   // & takes the address, &b is a pointer to b
```

Print the result, wait for a keyboard input:

```
char ch;
cout << "Hit any key to continue\n";
cin.get( ch );
```

Then join them in opposite order and print the result.

1.5.4. Putting It Together

Let us now settle on a command language for the flowchart plotter. For simplicity, assume that all boxes are 9 × 5 units and all diamonds have a radius of 4. The user can place a node, box, or diamond by typing N, B, or D followed by the coordinates of the center. For example,

```
D  6  20
```

places a diamond with center at row 6, column 20. It also places a pointer to a Diamond on the stack. Typing J joins the two shapes on the top of the stack, P pops the top of the stack, X exchanges the top two items on the stack, and L lists the stack. S shows the current contents of the grid buffer, and Q quits. Here is the code for the stack routines.

```
const int STACKSIZE = 20;

Shape* stack[ STACKSIZE ];
int stackPointer = 0;

void push( Shape* n )
{ if ( stackPointer < STACKSIZE )
  { stack[ stackPointer ] = n;
    stackPointer++;
  }
}

Shape* pop()
{ if ( stackPointer > 0 )
  stackPointer--;
  return stack[ stackPointer ];
}
```

```
int stackEmpty()
{ return stackPointer == 0;
}

void stackShow()
{ for ( int i = 0; i < stackPointer; i++ )
   stack[ i ]->print();
}

void xchg()
{ if ( stackEmpty() ) return;
  Shape* second = pop();
  if ( stackEmpty() ) { push( second ); return; }
  Shape* first = pop();
  push( second );
  push( first );
}

void joinTop2()
{ if ( stackEmpty() ) return;
  Shape* second = pop();
  if ( stackEmpty() ) { push( second ); return; }
  Shape* first = pop();
  join( first, second );
  push( first );
  push( second );
}
```

Of course, the push and pop functions look precisely like the ones in previous examples, except that we are now stacking Shape* s. We cannot simply pack the various objects with types derived from Shape; they have varying sizes. However, the pointers to them have uniform size and can be stacked.

Finally, here is the main function.

```
int main()
{ char ch; // next input token

  gridClear();
  cin >> ch;
  while ( ch != 'Q' )
  { int x, y;
    Shape* p;

    switch ( ch )
    { case 'B':
        cin >> x >> y;
        p = new Box( x, y, 9, 5 );
```

```
        push( p );
        p->plot();
        break;
      case 'D':
        cin >> x >> y;
        p = new Diamond( x, y, 4 );
        push( p );
        p->plot();
        break;
      case 'N':
        cin >> x >> y;
        p = new Node( x, y );
        push( p );
        p->plot();
        break;
      case 'J':
        joinTop2();
        break;
      case 'P':
        if (!stackEmpty() )
        { p = pop();
          delete p;
        }
        break;
      case 'X':
        xchg();
        break;
      case 'S':
        gridShow();
        break;
      case 'L':
        stackShow();
        break;
      default:
        cout << "Input error.\n";
        return 1;
    }
    cin >> ch;
  }
  return 0;
}
```

The new operator gets storage space from the *free store*. For example, new Diamond(x, y, 4) allocates the appropriate number of bytes to hold a Diamond and causes the constructor to fill the newly obtained storage area with x, y, and 4. It returns a pointer to the storage, which is then pushed onto the stack. When the stack is popped, the pointer is given to delete, which recycles the storage block and marks it as available for further allocation.

Pascal Note

new is similar to the Pascal **new**, except that in Pascal **new** takes the pointer as a **var** argument, as in **new(p)**, and manages to deduce the size of the object to be allocated from the type of the pointer. Of course, the Pascal **new** cannot thread a constructor invocation in. delete is the analog of **dispose**.

C Note

new and delete are super-versions of malloc and free. p = new Box is equivalent to p = malloc(sizeof Box). The major difference is that new and delete can invoke constructors and destructors. *They are not functions* but built-in language constructs. As with return or sizeof, parentheses are not necessary.

The user input

D 20 6	Make a diamond
B 30 10	Make a box
J	Join them
N 20 14	Make a node
X	Exchange the node and box
J	to join them in opposite order
P	Pop the box
J	Join the diamond and the node
S	Show the flowchart
Q	Quit the program

results in the following chart.

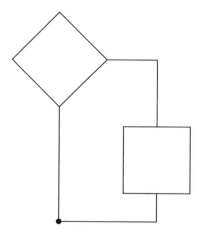

More complicated charts can be printed. For example,

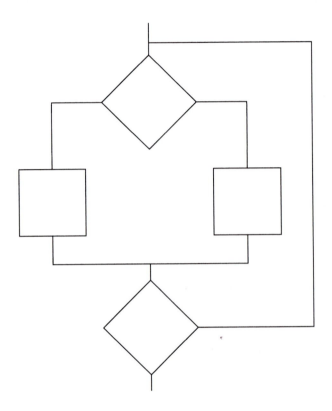

is the result of

```
N 20 0
N 20 1 J X P
D 20 6 J
B 10 10 J X
B 30 10 J X P
N 20 14 X J P
X J P
D 20 19 J X P
N 20 23 J P
N 40 10
J X P
J P P S Q
```

Because >> ignores any kind of white space, commands need not be typed on separate lines. If you try out this example, issue an occasional S or L command to watch the intermediate results.

● **Exercise 1.5.4.** Implement the flowchart plotter and test it. For testing, place the command lines in a file (maybe named infile) and redirect keyboard input to that file:

```
flow  <infile
```

We assume that you named the executable program flow. You can redirect output as well, capturing it in a file.

```
flow  <infile >outfile
```

That gives you a chance to edit the output before handing it to the grader.

● **Exercise 1.5.5.** What input produces the mirror image of the foregoing chart? A 90° clockwise rotation? Test your answers.

We are not proposing this as a serious aid to producing flowcharts. Clearly, it is difficult for a human user to come up with the correct command sequence to produce a desired chart. However, it is conceivable that the commands are generated by another computer program. Some printer control languages, notably PostScript, do use a stack for holding intermediate results during page composition, and PostScript code is usually generated by software and transmitted to the printer, untouched by human hands. Of course, PostScript is a lot more sophisticated than our command code, and we have resisted the temptation to call it FlowScript.

The reader who has followed this far may well wonder what is so fundamentally different about the programming method employed in this example that it deserves to be called object-oriented. Let us outline a more traditional solution. To distinguish between the different objects, each one would carry a type field.

```
struct Shape
{ char type; // contains an 'N', 'D', or 'B'
  int xcenter;
  int ycenter;
  int xsize;  // 0 for points, radius for diamonds
  int ysize;  // 0 for points and diamonds
}
```

The virtual functions' code would have to be rewritten. For example, the bottom of a shape would have to be computed as

```
switch( type )
{ case 'B': return ycenter + ysize / 2;
  case 'D': return ycenter + xsize - 1;
  default:  return ycenter;
}
```

and similarly for all other virtual functions. The real difference between the procedural and object-oriented style becomes apparent when the program is enhanced. Suppose we want to add circles to the flowchart. In the procedural model the code needs to be searched for all occurrences of switch(type), and a case 'C' has to be provided each time. That is tedious and error-prone. In the object-oriented model, a new Circle type is merely derived from Shape, which specifies how to do the margin computations and plotting. *No further change* to the existing code is required.

● **Exercise 1.5.6.** Implement the flowchart plotter without virtual functions.

● **Exercise 1.5.7.** Add a "stop-sign" shape

to the flowchart plotter. Note that all changes are localized in the StopSign structure and its member functions. No existing code needs to be modified!

● **Exercise 1.5.8.** Add the stop sign shape to the program of Exercise 1.5.6 that does not use virtual functions. What existing code do you need to modify? Contrast with Exercise 1.5.7.

C H A P T E R   2

DATA

2.1. BASIC TYPES

Like every programming language, C++ has certain built-in types that are handled very efficiently by the underlying hardware. These types are

int	Integers of the size most conveniently handled by the machine
char	Integers in a range sufficient to hold a single character
float	Single-precision floating-point numbers
double	Double-precision floating-point numbers

The size of an integer depends on the underlying machine. On larger processors, integers are typically 4-byte quantities, but on smaller machines (for example, personal computers) they are often 2-byte quantities. The char type just stands for a very short int, almost universally 1 byte. However, whether the range is $-128\ldots127$ or $0\ldots255$ is system-dependent.

The most common type for floating-point operations is double, not float. The math library functions use double, and the limited precision of float (typically only 6 or 7 significant digits) makes it unsuited for many computations. Of course, float only needs half the storage space, which can be a consideration in storing large amounts of data.

Pascal Note

In Pascal there is a separate character type, and you need the functions **ord** and **chr** to go between characters and integers. C treats characters as numbers that happen to fall into a small range. Characters coming from the keyboard or going to the screen are represented as small integers, namely the ASCII code (or other encoding used by the machine, such as EBCDIC) of the character.

Additional basic types can be produced with the modifiers

unsigned
long
short

An unsigned `int` is a type that occupies the same amount of space as an `int` does but has no sign bit. For example, if the processor has 2-byte `int`s in the range −32768...32767, `unsigned int` has the range 0...65535. The range of `unsigned char` is 0...255. A `long int` is a type that is somewhat longer than a regular `int`. A `short int` is somewhat shorter. How much longer or shorter depends on the implementation. For example, if an `int` is a 4-byte quantity, a `long int` can be 8-byte (but often still is 4-byte), and a `short int` can be 2-byte. If `int` is 2-byte, `long int` can be 4-byte and `short int` still 2-byte.

As a shorthand, you can drop an `int` after these modifiers. For example, `short` is the same as `short int`, and `unsigned long` is the same as `unsigned long int`. Finally, there is a type `long double`.

Constants ending in L are long (e.g., 16777216L), and constants ending in U are unsigned (e.g., 65535U). Numbers starting with 0x or 0X are hexadecimal, whereas numbers with 0 (zero) are octal. The latter is a truly bizarre convention. For example, 010 is 8!

There is a `sizeof` operator, which gives the size of each type as multiples of the size of a character. That is, we always have

```
1 = sizeof( char ) ≤ sizeof( short ) ≤ sizeof( int )
  = sizeof( unsigned ) ≤ sizeof( long )
```

and

```
sizeof( float ) ≤ sizeof( double ) ≤ sizeof( long double )
```

but it is unwise to assume anything further if we want to write programs that can easily be moved between different processors.

In arithmetic operations with operands of mixed types, operands are converted to prevent information loss whenever possible. For example, consider the computation of `m + n` where `m` is an `int`. If `n` is a `long`, `m` is converted to a `long`. If `n` is `unsigned`, `m` is converted to `unsigned` as well. Actually, converting an integral type to a floating-point type can cause information loss as well (e.g., `long` to `float`). Nevertheless, in mixed expressions the integer types are converted to floating-point.

It is sometimes necessary or convenient to convert from one type to another explicitly. For example, if `n` is an `int`, then `double( n )` and `char( n )` denote the equivalent floating-point value or character value. This is called a *cast*. Casting an integer into a character can involve information loss; for example, `char( 288 )` is likely to be 32.

C Note

The C style notation, such as `(char) n`, is also available in C++, but the functional notation `char( n )` seems clearer. Unfortunately, it does not work for pointers: `(char*) p` cannot be written as `char*( p )`. But `(char*)( p )` is legal and reasonably consistent.

● **Exercise 2.1.1.** Write a program that prints the sizes of all basic types on your computer. Use `sizeof`. Is char signed or unsigned on your machine?

● **Exercise 2.1.2.** Write a program that determines the ranges of all basic types on your computer (for example, int between −32767 and 32768). Your program should be portable (that is, run without modifications on other computers) and show the correct values there. Do not use sizeof. This is hard for floating-point numbers.

● **Exercise 2.1.3.** Write a program that prints an ASCII table:

	4	5	6	7	10	11	12	13	14	15	16	17
0|		(	0	8	@	H	P	X	'	h	p	x
1|	!	)	1	9	A	I	Q	Y	a	i	q	y
2|	"	*	2	:	B	J	R	Z	b	j	r	z
3|	#	+	3	;	C	K	S	^	c	k	s	~
4|	$	,	4	<	D	L	T	[	d	l	t	{
5|	%	-	5	=	E	M	U	\	e	m	u		
6|	&	.	6	>	F	N	V	]	f	n	v	}
7|	'	/	7	?	G	O	W	_	g	o	w	

Your program should consist of a loop traversing all printing characters between 040 and 0176 (octal).

2.2. VARIABLE AND CONSTANT DECLARATIONS

Here are a few declarations.

```
int m;
double x,y;
int daysPerMonth[ 12 ];      // an array of 12 integers
int calendar[ 12 ][ 31 ];    // a 2-dimensional array of int
```

Pascal Note

In C++, variables are declared "backward"—first the type, then the variable name. Arrays *always* start at 0, and the number in brackets gives the number of elements, *not* the highest permitted index. For example, daysPerMonth has 12 elements: daysPerMonth[0] ... daysPerMonth[11]. Two-dimensional arrays are written with a separate set of brackets for each dimension. The calendar elements range from calendar[0][0] to calendar[11][30].

There is *no* run-time array bounds checking. Setting daysPerMonth[100] to 0 will neither be flagged by the compiler nor cause a run-time exception—the 0 will simply be written 100 integers from the start of daysPerMonth, overwriting whatever happens to be there. Actually, as we will see later, it is possible to design a safe array type by overloading the [] operator to incorporate the out-of-bounds checking. (We can define a new data type in which the [] operator has a new meaning, just as we redefined the meanings of +, -, and so on for fractions in the first chapter.)

Variables can be initialized when declared, for example,

```
int m = 2;
double x, y = 1;      // only y is set to 1
int daysPerMonth[ 12 ] =
        { 31, 28, 31, 30, 31, 30, 31, 31, 30, 31, 30, 31 };
char ch = '1';
char s[ 6 ] = "Hello";
```

In C++, strings are arrays of char, terminated by a zero byte. For example, the string s in the foregoing declaration contains the six bytes 'H', 'e', 'l', 'l', 'o', '\0'. The last byte is a zero code, *not* the character code '0'. The zero terminator allows functions to find the end of a string. This does mean that a string cannot contain a zero byte as information. Because zero does not represent a printable character in most encoding schemes, this is not a real limitation. Also note that strings are enclosed in double quotes ("Hello"), whereas individual character codes are enclosed in single quotes ('H'). Those character constants are just a convenient notation for their integer codes. For example, '1' is equal to (and not just equivalent with) the number 49 under the ASCII encoding scheme. The types are different, though: '1' is of type char, 49 of type int. Furthermore, '1' is not at all the same as "1", a string of two bytes (a 49 followed by a 0) placed somewhere in memory. Nonprinting characters are coded with a backslash control sequence—for example, a newline is '\n' and a zero byte is '\0'. These are still single characters, not strings.

● **Exercise 2.2.1.** Write a function that reads in a string from standard input:

```
char s[ 20 ];
cin >> s;
```

and prints all values of the string in decimal (cout << int(s[i])), up to and including the terminating 0. What happens if you enter a string with 20 characters or more? Write another program that prints all 20 characters in s.

The sizeof operator can be applied to variables. For example, sizeof(x) = sizeof(double) and sizeof(daysPerMonth) = 12 * sizeof(int). Constants can be declared with the prefix const:

```
const int DAYSPERYEAR = 365;        // different on Mars
const double PI = 3.1415926535897932385;
const int daysPerMonth[ 12 ] =
  { 31, 28, 31, 30, 31, 30, 31, 31, 30, 31, 30, 31 };
const unsigned char MASK = 0xF0; // numbers starting with 0x
                                 // are hex
```

C Note

The C++ const differs slightly from its ANSI C counterpart. When applied to a basic type, it is inline-replaced with the constant, and no storage is allocated. It should be used rather than #define because it is type-safe.

Enumerated types can be defined with an enum declaration:

```
enum Bool { FALSE, TRUE };
enum Color { RED = 4, GREEN = 2, BLUE = 1 };
```

This defines Bool and Color as enumerations and constants FALSE = 0, TRUE = 1, RED, GREEN, and BLUE. Specific values for the constants can be provided. They need not be distinct, increasing, or positive. If not provided, the enumeration constants are assigned 0, 1, 2, ... Variables of enumerated types are defined in the usual way.

```
Bool more;
Bool done = FALSE;
```

C Note

In C there is *no* type checking for enumerations. Bool is not a type distinct from int; it is merely a synonym. A Bool variable can hold any integer value, such as −1, 2, or RED. In C++, explicit casts must be used to convert between enum and from int to enum. The conversion from enum to int is still automatic.

2.3. ARITHMETIC

C++ has the usual complement of arithmetic operators: +, -, *, /, %. The / operator is integer division if both arguments are integers and floating-point division if at least one of them is floating-point. For example, 14 / 4 is 3, 14.0 / 4 is 3.5. The % operator is the remainder of an integer division; for example, 14 % 4 is 2. It is undefined for floating-point arguments. There is no exponentiation operator, but there is a function pow in the math library.

Pascal Note

For integer arguments / and % correspond to the Pascal div and mod operators. Do not use ∧ for computing powers—it denotes "bitwise XOR."

There are *bitwise operators* that operate on the binary representation of integers:

x & y	Bitwise AND
x | y	Bitwise OR
x ∧ y	Bitwise XOR
x << n	Left shift by n
x >> n	Right shift by n
~x	Bitwise complement

● **Exercise 2.3.1.** Write a function binPrint that prints a number in binary. To convert a number into binary, repeatedly divide by 2 and store the remainders in an array. Then print that array in reverse order. Assume the number has 8 * sizeof(int) binary digits.

● **Exercise 2.3.2.** Modify the cheap calculator from Section 1.2 to a cheap bitwise calculator that implements AND, OR, XOR, shift, and complement. Use the < and > keys for shift. If you solved the preceding exercise, print the answers in binary.

Finally, there are the famous increment and decrement operators that give C++ its name. The statement

```
n++;
```

adds 1 to the value of n, and, of course, n-- subtracts 1. These operators have two aspects: (1) the side effect of incrementing or decrementing and (2) a value that can be used in expressions. The value depends on the placement of the ++ before or after its argument. For example,

```
2 * n++
```

evaluates to twice the value of n *before it was incremented,* whereas

```
2 * ++n
```

is twice the new value of n after increment. It is easy to remember which does which. In the expression n++, the n comes before the ++; hence its value is used before it is incremented. Conversely, in ++n the ++ comes first, so n is first incremented, then used. (It can therefore be argued that C++, the incremental improvement to C, should really have been called ++C; after all, we want to use it after it is improved.)

It is very common to step through an array with code like

```
const int ASIZE = 10;
int i = 0;
int a[ ASIZE ];
while( i < ASIZE )
    cin >> a[ i++ ]; // read the next array element in
```

and the placement of the ++ is crucial for the functioning of the loop. For example,

```
while( i++ < ASIZE )
    cin >> a[ i ]; // read the next array element in
```

would never read a[0] in but would read the out-of-range a[ASIZE]!

The original motivation for the introduction of the ++ and -- operators may have been to have the compiler generate efficient machine instructions. Many processors have an INC instruction that works much faster than fetching an operand, loading 1 in a register, performing an addition, and storing the result. Furthermore, a[i++] could take advantage of the fact that i is still in a register when a[i] is computed. Some processors even have a single machine instruction for a[i++]. With modern optimizing compilers, these considerations should *not* overly affect one's coding style. Modern compilers are devilishly clever about optimizing operations (for example, replacing a * 8 with the faster a << 3) and keeping frequently used variables in registers. Always code in the clearest possible fashion. Short code is clearer than long code, because the reader has to digest less information. The rich collection of C++ operators is a great help in this respect. However, stay away from convoluted code. Use good taste with nested assignments and increment/decrement operations, or the next person to maintain your code must waste time playing "C++ puzzles." C++ has the undeserved reputation of being a "write-only" language, but a skilled coder with good judgment can write programs that are easier to read than the best equivalent versions in wordier languages such as Pascal or Modula 2.

2.4. ASSIGNMENT

Assignment is written using =, as in a = 2 * b. The assignment is an *operator*; that is, an assignment a = 2 * b has a *value* (namely the value placed into a). This allows for multiple assignments: a = b = 1 places the value of b = 1 into a. The = operator binds right to left to make this work. The value of an assignment can be used in other subexpressions as well. For example,

```
while( !isupper( ch = s[ i++ ] ) && ch != '\0' )
    ;
```

sets ch to the first uppercase letter in the string s. This construction can simplify loops, but it should be used with caution. Mixing tests and actions can yield code that is quite difficult to understand and maintain.

Pascal Note

For Pascal programmers the choice of the = symbol rather than := for assignment takes getting used to. Being able to nest assignments inside arithmetic expressions is quite useful, though. You can casually store an intermediate result in a variable without breaking up an expression.

Arithmetic operators can be combined with the assignment operator; for example,

```
x += 2;      // same as x = x + 2
x <<= 2;     // shift x to the left twice (multiply by 4)
```

The operators += -= *= /= %= &= |= ^= <<= >>= can be similarly used. This corresponds rather nicely to the way a person often thinks. It is more natural to say "increment x by 2" than "take x, add 2 to it, and place the value back into x". This is especially true for complicated expressions such as

```
yyval[ yypv[ p3 + p4 ] + yypv[ p1 - p2 ]] += 2;
```

The reader does not have to check that two lengthy expressions on the left and right side of an = are identical or, if they are not, wonder whether that is a bug.

The assignment operator cannot copy arrays:

```
int a[ 10 ];
int b[ 10 ] = { 1, 1, 2, 3, 5, 8, 13, 21, 34, 55 };

a = b; // ERROR
```

Arrays must be copied with an explicit loop:

```
i=0;
while ( i < 10 )
{ a[ i ] = b[ i ];
   i++;
}
```

There are important differences between the assignment operator = and the role of = in variable initialization. For example,

```
char s[] = "Hello";
```

allocates six characters (including a '\0') of contiguous storage and gives this storage area the name s. No copying of characters takes place. This is not an assignment but an initialization. A subsequent statement

```
s = "Henry"; // ERROR
```

is illegal.

2.5. RELATIONAL AND BOOLEAN OPERATIONS

Currently, there is no Boolean type in C++. (However, it is likely that a type bool will be added to the language eventually.) All Boolean operations and flow-control statements operate on integers, under the convention that 0 is false and any nonzero value is true. The comparison operators

```
<    <=    >    >=    ==    !=
```

yield 0 if the comparison is false, 1 if it is true; for example, 3 < 4 has the value 1. It is possible to use these operations in arithmetic expressions:

```
sign = ( x > 0 ) - ( x < 0 )    // 1 if x > 0, 0 if x == 0,
                                // −1 if x < 0
```

The proposed bool type has values false and true that are automatically converted to 0 and 1 in expressions.

Pascal Note

This completes the confusion for the Pascal programmer. Pascal :=, =, <> correspond to C++ =, ==, !=. Using = when == is intended can have disastrous effects.

```
if( x = y )    // assigns y to x
{ // always gets here unless the value of y is 0

   ...
}
```

This is a legal construct, and most compilers issue no warning. (Some compilers *do* warn, which is annoying whenever you actually do want to assign and test whether the assigned value is 0.)

Just as arrays (and in particular strings) cannot be copied with =, the comparison operators cannot be used for comparison testing. For example,

```
char s[] = "Harry", t[] = "Hong";

if( s > t ) // NOT a lexicographic comparison!
```

does not test whether s comes lexicographically after t. As we will see later, the code is nevertheless legal, and it tests whether the *starting address* of s is larger than the one of t—a much less useful comparison in most circumstances. The strcmp function in the string library performs lexicographic comparison of strings.

● **Exercise 2.5.1.** Write a program that reads in two strings:

```
char s[ 20 ],t[ 20 ];
cout << "Enter string followed by [Return]: ";
cin >> s;
// ...
```

and prints out the result of the comparison s < t (this should be 0 or 1), strcmp(s, t), and the integer values of s and t. (Use (unsigned long)(...) to convert.) You must #include <string.h>.

Boolean conditions can be joined with

&&	Boolean AND
||	Boolean OR
!	Boolean NOT

These operators interpret 0 as false and any nonzero quantity as true, and they return a 0 or 1. For example, 3 || 0 is 1. Arguments are evaluated only until the truth value of the expression is determined. When the first true expression in an || or the first false expression in an && is encountered, the remaining arguments are not evaluated. It is therefore safe to write

```
if( x != 0 && y / x < eps )     // y/x only evaluated if x != 0
    // ...
```

Pascal Note

&&, ||, and ! are equivalent to the Pascal **and, or,** and **not** operators. However, the Pascal operators do not have the *short-circuit* feature. Writing **if** x<>0 **and** y/x < **eps then** ... will cause an error whenever x is zero, because Pascal first computes the values of all subexpressions before applying the **and** operator. Ada has **and then** and **or else** operators for short-circuit evaluation.

Do not confuse the Boolean and logical operators. & operates on the bit patterns of its arguments, whereas && only looks whether they are zero or not.

● **Exercise 2.5.2.** Write a program that reads in a date in the form 6 16 1959 and computes how many days it is away from January 1 of the same year. Recall that a year is a leap year if it is divisible by 4 but not by 100, or if it is divisible by 400.

Finally, there is a ternary selection operator. *expr1* ? *expr2* : *expr3* evaluates to *expr2* or *expr3*, depending on whether *expr1* is true (non-0) or not. For example,

```
x = a > b ? a : b;        // set  x to the maximum of a and  b
```

Conditional expressions are indeed expressions and can be nested inside other expressions, as in sqrt(a > 0 ? a : -a). This feature distinguishes them from if ... else statements.

● **Exercise 2.5.3.** Write toupper and tolower functions converting lowercase letters to uppercase and conversely and leaving all other characters unchanged. Use ?:.

2.6. OPERATOR PRECEDENCE AND ORDER OF EVALUATION

The following table summarizes the precedence of all C++ operators, including the ones we have not yet discussed. Operators are listed in decreasing strength. Operators on the same line have the same strength and are evaluated in the order indicated in the right-hand column.

Operators	Associativity
: :	Left to right
[] () -> .	Left to right
! ~ ++ -- unary + - * & (*type*) sizeof new delete	Right to left
* / %	Left to right
+ -	Left to right
<< >>	Left to right
< <= > >=	Left to right
== !=	Left to right
&	Left to right
^	Left to right
|	Left to right
&&	Left to right
||	Left to right
?:	Left to right
= += -= *= |= %= &= ^= <<= >>=	Right to left
,	Left to right

The *scope resolution* operator :: will be introduced in Chapter 5. The []
and () operators stand for array access and function call. The unary * and &
will be discussed in Chapter 4, and the . and -> in Chapter 5. The , operator
is a curious *sequencing* operator that executes its subexpressions one at a time
and returns the value of the last one. For example, the value of n = 5, a[n] is
a[5]. It is most commonly used in loop headers,

```
while( n = k, a[ n + 1 ] > 0 )
    // ...
```

to shoehorn multiple actions into a single expression. I recommend that you not
use this construction. Note that its precedence is below that of =. The commas
in a function call are *not* comma operators; after all, you would not want all but
the last value discarded.

This table says *nothing* about the order of evaluation. Like most programming languages, C does not guarantee the order in which the operands are
computed before an operation is applied. For example, in

```
n = 2;
x = a[ n++ ] - 2 * n++;
```

the precedence rules guarantee that parentheses are set like

```
x = ( a[ n++ ] - ( 2 * n++ ));
```

leaving no doubt that the 2 is multiplied by n++ (rather than subtracted from
a[n++]), but it is not clear when it happens. Will the operation be evaluated
left to right, with a[n++] computed and parked somewhere, followed by the
computation of 2 * n++ and finally the subtraction? Or will the subexpression
2 * n++ be computed first and subtracted from a[n++]? It is up to the
discretion of the compiler. The results are, of course, very different:

```
x = a[ 2 ] - ( 2 * 3 ) ;
```

or

```
x = a[ 3 ] - ( 2 * 2 ) ;
```

It is the responsibility of the programmer to organize the code in an unambiguous manner by breaking up the computation into two steps. Even if your
current compiler performs an ambiguous computation in the desired order,
break it up. Another compiler, or even another release of your compiler, might
act differently. In practice, such situations are rare and easily handled.

The difference between operator precedence and order of evaluation is
subtle. Operator precedence determines *how* the components are combined.
Order of evaluation specifies *when* this happens. Only four operators have a
guaranteed order of evaluation:

```
&&  ||  ?:   ,
```

We have discussed the short-circuit evaluation of && and || earlier. The first
argument of ?: is guaranteed to be evaluated first to enable the choice between

the second and the third. The arguments of the , operator are guaranteed to be executed left to right. Note again that the , in function calls is not the , operator. In a function call

```
pow( a[ n ], n++ );
```

there is *no guarantee* whether a[n] or n++ is evaluated first. Again, you should never write code that is sensitive to the order of evaluation. The best policy is to avoid subexpressions with side effects whenever possible.

● **Exercise 2.6.1.** Write a program that tests in which order your compiler evaluates expressions such as a[n++] - (a[n++] - (a[n++] - a[n++])). Also test in which order function arguments such as pow(a[n], n++) are evaluated.

● 2.7. PITFALLS

Welcome to the first "pitfalls" section of this book. In C++, almost every properly formatted expression has *some* meaning, but not necessarily the one you have in mind. It is easy to write code that is legal and accepted by the compiler but does not quite do what you think it does. Read through these "horror stories" even if you do not intend to program right away. Seeing how uncommon expressions are evaluated by the compiler can be very illuminating.

Most of these pitfalls are not indications of "design flaws" in C++. They are just consequences of a rich set of operators and a concise set of rules that occasionally clash with intuition. The language designers are to be applauded for sticking to general and elegant concepts rather than cluttering the language with exceptions. The appearance of some pitfalls, which are easily mastered with some practice, is a small price to pay.

2.7.1. = vs. ==

```
if( n = 10 )
    k = 0;
else
    a[ n ] = k;
```

always sets k to 0 and n to 10. The expression n = 10 has the value 10, because the value of an assignment is the value being assigned. The if statement considers 10 as true because it is nonzero.

Of course, once you are used to typing ==, you might make the opposite mistake:

```
n == 10;
a[ k ] = n;
```

This does not put a 10 into a[k]. The value of n == 10 is computed (it is 1 if this code immediately follows the previous example) and quietly ignored because you did not provide code to do anything with it. It is legal to write statements that do nothing with their values. For example,

```
n + 2;
```

is correct (but useless).

2.7.2. Operator Precedence

Stashing away a value inside an expression can be useful, but it is important to observe that = has very low precedence. For example,

```
while( ch = a[ i++ ] != '\0' ) ...
```

does not place a[i++] into ch but a 1 or 0, depending on whether a[i++] was the terminating '\0' or not. The correct syntax is

```
while( ( ch = a[ i++ ] ) != '\0' ) ...
```

Most operators have reasonable precedence, but the bitwise operators do not. To test for presence of a bit, you cannot write

```
int mask = 0x1000;
if( n & mask != 0 ) ...
```

because & has lower priority than !=, and you do not want to compute n & (mask != 0), which is n & 1. And n << 3 + 1 does not multiply n by 8 before adding 1; instead it adds 3 and 1 first and hence multiplies by 16.

2.7.3. Overrunning Array Boundaries

Unlike Pascal, C++ does not check indices before array access. If an array index is out of range, the access is performed anyway, fetching or modifying the memory location that happens to be at the specified distance from the start of the array. The most dangerous location is the one right after the end of the array. When an array of 10 ints is declared,

```
int a[ 10 ];
```

legal values are a[0], a[1],..., a[9]. a[10] would be the eleventh element and is therefore out of range. Consider the following code to fill an array with zeroes:

```
int a[ 10 ];
int i = 0;

while( i <= 10 ) { a[ i ] = 0; i++; }
```

On many machines this code will run into an infinite loop because i is located right after the array a, and the assignment a[10] = 0 actually stores a 0 in i. Of course, there is no guarantee how the compiler allocates the variables, and the same code might create some other damage.

2.7.4. Order of Evaluation

The order in which subexpressions are evaluated is largely left to the discretion of the compiler. This can lead to problems when using ++, --, or assignments inside expressions. For example,

```
n = 2;
x = pow( a[ n ], n++ );
```

will most likely not compute a[2]^2 but a[3]^2 because most compilers push function arguments onto the stack from right to left.

2.7.5. char **Can Be** signed

Here is just one example that can occur in practice. Many ASCII code extensions use the characters above 127 for international characters. For example, an IBM extension uses 129 for ü.

```
char ch = 129;
if( ch == 129 )
    cout << "u\b\""; // \b: backspace,  \":  " inside string
```

This will not work with many machines because char is often signed. The 129 is changed into the 2's complement equivalent −127 and the comparison fails: −127 ≠ 129.

2.7.6. int **Is Promoted to** unsigned

unsigneds are often useful for quantities that cannot be negative, for example, memory block sizes. But computations may involve subtractions, so great care must be taken.

```
int n = -1;
unsigned baseSize = 40000;
const unsigned adjust = 100;

baseSize += n * adjust; // WRONG
```

The int value n is "promoted" to an unsigned number (for example, 65535 if integers occupy 2 bytes) and that number is multiplied by 100. The result is truncated to fit into sizeof(unsigned) bytes and added to 40000.

If you need unsigned, you must explicitly avoid negative numbers in subexpressions:

```
if( n < 0 )
    baseSize -= ( -n ) * adjust;
else
    baseSize += n * adjust;
```

2.7.7. Boolean Values Are Converted to `int`

Consider the condition

```
if ( -0.5 <= x <= 0.5 )...
```

Unfortunately, this does not test whether x is between −0.5 and 0.5. Instead, -0.5 <= x evaluates to 0 or 1, depending on the comparison between −0.5 and x. That value of 0 or 1, and not x, is then compared against 0.5.

Most programming languages strictly separate Boolean and numeric types and would never permit the comparison of the Boolean value -0.5 <= x with the numeric value 0.5. This is a good idea because it allows the compiler to flag the condition as an error.

At the time of this writing, C++ has no Boolean type. It is contemplated that a type bool will be added in the eventual language standard. But for compatibility reasons, the proposed bool type will automatically convert to int, making the same pitfall possible.

FUNCTIONS

3.1. FUNCTION DECLARATIONS

A function declaration typically has the format

type funcname(type argname, type argname, ...)

For example,

```
double power( double x, int n )
```

The declaration lists the return type, the function name, and the types and names of all arguments. It is followed by the function body, describing the function's action. For example, a complete definition of power is

```
double power( double x, int n )
{ double r = 1;

  if( n == 0 ) return 1;
  if( n < 0 )
  { if( x == 0 ) return 0; // not mathematically correct
    x = 1/x;
    n = -n;
  }
  while( n-- > 0 ) r *= x;
  return( r );
}
```

Pascal Note

From the point of view of the Pascal programmer, C++ declarations are "backward", so it should come as no surprise that the return type comes before the function name.

An important difference is the way the function value is assigned. In Pascal the return value is assigned to a dummy variable with the same name as the function, and execution continues even after this assignment until the function body is exited. In C++ the return value is assigned via the `return` statement, and the function exits *immediately* whenever a `return` statement is encountered. This is very convenient for treating abnormal cases, such as the case of a zero exponent just illustrated, without yet another `else` and another indentation level.

There are no procedures in C++. A procedure is simply a function returning `void`.

C Note

Are you still using pre-ANSI C–style function declarations?

```
double power( x, n )
double x;
int n;
```

You will have to change your habits. These declarations are not acceptable in C++. The new style is a major convenience, catching argument mismatch bugs during compilation. It is also essential for overloading of functions.

If a function does not take any arguments, you must still supply the parentheses. For example,

```
x = rand(); // get a random number
```

It is legal (but uncommon) to omit the parentheses. When that happens, the function name without the parentheses denotes the *starting address* of the function, *not* the return value from the function. This address can be passed to other functions, for example,

```
x = integral( -1, 1, exp );
    // pass address of exp
```

This will be discussed later in Chapter 6.

C Note

The ANSI standard requires that a function with no argument have an argument list `f( void )` to distinguish it from an old-style `f()`. In C++ explicit argument lists are required, so `f()` denotes a function without arguments.

Unless specified otherwise, function arguments are passed by *value*. The function allocates local variables on the stack for each argument. They are *initialized* with the values passed to the function in the call. Once they are initialized, they behave the same way as any other local variables of the function. The values of argument variables can be modified (for example, `n--` in the power function in the foregoing example). The contents are forgotten when the function exits. They are *not* copied back in any way to the caller. For example, if power is called as

```
y = power( 2.0, n );
```

the n in the scope of the call is unaffected, although the local n inside the function is counted down to zero.

● **Exercise 3.1.1.** Rewrite the power function to compute the result faster. When n is even, multiply x by itself and divide n by 2. If n is odd, multiply r by x and decrement n. Write down and verify a *loop invariant* for your code. Discuss the improvement in execution time.

Arguments passed by value can never be modified by a function. However, array arguments *can* be modified. For example, this function clears an array:

```
void clear( int a[], int n )
{ int i = 0;
  while( i < n )
    a[ i++ ] = 0;
}
```

Note the omission of the array limit in a[]. The function can clear arrays of any length. The number of elements to clear is explicitly passed as a second argument.

Pascal Note

This is patently impossible in Pascal. The array limits are part of the array type. We cannot write a single Pascal function that can clear arrays of different lengths.

In contrast, a function cannot clear a single integer. It appears inconsistent that nonarray arguments are passed by value and cannot be changed, whereas array arguments can be modified. But there is actually a logical explanation. The array is not copied in and out of the function, but the function allocates a local pointer variable that gets initialized with the starting address of the array. Because the location of the array, not merely the contents, is communicated to the function, the array values can be modified. This will be explained in detail in Chapter 4.

Pascal Note

Think of array arguments as automatically **var** and all others as value arguments.

If you wish to protect an array argument from modification, it must be explicitly declared const:

```
int max( const int a[], int n );
```

Certain functions cannot be implemented using value arguments. For example, the following function does not swap two integers:

```
void swap( int x, int y )      // WRONG
{ int temp;

   temp = x; x = y; y = temp;
}
```

When called with swap(a, b), the local variables x and y are created and initialized with the current values of a and b. The values of the local x and y are swapped and forgotten on function exit. The values of a and b are unaffected. To change the contents of a variable, use a *reference* argument. The C++ syntax is as follows:

```
void swap( int& x, int& y )      // OK
{ int temp;

   temp = x; x = y; y = temp;
}
```

Now when swap(a, b) is executed, the addresses of a and b (and not their values) are passed to the function, and the function swaps the contents of the memory location referenced by those addresses. What happens behind the scenes is similar to array parameters. x and y are actually pointers, initialized with the addresses of a and b. We will discuss the relationship between pointers, arrays, and references in the next chapter.

Pascal Note

For Pascal programmers, this offers no surprise (except for the odd placement of the & operator). It is simply the **var** argument-passing mechanism. However, because array arguments are automatically **var**, do not use f(int& a[]).

C Note

In C we have to use pointers to achieve this effect.

```
void swap( int* x, int* y )
{ int temp;

   temp = *x; *x = *y; *y = temp;
}
```

and call the function as swap(&a, &b). The C++ reference mechanism merely takes care of placement of the * and & operators for you.

The following table summarizes the behavior of function arguments.

Function	Behavior
f (int n)	Modification of n affects local copy only
f (int& n)	Modification of n affects variable from call
f (int a[])	Modification of a[i] affects array from call
f (const int a[])	No modification of a[i] is possible

● **Exercise 3.1.2.** Write a function that sorts an integer array of arbitrary length. Use quicksort.

● **Exercise 3.1.3.** Write a function s3 that arranges three integers in ascending order. For example,

```
x = 3; y = 1; z = 2;
s3( x, y, z );
// now x == 1, y == 2, z == 3
```

● **Exercise 3.1.4.** Write a function int median(const int a[], int n) that computes the median of an array (of course, without modifying it).

Often it is convenient to specify *default values* for function arguments. Let us rewrite the clear function to fill an array with zeroes, if no other value was requested, or with a specified value, if desired:

```
void clear( int a[], int n, int value =0 )
{ int i = 0;
  while( i < n )
    a[i++] = value;
}
```

The call clear(a, sizeof(a)) fills a with zeroes, whereas

```
clear( a, sizeof( a ), -1 )
```

fills the array with −1. A function can have any number of default arguments, but they must all be grouped at the end of the argument list. Whenever there are fewer arguments in a call, the remaining ones are set to the default.

● **Exercise 3.1.5.** Write a function print that prints an integer in a given base between 2 and 36, with a default of base 10. For example, print(10) prints 10 and print(10, 3) prints 101. If the base is > 10, use 0,..., 9, A, ..., Z for digits. Be sure to handle negative numbers.

Sometimes functions are very short, and a function call may take more space and time than direct coding. For example, to compute the larger of two integers, one can write

```
int max( int m, int n )
{ return m > n ? m : n;
}

c = max( a, b );
```

or simply

```
c = a > b ? a : b;
```

The first method is definitely slower, but the second one is harder to read. The compiler can be instructed not to generate code for a function call but to replace the function invocation with the actual code by declaring the function `inline`:

```
inline int max( int m, int n )
{ return m > n ? m : n;
}
```

This is fine for functions with very small bodies, but it should be avoided otherwise. For all but the shortest functions, it takes more code to do the computation "on the spot" each time a function is invoked rather than having the code occur only once in a true function. This is simply a run-time versus code-size trade-off.

The `inline` attribute is merely a recommendation to the compiler that may be ignored at the compiler's convenience. Many compilers cannot or will not make functions containing loops inline.

C Note

Default arguments and inline expansion are new features of C++. Inline expansion is much safer than preprocessor macros. For example, using the inline function call `max( a[ n++ ], b )` truly computes the maximum of `a[ n ]` and b and increments n once. In contrast, the macro

```
#define max( x, y ) (( x ) > ( y ) ? ( x ) : ( y ))
```

causes computation of the expression `a[ n++ ] > b ? a[ n++ ] : b`, which can increment n twice.

The preprocessor simply performs lexical replacement without any knowledge of the language, whereas inline functions are clever enough to replace `c = max( a,b )` with `c = a > b ? a : b` and `c = max( a[ n++ ], b )` with

```
int temp1 = a[ n++ ]; c = temp1 > b ? temp1 : b;
```

On the other hand, the macro is typeless and can compute the maximum of `double`s as well, whereas the inline function can handle only `int`s. We will see later how a function template can overcome that problem.

● **Exercise 3.1.6.** Write an inline version of `toupper`, a function converting lowercase characters to uppercase. Write a program containing 100 calls to `toupper` and a loop that executes them 100 times. Measure how removing the `inline` attribute affects its space and time behavior.

Pascal Note

In Pascal you can define procedures that are nested inside other procedures. In C++ that is not possible.

3.2. CONTROL FLOW

In C++, each simple statement ends in a ;. Statements can be grouped together by { ... }. It is our style to have matching braces either on the same line or lined up vertically, as in

```
{  ... ;
     ... ;
}
```

Other authors follow different conventions. Some programmers prefer not to place code on the same line after an opening brace, but that wastes space. If you are free to choose a style for yourself, observe others and select the method that appeals to you the most.

Pascal Note

The { and } correspond to Pascal **begin** and **end**. In Pascal the ; is a statement separator, not a terminator. That is, the last statement before an **end** does not carry a ; in Pascal whereas in C++ all statements, including the one just before the }, end in a ;.

The `if` statement has the form

```
if( expression )
   statement
else
   statement
```

The statements can be simple or a sequence of simple statements enclosed in braces. The `else` part can be missing. The *expression* is evaluated, and if it is nonzero, the first statement is executed; otherwise the second statement is executed. In a situation such as

```
if( ... ) if( ... ) ... else ...
```

the `else` groups with the closest `if`. If another grouping is desired, braces must be used. However, it seems wise not to rely on readers of your code to remember this rule; therefore, use braces either way. A common situation is a multiple decision structure like

```
if( ... )
    ...
else if( ... )
    ...
else if( ... )
    ...
else
    ...
```

which performs as expected without requiring braces.

There are two loop formats, one with condition testing at the top:

```
while( expression )
    statement
```

and one with testing at the bottom:

```
do
    statement
while( expression ) ;
```

You will often encounter loops with empty bodies. For example,

```
i = j = 0;
while( ( b[ j++ ] = a[ i++ ] ) != '\0' )     // copy the string  a
    ;                                         // to  b
```

has no loop body—all the work (copying characters and incrementing indices) is already performed in the termination condition as a side effect of testing for the end of the string. This is quite normal, and it is customary to place the ; on a line by itself to amplify the intent. That way, a ; on the same line as the while is sure to arouse suspicion. For example, the code segment

```
while( a[ i ] != '\0' ) ;          // TYPO
    n = 10 * n + a[ i++ ] - '0';
```

does not do what the indentation level suggests. The ; behind the while is the sole body of the while loop. Because semicolons are so frequent in C++, such an error is easily made.

Pascal Note

The do ... while loop is very similar to the Pascal **repeat** ... **until** loop, except that the termination condition is reversed.

C++ has a very general for loop facility. The most common form looks like

```
for( i = 0; i < n; i++ )
    a[ i ] = 0;
```

There are three parts: an initialization, a termination condition, and a reinitialization. The for loop

```
for( expression1; expression2; expression3 )
    statement
```

is completely identical to

```
expression1
while( expression2 )
{ statement
    expression3
}
```

There is no limit to what these expressions are, and it is easy to write inscrutable code such as

```
for( r = i = 0; s[ i ] != '\0'; r += s[ i++ ] - '0' ) r *= 10;
```

This should be discouraged, because the sequence in which the instructions are executed is not intuitive. A `while` loop is much clearer:

```
i = r = 0;
while( s[ i ] != '\0' )
{ r *= 10;
    r += s[ i++ ] - '0';
}
```

I recommend you use `for` loops only when a variable runs from somewhere to somewhere with some constant increment/ decrement.

```
for( i = 0; i < N; i += 4 )
    // ...
```

Occasionally, a `for` loop traversing a linked list can be neat and intuitive:

```
for( l = head; l != 0; l = tail( l ))
    // ... ;
```

That is fine—use your judgment and good taste.

Some of the expressions in the `for` header can be missing. If the second expression is missing, the continuation condition is construed to be always true. In particular, an infinite loop, presumably to be broken by a `return`, can be written as

```
for( ;; )
    // loop never terminates
```

Think of it as "forever". If you need to squeeze two unrelated actions into a `for` header expression, you can use the sequencing operator.

```
for( i = n, j = 0; ( b[ i ] = a[ j ] ) != '\0'; i--, j++ )
    ;
```

The need for the sequencing operator could be a signal that a `for` loop may not be the optimal control structure. In that case, rewrite it as a `while`.

Pascal Note

Pascal programmers will particularly welcome the possibility of controlling the step size of a for loop. The Pascal **to** and **downto** can be easily realized with i++ and i-- in the third slot of for, and the more general for(i = 0; i < N; i += 2) has no convenient Pascal counterpart.

● **Exercise 3.2.1.** There are an endless number of C++ puzzles of the form: "What does this for loop do?" Describe what the following loops do:

```
for( i = 0, r = a[ 0 ]; r = r > a[ ++i ] ? r : a[ i ]; )
    ;
for( i = c = 0; i < n; c += a[ i++ ] != 0 )
    ;
```

These are fun, but before putting them into your programs, ask yourself whether you want your colleagues to remember you for your clever puzzles or for your well-crafted, readable code.

Finally, there is a multiple branching statement of the form

```
switch( expression )
{ case  constant:
     statements
  case  constant:
  case  constant:
     statements
  default:
     statements
}
```

If the expression matches the value of one of the constants, execution starts there. If none of the constants match and there is a default, execution starts there. If there is no default, no action is taken at all. Once started, execution continues, possibly *falling through* one or more case labels, until explicitly stopped with a break statement or the closing }. Here is an example:

```
switch( ch )
{ case '0': case '1':
    x = 2 * x + ch - '0';
    break;
  case '\n'
    linecount++;
    // fall through to next case
  case ' ':
    return( x ); // exit current function
  default:
    cout << "Error"; // print error message
    break;
}
```

A break statement exits the switch; a return statement exits the enclosing function. Each branch of a switch should end in either a break, a return, or an explicit comment "fall through". Strict adherence to this rule makes it easy to flag a forgotten break, a common error.

Pascal Note

It takes some effort to switch from the Pascal **case** to the C++ switch construct. There are few opportunities for the "fall through" behavior, certainly not enough to compensate for the grief caused by the common error of omitting a break. There is no way of specifying a subrange like **case** **'A'..'Z'**, making the switch useless for such a test because the alternative of writing 26 case labels is ridiculous. On the other hand, a default clause is supported. It is obviously useful, but missing from standard Pascal. It is present in many actual Pascal implementations as **else** or **otherwise**.

● **Exercise 3.2.2.** Write a function that uses a switch with fall-through in a useful and realistic way.

C++ also has three forms of nonlinear flow control. break can be used inside while, do, and for loops to exit the innermost enclosing loop. This is completely analogous to the break action inside a switch statement. A continue statement causes the next iteration of the innermost enclosing while, do, or for. Finally, goto label jumps to label:, which must be in the same function. We recommend against using these constructs. It is just too difficult to understand code behavior if one cannot easily answer the question "How did the program get to this spot?" The goto statement is not completely useless—it sometimes occurs in programs written by other programs.

3.3. VARIABLES

Variables can be declared *anywhere* inside a function. Their *scope* ranges from the point of declaration to the end of the enclosing block. It is good programming practice to declare variables at the time they are first needed and initialize them at the same time. This minimizes problems with forgotten initializations. It is even possible to declare a variable in the header of a for loop, such as

```
for( int i = 0; i < 10; i++ ) ...
```

This is completely equivalent to

```
int i = 0;
for( ; i < 10; i++ ) ...
```

and i is known until the end of the block enclosing the for.

Normally, variables are allocated on a run-time stack. Whenever a block is left, all variables that are local to that block are forgotten and the space they occupied on the stack will soon be reused by other variables. Such variables are called *automatic*. They are created and reinitialized every time their scope is entered and forgotten whenever their scope is left. For example, the variable j in

```
for( int i = 0; i < 10; i++ )
{ int j = i;
   ...
}
```

is created and initialized 10 times, once at each loop entry, and forgotten at each loop end.

The function arguments are automatic variables as well, initialized by the values passed to the function in the call. In fact, the only difference between them and other variables is initialization. In all other aspects, they are ordinary variables whose scope extends until the end of the function. They can be modified in any way. On function exit, their values are forgotten.

Sometimes it is not desirable to have the value of a variable forgotten at function exit. Declaring a variable as static makes it persistent. When the function is reentered, the old value is still there. For example,

```
void getword( char buffer[], int buflen )
{ static int linecount = 0;
   int ch;

   cin.get( ch );
   if( ch == '\n' ) linecount++
   ...
}
```

The linecount variable is initialized only *once*, at the beginning of the program (before main starts). Thereafter, it is incremented inside getword, and its value is retained whenever getword exits. Of course, the scope of the variable is still the getword function. It is inaccessible from outside. Applying the static attribute to a local variable changes its lifetime but not its scope.

In recursively called functions, there can be multiple copies of the same automatic variable in existence, one for each invocation. But there is only one copy of each static variable, shared by all invocations.

Variables declared outside functions are accessible to all functions from the declaration on until the end of the file. Such variables are called *global*. They can be initialized as well, and initialization takes place before main starts. It is good programming practice to minimize the number of global variables. Global variables are error-prone, because they can be modified by many functions and it can be difficult to find the culprit if a global variable has been set to an improper value.

Static variables (all globals and static locals) that are not explicitly initialized are guaranteed to be filled with 0. Automatic variables without explicit initialization are guaranteed to be filled with garbage (whichever value happened to be on the stack when their space is allocated there).

To summarize, variables have two distinct attributes: their *scope* and their *lifetime*. Automatic variables get created whenever their scope is entered, forgotten when it is left. They always have local scope. Static variables get created once before the start of main. They can have local or file scope. Any variable can be initialized at its time of creation.

● **Exercise 3.3.1.** static local variables are uncommon because it is not possible to reset their value from outside. Here is an example of the problem: a recursive program for counting the number of nodes of a binary tree.

```
int countNodes( Tree t )
{ static int count = 0;  // shared by all recursive invocations

  if( t != 0 ) // not the null pointer
  { count++; // found a node
    countNodes( t->left ); // do the same with both subtrees
    countNodes( t->right );
  }
  return count;
}
```

Explain why this function is not useful.

● **Exercise 3.3.2.** Give a useful example of a function with a static local variable.

● **Exercise 3.3.3.** Explain the difference between

```
void main()
{ int a[ 100 ];
  // ...
}
```

and

```
void main()
{ static int a[ 100 ];
  // ...
}
```

● 3.4. PITFALLS

3.4.1. return Returns Immediately

Pascal programmers often make the mistake of equating *functionName* := *value* and return(*value*). For example, suppose your job is to write a function

```
int reverse( char s[] )
```

that reverses a string and returns the number of characters in the string.

```
{   int n = 0;
    while( s[ n ] != 0 ) n++; // find end of string
    // now n = #characters in s
    return( n ); // WRONG—returns immediately
    for( int i = 0, j = n - 1; i < j; i++, j-- )
    { char temp = s[ i ]; // swap s[ i ] and s[ j ]
      s[ i ] = s[ j ];
      s[ j ] = temp;
    }
}
```

The return(n) statement should be moved to the end of the function.

3.4.2. Functions Cannot Modify Arguments

The arguments of a function are local variables, initialized with the values used in the call. Any modifications affect the local copies only and do not propagate back to the caller.

```
int vscan( char s[], int v ) // WRONG
// return length of string, compute #vowels in v
{ int i = 0;
  v = 0;
  while( s[ i ] != 0 )
  { char ch = tolower( s[ i ] );
    if( ch == 'a' || ch == 'e' || ch == 'i' ||
        ch == 'o' || ch == 'u' ) v++;
    i++;
  }
  return i;
}
```

```
nchars = vscan( "Hello", nvowels ); // nvowels not set to 2
```

To have a function modify a value, use pointers (see Chapter 4) or references. References are easier:

```
int vscan( char s[], int& v ) // OK
```

3.4.3. Omitting ()

Some functions take no arguments, such as the random number generator rand. Contrary to Pascal, the () must nevertheless be supplied in the call.

```
n = rand(); // OK
```

Unfortunately,

```
n = rand; // WRONG
```

will be flagged by some compilers as a warning, not an error, because it has a legal meaning. rand without the () denotes the starting address of the rand function, which is a number (although not an integer). The compiler may generate code to force that number into an integer. Always pay attention to compiler warnings and treat them just as seriously as errors.

3.4.4. Missing return Values

It is easy to forget a return at the end of a function.

```
int pow( int a, int n )
{ r = 1;
  if( n >= 0 )
  { for( int i = 1; i <= n; i++ )
      r *= a;
    return( r );
  }
  // no return value for n < 0;
}
```

A random value will be returned for n < 0.

● **Exercise 3.4.1.** What value should be returned? Note that a and the return value are int.

3.4.5. Mismatched Arguments

Be extremely careful when using a function that is known to the compiler only as f(...), for example,

```
int printf( char*, ... );
```

The compiler cannot check the arguments at compile time or perform conversions, and you are responsible for *exactly* matching the types. For example,

```
int n = 2;
printf( "%8.2f", n ); // WRONG—won't print "    2.00"
```

It will print something, because the function has no way of checking the type of a bit pattern on the stack at run time. It will just take what it finds and print it as a double.

3.4.6. Misplacing ;

There are so many semicolons in C++ code that it is easy to add one accidentally at the end of an if, for, or while statement:

```
for( i = 0, j = n - 1; i < j; i++, j-- ) ; // WRONG
{ char temp = a[ i ]; // swap a[ i ] and a[ j ]
  a[ i ] = a[ j ];
  a[ j ] = temp;
}
```

The for loop has an empty body and will be executed until i ≥ j. Then the code inside the {} block is executed only once.

These are mean bugs that can be very hard to detect. We recommend *never* to place a ; in the same line as a for or while, even if the loop body is empty on purpose:

```
while( ( ch = s[ i++ ]) != 0 && ( s += ch == ' ' ) < 10 )
  ; // place on separate line
```

3.4.7. Omitting break in a switch

It is easy to omit a break in a switch statement accidentally.

```
switch( ch )
{ case '+': sign = 1;      // WRONG—no break
  case '-': sign = -1;
  default: cin.putback( ch );
}
```

If ch is '+', execution starts at sign = 1 and continues until the next break or the end of the switch block. The lines sign = -1 and cin.putback(ch) are executed!

Always end each branch of a switch with a break, return, or an explicit // FALL comment, even the last one! One day, someone will add another branch beyond it.

C H A P T E R   4

POINTERS, ARRAYS, AND REFERENCES

4.1. POINTERS ARE ADDRESSES

Pointers are a central and rather technical concept of C++. The declaration

```
int* p;
```

declares a variable p that can contain the address of an integer. Then *p is the integer whose address is stored in p. For example:

```
int n = 5;
p = &n;          // store the address of n in p
*p += 2;         // increment n by 2
```

Here & is the address operator, which yields the memory location of a variable. It is not too common to have a pointer to a single integer. More often a pointer points to an element in an array, for example,

```
int a[ 10 ];     // an array of 10 integers;

p = &a[ 0 ];     // store the address of the 0 location of a in p
*p = 5;          // and store a 5 into the 0 location
p++;             // now p points to the next location in the array
```

If a pointer points into an array, one can move it to point to other memory locations in that array by adding or subtracting integer values. This *pointer arithmetic* takes into account the sizes of objects pointed at. Adding 1 to an int* actually adds sizeof(int) to the address; adding 1 to a double* increments it by sizeof(double) instead. In general, if p and q are pointers to a type X (that is, p, q are of type X*), it is legal to add or subtract an integer and to compute the pointer difference: p + n is the address of the nth X away from *p, and q - p is an integer denoting how many Xs are between *p and *q . (This makes sense only if p and q point to the same array.) The arithmetic is simply address computation, scaled by sizeof(X).

By the way, note that `sizeof( int* )` is the same as `sizeof( double* )`, because both an `int*` and a `double*` hold a memory address. Generally, all pointer variables have the same size. (Actually, this is not always true. Depending on the processor and the selected memory model, some classes of pointer variables might be larger than others.) No assumption should be made whether `sizeof( X* )` equals the size of some basic type.

In pointer declarations, I prefer to group the `*` with the type name: `int* p`. This appears to declare an object p to be of type `int*`. However, this does not accurately reflect the compiler's point of view. The compiler groups the `*` with the variable name: `int *p`. This declares "p is an object whose `*` is an `int`". (White space is completely ignored by the compiler, except when necessary to separate tokens—`int*p` and `int * p` would be legal, too.)

If you decide to follow my convention for placement of the `*`, be careful not to declare two pointers in the same line! The declaration

```
int* p,q;
```

does *not* declare two pointers p and q but one pointer p and one *integer* q. The `*` really groups with the p, not with the `int`. It is correct to declare

```
int *p, *q;
```

But I prefer to use two lines and declare the pointers separately:

```
int* p;
int* q;
```

The keyword `const` also interacts strangely with pointer declarations:

```
const int* p;
```

declares a pointer to a `const int`, not a constant `int*`. That means it is okay to look at `*p` but not to modify it. `*p = 0` is an error. Because p is not a constant, `p++` is legal and makes p point to the next `const int`. To declare a pointer that is itself constant, place the `const` to the right of the `*`, next to the pointer name:

```
char* const q = "Version 12.3d";
```

This means that q may not be modified in any way, but the character it points to may be. Of course, both may be held unchangeable:

```
const char* const r = "Version 12.3d";
```

means that neither r nor `*r` may be changed. The most frequent case is the first one. For example, the function

```
int max( const int* p, int n )
```

receives a pointer to an integer (and more integers following that one, n in all). The function may not touch the integers, only look at them. But p may change; for example, repeated execution of `p++` makes p traverse the array.

Pascal Note

Pointers do occur in Pascal, and they are dereferenced with the ˆ operator rather than *. In Pascal there is no concept of pointer arithmetic. The only legal operation on a Pascal pointer is to dereference it. Pascal does not have an address operator either. The only way of obtaining a memory address is from the heap via **new**.

Pascal pointer variable declarations cleanly separate the type name from the variable name.

● **Exercise 4.1.1.**   Find out what sizeof(X*) is on your system. Does your compiler have different "memory models"? If so, find the size of a pointer in each one of them.

● **Exercise 4.1.2.**   Pointers are addresses, that is, numbers. You can print out the value of a pointer, simply as cout << (unsigned long) (p). Write a program to compare p, p+1 and q, q+1, where p is an int* and q a double*.

4.2. ARRAYS AND POINTERS

There is an intimate connection between arrays and pointers in C++. When an array is declared, for example,

```
int a[ 10 ];
```

the name of the array a denotes a pointer (constant), namely the address of the 0 element of the array. Similarly, a + 1 is the address of the next array element. *(a + 1) is the integer stored at that location, a value customarily referred to as a[1]. In fact, the C++ compiler always translates all array references a[n] into the pointer computation *(a + n). Conversely, if p is a pointer variable, for example,

```
int* p = a + 3; // p points to a[ 3 ]
```

p[4] is legal, and it means simply *(p + 4), that is, the contents of 4 integers away from p, or a[7] . Under all circumstances it is true that for all pointers p and all integers n,

$$p[n] \text{ equals } *(p + n)$$

This is the *array-pointer duality law.*

To summarize, if we declare an array of objects of type X,

```
X a[ N ];
```

then sizeof(a) = N * sizeof(X). From the declaration, it is apparent that the type of a is X[N], but if it is used in any expression except sizeof (which is computed at compile time), a is converted to type X* (or more precisely, X* const). All uses of a, such as computing a[n], are simply pointer arithmetic, via the array-pointer duality law. By the way, all C++ arrays start at zero to make the pointer arithmetic work.

Pascal Note

In C++ all array expressions become pointer expressions. In particular, the size of the array is ignored. Contrast this with Pascal, which suffers from the problem of having *too many* array types. When you declare an array, you must specify the lower and upper bounds, and these are inextricably tied to the type. You can write a sort routine that sorts arrays of type **array [1..20] of int**, but that routine cannot sort an array with 21 elements, or even an array with 20 elements numbered from 0 through 19.

Let us write a function that finds the largest number in an array of integers. The call

```
max( a, 10 );      // find the max of an array with
                   // 10  elements
```

computes the maximum of

```
int a[ 10 ]
```

The function should expect to receive an int* and an int:

```
int max( const int* p, int n )
```

This declares two local variables: p, which is initialized with the starting address of the array; and n, which is initialized with the number of elements. Note that the array is not copied into the function; merely its starting address is passed to the pointer variable p. To refer to the ith element of the array, we can nevertheless use the notation p[i], as if there were an actual array passed to max. Recall that p[i] is *(p + i), the contents of the memory location obtained by adding the size of i integers to the address stored in p.

In fact, there is another style of declaring a pointer argument that is permissible only in a function declaration:

```
int max( const int p[], int n )
```

This gives the illusion that p is an (open-ended) array. In fact, the array has not been copied, no large amount of space has been allocated, p is still an int*, and sizeof(p) = sizeof(int*). There is no difference between an argument int p[] and int* p, just as there is no difference between p[n] and *(p + n).

This empty-bracket notation has *no* relationship with an earlier use of empty brackets. At that time, we saw array declarations with an initializer that enables the compiler to count the elements.

```
int a[] = { 1, 1, 2, 3, 5 };
```

which is a convenient shorthand for

```
int a[5] = { 1, 1, 2, 3, 5 };
```

and really allocates five `sizeof( int )`s' worth of storage. Similarly,

```
char s[] = "Harry";
```

declares an array of six characters, not a pointer variable. However,

```
char* p = "Harry";
```

does declare a pointer variable and allocates six characters somewhere else, initializing p with the starting location of these characters.

Let us have a look at two distinct ways of writing the max function:

```
int max( const int p[], int n )
{ int m = p[ 0 ];
  int i = 0;

  while( ++i < n )
    if( m < p[ i ]) m = p[ i ];
  return( m );
}
```

This is an obvious and easily understood solution. The `p[ i ]` are actually pointer computations, but the convenient `[]` notation hides that. Another possible solution makes use of the fact that p is a local pointer variable, and we can modify it:

```
int max( const int* p, int n )
{ int m = *p;

  while( --n > 0 )
  { p++;
    if( m < *p ) m = *p;
  }
  return( m );
}
```

The pointer p steps through the array element by element.

In these solutions we have chosen the `int []` notation in the declaration of the version using `p[ i ]` in the body and the `int*` notation in the declaration of the version with `*p` in the body. This was dictated merely by good taste, not by any requirement of the language. It is permissible to switch freely between the `[]` and the `*` notation at any time. The programmer should choose the notation that makes the code most readable.

● **Exercise 4.2.1.** Write a function that computes the average value of an array of floating-point numbers.

```
double average( double* a, int n )
```

Use pointers, with the pointer variable a traversing the array.

● **Exercise 4.2.2.** Write a program that prints sizeof(a) in the following two situations:

```
int f( int a[], int n );
int a[] = { 1, 1, 2, 3, 5 };
```

4.3. STRING FUNCTIONS

To illustrate some pointer techniques, we will consider strings. (This section can be skipped if you are familiar with C-style string-handling functions. While a reading knowledge of the pointer tricks of this section is important for deciphering existing code, I don't advocate this style for new code.) *Strings* are arrays of characters, terminated by a zero byte. Here is a string and a buffer capable of holding a string:

```
char s[] = "Harry";      // same as s[ 6 ] = ...
char buffer[ 10 ];
```

Let us start with an easy function. strlen computes the string length, the number of nonzero characters in a string.

```
int strlen( const char* p )
{ int n = 0;
  while( *p++ != '\0' )
    n++;
  return n;
}
```

For example, strlen(s) is 5. The pointer p gets initialized with the starting address of the string. Inside the loop header, the curious expression *p++ is executed. Looking at the operator precedence table, we find that * and ++ have the same precedence and are executed right to left. p++ is executed first, incrementing p. But the *value* of p++ is the old value of p, before the increment. To this value the * operator is applied, resulting in the content of the old p location. As long as that content is not zero, we are not yet at the end of the string, and n is incremented. Once the terminating zero is encountered, we leave the function.

Note how the argument p was treated like an ordinary variable that happened to be initialized with the starting address of the string in the function call.

To copy s into buffer, we cannot simply write

```
buffer = s; // WRONG
```

and a moment's reflection on the material of the previous section will show why. buffer and s, written without the [], are pointers, pointing to the starting addresses of the array. In particular, buffer is a constant (because the array is at some fixed location) and cannot be modified. The foregoing statement is the pointer equivalent of attempting an assignment 10 = 6. It simply is not possible to modify the value of the pointer constant buffer.

Of course, what we really want to do is to copy the contents. Another function must be provided for this purpose.

```
char* strcpy( char* to, const char* from )
{ char* r = to;
   while( ( *to++ = *from++ ) != '\0' )
      ;
   return r;
}
```

Calling strcpy(buffer, s) performs the string copy. In this function, both the pointers from and to traverse the character arrays. The *to++ = *from++ assignment increments to and from, but the * is applied to the values of those increment operators, that is, to the pointer values before increment. Thus, the contents of the old from address gets copied to the old to address. As long as the value of the assignment is not zero, this process is repeated.

All the work is being performed simultaneously with the test for completion in the loop header, and the loop body is empty. Because any nonzero value is considered true, it is even possible to write

```
while( *to++ = *from++ )
   ;
```

Of course, the = really is assignment, not test for equality, and the loop continues until a zero is assigned. Because of the potential for error, many compilers issue a warning for this construct.

The function returns the original address of to. That seems unnecessary; after all, the caller of strcpy supplied that value and will not need it back. However, it is convenient for nesting calls, such as

```
n = strlen( strcpy( buffer, s ));
```

To concatenate two strings, the + operator cannot be used. Again, we need a function. The strcat function appends t to s.

```
char* strcat( char* s, const char* t )
{ char* r = s;

   while( *s != '\0' ) s++;   // go to the end of the first string
   while( *s++ = *t++ ) != '\0')
      ;                        // copy
   return r;
}
```

Why not simply while(*s++); to go to the end of s? The ++ is executed regardless of whether the loop test is true or false. When s points to the terminating zero of the first string, *s++ will be zero, but s now points one character beyond the zero. Because we want the zero to be overwritten with the first character in t, we would then have to move s back with an additional s--.

For both strcpy and strcat there is no check whatsoever for overrunning the space in the first array. The functions merely receive pointers to the character arrays to be filled, which give no indication of their size. Only the size of an already existing string can be determined by the location of the zero terminator. If a long string is copied into a buffer with not enough space, adjacent memory locations will be overwritten.

```
char buffer[ 10 ];
char s[] = " Harry";
char t[] = " Hacker";
strcpy( buffer, s );   // OK
strcat( buffer, t );   // WRONG—buffer can only hold
                       // 10  chars
```

The following is worse:

```
char* p;
strcpy( p, s );        // WRONG—memory will be overwritten
```

This causes placement of a copy of s into whatever area in memory p happens to point to, simply overwriting the previous contents of those memory cells. How could it do anything else? p itself is quite small, only 2 or 4 bytes, and cannot itself hold all the characters from the string s. And memory does not come for free. However, this is fine:

```
char* p;
p = buffer;            // p points to buffer
strcpy( p, s );        // places a copy of s in buffer
```

When writing down a string such as "Harry", that too has a value (like most things in C++). The value is the starting address of the string that has been placed somewhere in memory. For example, the call

```
strcpy( buffer, "Harry" )
```

causes the string "Harry" to be allocated somewhere in memory, and its starting address is given to strcpy. Note the difference between

```
char s[] = "Harry";
```

and

```
char* p = "Harry";
```

The first declares s to be an array with six characters. The second declares p to be a pointer variable; in addition, it allocates six characters somewhere and places the location into p. s will always denote the address of the same block. p can be changed simply by assigning it another address.

● **Exercise 4.3.1.** Write a function char* strchr(const char* s, char c) that returns a pointer to the first occurrence of c in s, 0 if none is found. Use pointers, not arrays.

Note: In conformance with the standard C string library, the function receives a const char* (because one might be passed to it) and returns a char* (because it might be used to modify the string). You will need to cast the return value. Ideally there should be two functions

```
const char* strchr( const char* s, char c )
```

and

```
char* strchr( char* s, char c ).
```

● **Exercise 4.3.2.** Write a function char* strstr(const char* s, const char* t) that returns a pointer to the first occurrence of the string t in s, 0 if none is found. Use pointers, not arrays.

● **Exercise 4.3.3.** Write a function unsigned strspn(const char* s, const char* t) that returns the length of the prefix of s consisting of characters in t (in any order). Use pointers, not arrays.

● **Exercise 4.3.4.** Write a function void reverse(char* s) that reverses a character string (for example, "Harry" becomes "yrraH").

Strings cannot be compared lexicographically using the standard relational operators.

```
if( s == "Harry" ) ...
```

tests whether the *starting address* of s is the same as the starting address of a freshly allocated string "Harry". It certainly is not. The function strcmp compares two strings. It returns some negative number if the first string comes before the second, zero if they are identical, and some positive number otherwise:

```
int strcmp( const char* s, const char* t )
{ while( *s ! = '\0' && *s == *t ) { s++; t++; }
  return int( *s ) - int( *t );
}
```

The cast to int is necessary because char is unsigned in some implementations. For example, strcmp("Harry", "Hong") returns int('a') - int('o'), a negative number, because the strings differ at that position for the first time.

● **Exercise 4.3.5.** Write a function strncmp(const char*, const char*, int n) that compares two strings but only looks at the first n characters.

● **Exercise 4.3.6.** Write a function strncpy(char*, const char*, int n) that copies the second string into the first but copies at most n characters. If the second string is longer than that, there will not be a terminating 0.

Suppose you need to convert a string containing digits only (such as "159") into its numerical equivalent (the integer 159). The following does not work:

```
char a[4] = "159";
int n = int( a ); // WRONG
```

This code takes the starting address of the array a, interprets that number as an int, and places it in n. Instead, the library function atoi ("ASCII to integer") can be used:

```
int n = atoi( a ); // OK
```

atoi takes any string and computes the decimal equivalent. Conversion stops when the first nondigit (not necessarily the zero terminator) is encountered.

```
int atoi( char* s )
{ int r = 0;
  while( '0' <= *s && *s <= '9' )
    r = 10 * r + *s++ - '0';
  return r;
}
```

The functions introduced in this section are part of the standard string library. To use them in your programs, you need not retype them. Just place the line

```
#include <string.h>
```

in the top of your program file. atoi is declared in stdlib.h.

The *p++ idiom is common in older code because the first C compilers had very poor optimizers. Today, you should write p[i]; i++; instead.

4.4. REFERENCES

References were briefly introduced in Chapter 3 as a way of implementing reference (Pascal **var**) parameters. If a function modifies regular arguments, the modification extends to the local copy only and is not communicated back to the variables in the function call. If modification of a variable in the function call is desired, reference arguments should be used. This situation frequently arises when a function computes two values simultaneously. Consider a function computing the mean

$$\bar{x} = \frac{1}{n} \sum x_i$$

and standard deviation

$$\sigma = \sqrt{\frac{\sum x_i^2 - \frac{1}{n}(\sum x_i)^2}{n}}$$

of a set of data $x_1, \ldots, x_n$.

```
void parameters( double x[], int n,
  double& mean, double& std )
{ double sum = 0, squaresum = 0;

  for( int i = 0; i < n; i++ )
  { sum += x[ i ];
    squaresum += x[ i ] * x[ i ];
  }
  if( n > 0 )
  { mean = sum / n;
    std = sqrt( ( squaresum - sum * sum / n ) / n );
  }
}
```

When called with

```
const int NSTUDENT = 35;
double classgrades[ NSTUDENT ], m, s;

// ...

parameters( classgrades, NSTUDENT, m, s );
```

the mean and standard deviation are deposited into m and s.

Behind the scenes, all references are translated to pointers, according to the following two rules:

- Whenever a reference variable p is used, replace p by *p.
- Whenever a reference variable is initialized with a, replace a by &a.

Initialization can occur directly through a reference declaration:

```
double& p = m;        // really means double* p = &m;
```

Much more frequently, though, function arguments are initialized through call values. For example, the function parameters is translated to

```
void parameters( double x[], int n,
  double* mean, double* std )
{ //...

  if( n > 0 )
  { *mean = sum / n;
    *std = sqrt( ( squaresum - sum * sum / n ) / n );
  }
}
```

and *each* call to parameters is modified by adding & operators:

```
parameters( classgrades, NSTUDENT, &m, &s );
```

The function actually receives the addresses of m, and s and places the values directly into those addresses (*mean = sum / n...).

References are a convenience. It is easier to use a reference argument than a pointer argument because the compiler automatically supplies the necessary & and *. You do not even have to be conscious of this process when using references simply to implement Pascal-style **var** parameters. On the other hand, many C++ programs use references in other ways for which it is helpful to understand the precise mechanism.

Not only can functions take reference arguments—they can *return* a reference! To give a realistic example, consider the problem of efficiently storing the values of a sparse matrix, a matrix whose entries are mostly zero. In particular, we will consider square matrices of the form

$$\begin{bmatrix} * & * & & & & & & & \\ & * & * & & & & & & \\ & & * & * & & & & & \\ & & & * & * & & & & \\ & & & & * & * & & & \\ & & & & & * & * & & \\ & & & & & & * & * & \\ & & & & & & & * & * \end{bmatrix}$$

with zero entries except for the main diagonal and the diagonal above (as in Jordan canonical forms). To store a 10×10 matrix of this shape it would be wasteful to allocate 100 doubles, most of them 0. It suffices to store the 19 values on the diagonals. A simple function elem can be written to access the (i,j)th element:

```
double diag[ 10 ];
double above[ 9 ];

double elem( int i, int j )
{ if( i == j ) return( diag[ i ]);
  else if( i+1 == j ) return( above [ i ]);
  else return 0;
}
```

Although elem(i, j) reports the matrix entry at that location, a different function must be written to change an entry. However, modifying elem to return a reference makes it possible to write

```
elem( 2, 3 ) = 3.14;
```

The elem function needs to be rewritten:

```
double& elem( int i, int j )
{ if( i == j ) return( diag[ i ]);
  else if( i + 1 == j ) return( above [ i ]);
  else // ...
}
```

Because the function returns a double&, it actually returns the address of above[2] (and not the value stored there). In each function call, a * is supplied.

> * (*returned pointer*) = 3.14;

The * is also supplied when the function value occurs on the right side of an =. Consider

> x = elem(2, 3);

Again, elem(2, 3) returns a pointer, and the assignment sets

> x = * (*returned pointer*)

In the elem function, we have left open the case of accessing a 0 element ($j \neq i, i + 1$). What is wrong with returning 0?

```
double& elem( int i, int j )
{ // ...
   else return 0;
}
```

Recall that the function actually returns an address. It must therefore create a double, place 0 in it, and return the address of that double. However, the storage for the 0 will be allocated on the stack of elem. Being a local variable of that function, the zero no longer exists after elem returns. Using that value—or, worse, writing to it—can cause disaster. Instead, we will explicitly allocate a variable zero and return a reference to it:

```
double zero = 0;

double& elem( int i, int j )
{ // ...
   else
   { if( zero != 0 )
     { warn( "Illegal access occurred previously" );
       zero = 0;
     }
     return zero;
   }
}
```

We check whether zero is 0 every time because it might have been changed by an (illegal) call such as elem(4,1) = 3.14. Unfortunately, elem does not know whether it is called on the left or right side of an =, and it cannot report an error when a zero element is being modified.

● **Exercise 4.4.1.** Model a triangular matrix containing elements a_{ij} for $i \geq j$ only. Store them in a linear array, in a sequence $a_{00}\ a_{10}\ a_{11}\ a_{20}\ a_{21}\ a_{22}$ ... and write an elem access function. Test your code by computing the Pascal triangle:

```
for( i = 0; i < n; i++ )
  for( j = 0; j <= i; j++ )
    elem( i,j ) = j == 0 || j == i ? 1 :
        elem( i - 1, j - 1 ) + elem ( i - 1, j );
```

● **Exercise 4.4.2.** Implement an *associative array* that can store pairs of floating-point numbers, for example,

Key	Value
4.0	1
3.7	2
3.3	2
3.0	5
...	

such that assoc(3.3) returns 2, and assoc(3.3)++ increments the entry to 3. Store the keys and values in parallel arrays of double and have assoc return the appropriate reference in the value array. If a new entry is referenced (for example, assoc(3.8)), append it to the key list and set its corresponding value to 0. You may assume that there are at most 100 keys.

● **Exercise 4.4.3.** The most common use for references is the implementation of **var** parameters. We know that all array parameters are **var** anyway. Explain what happens if such a parameter is declared as a reference argument, such as

    void reverse(char*& s)

Explain the meaning of

    void reverse(char& s[])

● 4.5. PITFALLS

4.5.1. Copying without Allocating Storage

This is the most common beginner's bug:

    char* p;
    strcpy(p, "Harry");

There is no syntax error. strcpy expects two char*. However, where is the string copied to? The declaration char* p allocates a variable p. It can hold an address and is not initialized. It points to a random location in memory. The string "Harry" is copied to that random location, overwriting whatever was there before.

There is an easy method to avoid this bug. Whenever declaring anything, ask yourself: What is sizeof(...)? sizeof(p) is 2 or 4 bytes on most systems. There is *no way* that a 6-byte string can be placed into it. In C++, storage is never allocated automatically. (This does not mean that a very short string of

2 or 4 bytes might be profitably stored in a pointer variable. The point is that a pointer variable has a fixed small size and that string storage is variable and potentially large.)

4.5.2. Pointing to Data That No Longer Exists

Never have a function return a pointer or reference to a local object!

```
char* num2str( int n ) // number to string conversion
{ char buffer[ 10 ];

    // compute answer in buffer

    return buffer; // WRONG
}
```

The storage space for buffer is forgotten and overwritten with other information when num2str exits. The same holds for references.

```
double& elem( int i, int j )
{ double r = 0;

    // compute answer in r

    return r; // WRONG
}
```

If the function were to return a double instead of a double&, there would be no problem.

There are three remedies for this problem:

1. Return a pointer to a static object (Section 3.3).
2. Return a pointer to an object on the free store (Section 10.1).
3. Have the caller pass a pointer or reference to storage for the result (num2str(int, char*)).

4.5.3. Forgetting a String Terminator

All C++ string-handling functions expect a string to be terminated with a zero byte. If it is not, the functions will continue searching through memory until a byte that happens to be zero is encountered.

```
char buffer[ 80 ];
for( int i = 0; i < 80; i++ ) buffer[ i ] = '-';
cout << buffer;
    // WRONG–prints 80 dashes + random characters
```

4.5.4. Using Omniscient `sizeof`

If a is an array, declared as

```
int a[ 5 ];
```

or

```
int a[] = { 0, 1, 4, 9, 16 };
    // size determined by counting initializers
```

then `sizeof( a )` measures the number of bytes in a: $5 \times$ `sizeof( int )`. One might well wonder why a function operating on arrays cannot use the `sizeof` operator to determine the size of the array passed to it:

```
int max( const int p[] )
{ int m = p[ 0 ];
   int i = 0;

   while( ++i < sizeof( p )) // WRONG
      if( m < p[ i ]) m = p[ i ];
      return( m );
}
```

Here, `sizeof( p )` does *not* obtain the size of the array passed to the function (which after all is neither a constant value known at compile time, nor available at run time, as it is not stored with the array). It obtains the size of the pointer variable p (which is initialized with the starting address of the array passed to the function).

It is necessary to supply a second parameter `size` to the max function. The function can be called with

```
max( a, sizeof( a ) / sizeof( int ))
```

because the compiler can compute `sizeof( a )` at compile time.

C H A P T E R   5

STRUCTURED TYPES

5.1. STRUCTURES

An array collects objects of the same type, whereas a *structure* collects objects of different types. Here is the classic example:

```
struct Employee
{ char name[ 30 ];
  int age;
  double salary;
  char ssNum[ 12 ];
};
```

This structure defines a new type `Employee`, with *members* `name`, `age`, `salary`, and `ssNum`. Individual employees can be obtained by

```
Employee harry = { "Harry Hacker", 20, 34500,
                   "000-00-0123" };
```

and members can be accessed with the `.` operator:

```
if( harry.age < 21 ) ...;
```

Structures can be assigned:

```
Employee staff[ 100 ];
staff[ i ] = harry;
```

This makes a copy of all members of the structure. We call such a copy a *memberwise copy*.

Structures can be passed to functions as arguments, and they can be returned as function values. For example, if a `Date` structure is defined as

```
struct Date
{ int dy, mo, yr;
};
```

we can (with sufficient patience and observance of the variable number of days per month and leap years) write functions

```
int daysBetween( Date d1, Date d2 );
    // returns the number of days between d1 and  d2.

Date addDays( Date d, int n );
    // returns the date n days from d.
```

Pascal Note

Structures are called records in Pascal. Returning a record from a function is not possible in Pascal.

C Note

In C++ the struct keyword may be dropped when using the structure name as a type. In C, a new employee must be declared as struct Employee harry; or a new type must be produced with typedef. Structure assignment, passing structures to functions, and returning structure values are defined in the ANSI standard but are missing from some pre-ANSI compilers.

When a structure is passed to a function, the argument is a local variable of that function that gets initialized with a memberwise copy of the calling value. When a structure is returned with a return(r) statement (where r is a structure variable in the scope of the function), a memberwise copy of r is placed into a temporary location. These memberwise copies take time, especially for large structures. Therefore, it can be preferable to pass a (constant) reference:

```
Date addDays( const Date& d, int n )
{    // ...
     if( isleap( d.yr )) // access member via . operator
     // ...
}
```

Because of the const, the function cannot modify the date. However, the function receives a pointer to the argument, not the argument itself. (As explained in Section 4.4, the compiler generates code to supply a & in each call and *s in the body of the function.) The time-consuming copying of all members into a local variable is avoided.

The function can also be defined to receive the address of the structure explicitly:

```
Date addDays( const Date* d, int n )
{    // ...
     if( isleap( d->yr )) // access member via ->
                          // operator
     // ...
}
```

Then it must be called as

```
addDays( &d, n );
```

The expression d->yr is merely an abbreviation for (*d).yr. (The () around *d are necessary because . binds stronger than *.) The -> operator was introduced because the construct "take the member of a pointer to a structure" is so common, and the parentheses are awkward.

Pascal Note

In Pascal there is no special −> operator. The pointer-dereferencing operator comes *behind* the pointer, and we would simply write *d^.***days**.

Different structures can have members with the same name. For example, another structure besides Employee can have a name member, and there can even be a global name variable. The compiler can tell the difference simply by looking left of the . or -> operator.

● **Exercise 5.1.1.** Implement the addDays and daysBetween functions. Pass the Date arguments as const Date &.

● **Exercise 5.1.2.** Write a function readEmployee that reads an employee record from a text file in the format

```
Harry Hacker   20   34500   000-00-0123
Joe M. Conrad  49   84000  363-30-6330
...
```

Hint: Read one line of input with the command

```
char line[ 200 ];
//...
cin.getline( line, sizeof( line ));
```

where line is an array of char. The last three items (separated by spaces) are age, salary, and social security number. Everything before that must be the name. Transfer the information into a variable of type Employee (using atoi and atof to convert the digit strings to numbers) and return it.

● **Exercise 5.1.3.** Write a program that reads in a list of employees as in the previous exercise, places them into an Employee[] array, and prints out the information of the employees with the highest, lowest, and median ages and salaries.

5.2. MEMBER FUNCTIONS

In addition to data members, structures can have function members.

```
struct Date
{ int dy, mo, yr;
```

```
    void print();
    void advance( int );
    Date add( int );
    long diff( Date );
};

void Date::print()
{ cout << mo << "/" << dy << "/" yr;
}


Date bday = { 16, 6, 1959 };

    bday.print();
```

The `Date::` in the function definition indicates that the member `print` of the `Date` structure is being defined. Other structures could also have a `print` function. Within the definition of `print`, the data member names are used without a variable and without . or -> preceding them. The member names refer to the variable in front of the . in the function call `bday.print()`. This is called the *implicit argument* of the function. Each member function has at least one argument: the implicit argument. It may have explicit arguments as well, as does the advance function in the foregoing structure definition. To add a number of days to a date d, the function call is

```
    d.advance( 30 );
```

The implicit argument d comes before the ., and the explicit argument 30 is placed within parentheses. Here is the function.

```
    int daysPerMonth( int month, int year )
    { static int dpm[] = { 0, 31, 28, ... };
      if( month != 2 ) return dpm[ month ];
      return 28
        + (year % 4 == 0) - (year % 100 == 0) + (year % 400 == 0);
        // recall that the result of the == is 0 or 1
    }

    void Date::advance( int n )
    { int d;

      dy += n;
      while( dy > ( d = daysPerMonth( mo, yr )))
      { dy -= d;
        if( ++mo > 12 ) { mo = 1; yr++; }
      }

      while( dy < 1 ) // if n was negative
```

```
{ if( --mo < 1 ) { mo = 12; yr--; }
  dy += daysPerMonth( mo, yr );
}
}
```

Again, the members of the implicit argument are used without prefixing them with a dot. This function modifies its implicit argument.

● **Exercise 5.2.1.** Add member functions `print` and `raise` to the `Employee` structure. If e is of type `Employee`, `e.print()` prints it and `e.raise( x )` raises the salary by x percent.

● **Exercise 5.2.2.** Make the `readEmployee` function of Exercise 5.1.2 into a member function. Write a program that reads in an array of employees, raises each one's salary by 4 percent, and prints them.

Sometimes it is necessary or desirable to refer to the implicit argument in its entirety, or to pass its address to another function. Each member function gets a pointer `this` to its implicit argument. You can think of the use of dy in a member function as a shortcut for `this->dy`. A member function can use `this`, to refer to the address of the structure that appeared to the left side of the . in the call, or `*this`, to refer to the actual structure. Here is a function that returns a date + n days without modifying the original:

```
Date Date::add( int n )
{ Date r = *this; // make a copy of the implicit argument
  r.advance( n );
  return r;
}
```

```
Date e = d.add( 30 );   // d is unchanged
```

It is curious that the implicit argument appears like a reference argument in the call (no & is taken) and like a pointer argument (add(`Date* this`, ...)) in the function.

If a pointer to a structure is given, member functions are called with the -> operator. (This is entirely consistent with data-member access.)

```
struct Employee
{ //...
  void print();
}
```

```
Employee* staff[ 100 ]; // pointers only, actual info stored elsewhere
```

```
for( int i = 0; i < 100; i++ )
  staff[ i ]->print();
```

The fact that a function does not modify an (explicit) argument can be expressed with the `const` indicator; for example,

```
int Date::diff( const Date& );
```

But how does one indicate that a function does not modify the implicit argument? The const must be placed behind (!) the argument list, as in

```
Date Date::add( int n ) const;
int Date::diff( const Date& ) const;
```

Why use member functions? Any member function can be rewritten as a regular function by explicitly passing the implicit argument. There are several reasons:

- Member functions of different structures can have the same name. You can have print() members of Employee and Date. In a call to x.print(), the compiler can tell which one to use by looking at the type of x. Actually, member functions are not strictly necessary for this purpose, because, as we will see later, regular functions can behave in this way too.

- It is often convenient to package all functions that allow access to the data members of a data type together, giving the user of the data type a consistent user interface that remains stable even if the internal data representation changes. Member functions are not necessary for achieving this, but they come neatly packaged inside the structure declaration.

- It is sometimes intuitive to single out the implicit argument as something special. One can think of a function call car.accelerate(5) as sending a *message* to the *object* car. This terminology is used in some object-oriented programming languages: Structure variables are called objects, member functions are called methods, and member function calls messages. Whether it is more intuitive to send an "add 30 days" message to a date than making a function call add(d, 30) is probably a matter of taste.

- It is somewhat convenient to refer to the members of this just by their name because the prefix this-> is implicit. (This use is similar to the Pascal **with** construct.)

- Some functions necessary for memory management (so-called constructors and destructors), as well as operator =, operator->, operator[], and operator(), *must* be member functions.

- Functions dynamically selected at run time (so-called virtual functions) *must* be member functions.

Short member functions can be defined inside the structure definition.

```
struct Date
{ int dy, mo, yr;
  void print() const
  { cout << mo << "/" << dy << "/" yr; }
  // ...
};
```

This has the same effect as declaring Date::print to be inline. A call cout << bday.print() is literally replaced with

```
cout << bday.mo << "/" << bday.dy << "/" bday.yr;
```

rather than the code for a function call. Be aware that inline replacement can significantly increase code size, especially if one inline function calls another, and that inline replacement is only a recommendation to the compiler, which can ignore it. It is actually not terribly good practice to use this notation for inlines. If you later change your mind about the inline status, you have to move the function body outside the structure declaration. Because inline functions are not recognized by many debuggers, it is common to remove the inline attribute during debugging and restore it later. This is more easily achieved with a separately defined function.

Enumeration constants defined inside structures are considered members. When used by nonmember functions, they must be preceded by *structure name*::. For example, the following enumeration constants

```
struct Date
{ // ...
   enum Weekday {
      MONDAY = 1, TUESDAY, WEDNESDAY, THURSDAY,
      FRIDAY, SATURDAY, SUNDAY };
};
```

can be used as MONDAY inside a member function of Date but must be used as Date::MONDAY elsewhere.

Enumeration constants are commonly used to specify array sizes in structures:

```
struct Stack
{ enum { SIZE = 20 };
   int stack[ SIZE ];
   // ...
};
```

This is better than

```
const int SIZE = 20;

struct Stack
{ int stack [SIZE]
   // ...
};
```

because the enumeration is inside the scope of the structure. Stack::SIZE does not conflict with another constant SIZE. The prefix Stack:: is not required when SIZE is used in the scope of the Stack structure.

● **Exercise 5.2.3.** Write a `Point` structure storing the x- and y-coordinates of a point. Write a `Line` structure with two data members of type `Point`, that is, two points on that line. Write member functions `Point::read()` that reads in a point in the format `(10.5,2)` and `Line::read` that reads in the line coordinates in the format `[(10.5,2),(-2.3,0)]`. Use `Point::read` in `Line::read`.

● **Exercise 5.2.4.** Write a member function `Line::isVert` returning 1 if the line is vertical and 0 otherwise, a function `Line::slope` returning the slope of a nonvertical line, and a function `Line::equation` that prints the equation of a line in the format $y = 6.4x + 3.7$ (or $x = 2$ for a vertical line). Write a member function `Line::isEqual( Line )` that tests whether two lines are actually the same (just defined by different pairs of points).

● **Exercise 5.2.5.** Write a member function `int Line::onLine( Point )` returning 1 if the point is somewhere on the line, 0 if not.

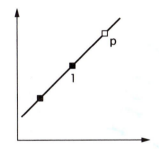

● **Exercise 5.2.6.** Write a function `Point Line::intersect( Line )` that computes the point of intersection between the lines. If the lines do not intersect (because they have the same slope), return (0,0).

5.3. CLASSES

Data representation can change. A major goal of object-oriented programming is to keep the code that uses the data completely unchanged when the internal representation is modified.

Even as simple a structure as `Date` is not immune from change. If a program performs a lot of date arithmetic, the repeated adjusting of month lengths can be time-consuming. Instead, it may be preferable to store dates as single integers that contain the number of days from some fixed point in the past, such as 1/1/1970. Many spreadsheets use this format internally, sometimes called *Julian date*. Now computing "date + integer" and "date − date" become trivial, but printing is more difficult. That trade-off will be beneficial if date arithmetic is much more frequent than printing.

Now consider a program P that uses `Date` a lot. How can we, the designers of the `Date` type, present to our client, the programmer of P, the `Date` type in such a way that we can switch between the two representations without changing a line of code in *P*? We can suggest to the client never to access the dy, mo, yr member data (which might be replaced by int julian), supplying member functions day(), month(), and year() (in addition to add(), diff(), print(),...) instead. Unfortunately, programmers do not always have a good track record in following such suggestions. For this reason, C++ enables the supplier of structures to enforce privacy of structure members. Such structures become *abstract data types*. In an abstract data type, the details of the implementation are hidden from the type user. The user accesses the data through an interface that is stable even if the internal representation changes.

This is achieved by separating member data and functions into a *private* and a *public* section. The private section is the representation, and the public section is the abstract data type. C++ uses the class construct for this purpose. A class is the same as a struct, except that all its members are hidden unless they are explicitly declared public. (It works the other way around, too. A struct is in fact a class with all its members public unless explicitly declared private.) For a Date type, it looks like this:

```
class Date
{ int dy, mo, yr;
public:
    int day() const;
    int month() const;
    int year() const;
    void print() const;
    int read();
    void advance( int );
    Date add( int ) const;
    int diff( const Date& ) const;
    // ...
}
```

If the private section is changed into

```
long julian;
```

the public section is completely unchanged. Any attempt to access the private portion,

```
Date bday;
bday.dy = 16; // WRONG
```

will be flagged by the compiler as an error.

It is a coincidence that this class has all member data private and all member functions public. Functions can be private, and data can be public.

The private member data of a class can be accessed by the member functions of the class only (as well as *friend* functions; see Section 5.5). Similarly, private member functions can be called only inside other member functions of the same class. For example, Date::print() can immediately access the data members. Other functions need to call *access functions* such as Date::year().

● **Exercise 5.3.1.** Implement the Date class using the day/month/year representation.

● **Exercise 5.3.2.** Implement the Date class using the Julian date representation using 1/1/1970 A.D. as day 1.

● **Exercise 5.3.3.** Present a class Employee with member functions for reading, printing, and data access, and for raising the salary by a percentage.

The next example, which will be used in later programs, abstracts a terminal display grid, as used in Section 1.5. We hide the representation (a double array of char) and allow access only via certain functions.

```
class Grid
{
  public:
    enum { XSIZE = 79, YSIZE = 24 };
    Grid();
    void clear(); // fill with ' '
    void show() const; // display current picture
    void set( int x, int y, char ch ='*' );
    void line( int xstart, int ystart, int xend, int yend );

  private:
    char g[ YSIZE ][ XSIZE + 1 ];
};
```

● **Exercise 5.3.4.** In our Employee class, we stored the age of the employees as an integer. That isn't smart, since we don't want to update the field every year. Change the implementation to store the birthday, but don't change the public interface. That is, keep the age member function in the interface and implement it to compute, not just return, the age. In the read member function, assume that the file format is changed to contain the birthday.

● **Exercise 5.3.5.** Implement the member functions of the Grid class. Be sure to write safe set and line functions that check for proper array indices. If you entered the code for the flowchart plotter program (Section 1.5), modify it by allocating a global Grid display and replacing calls to gridLine to display.line, and so forth, then test it.

It is possible to define a data member that is shared by all *instances* of a class (all variables of that type) by declaring it static. For execution profiling purposes, one might want to keep track of how many (time-consuming) calls to the date print function have been performed. Add a static field printCount to the Date structure:

```
class Date
{ long julian;
public:
  static int printCount;
  void print() const;
  // ...
}
```

```
int Date::printCount = 0;
```

There is only a single storage location `printCount` in the entire program, not one for each instance of `Date`. It can be accessed in any member function.

```
void Date::print()
{ printCount++;
  // ...
}
```

Since `printCount` has been declared in the public section, it can be accessed from anywhere as `Date::printCount`. Each static data member must be explicitly defined outside the `class`, even if the static member is private.

```
class Shape
{ static double trans[ 2 ][ 2 ]; // a transformation matrix
  // ...
};
```

```
double Shape::trans[ 2 ][ 2 ] = { 72, 0, 0, 72 };
```

Compare the use of the `static` keyword with the declaration of a `static` local variable. Such a variable also occurs only once, even if the function in which it is defined is recursive and has multiple invocations pending, each with its own set of automatic variables.

Finally, member functions can be declared as `static`. Such functions have no implicit `this` argument and can only operate on the static data members. For example,

```
class Shape
{ static double trans[ 2 ][ 2 ]; // a transformation matrix
  // ...
public:
  static void scale( double s ); // multiplies trans by s
};
```

Static member functions are accessed like static member data, as

```
scale( .5 )
```

inside other member functions of Shape and with the scope resolution operator

```
Shape::scale( .5 )
```

elsewhere.

● **Exercise 5.3.6.** Make the daysPerMonth function and the dpm array into private static members of the Date class. Write a public static function today that returns today's date.

● **Exercise 5.3.7.** Design a String class

```
class String
{ char s[ MAXSIZE ];
public:
  void read();  // reads a string from cin, delimited by
               //  white space
  int length() const;
  void print() const;
  String substring( int, int ) const;
              // extract a substring
  int find( const String& ) const;
              // find first occurrence of substring,
              // return −1 if none found
  String concat( const String& b ) const;
              // returns concatenation of *this and  b.
};
```

implementing strings with an upper bound on their size. For example, the following code adds the reverse of a string to its end:

```
String s;
s.read();
String r = s;
for( int i = s.length() - 1; i >= 0; i-- )
{ String t = s.substring( i, i );
  r = r.concat( t );
}
r.print();
// e.g., Harry becomes HarryyrraH
```

The following two exercises show that global variables can often be replaced by static members in C++. Static members have two advantages over global variables: The class mechanism protects them from uncontrolled modification, and the *names* used by them are not blocked. For example, users of the Date class in the foregoing example are free to use the name printCount elsewhere in their programs. This consideration is particularly important when designing class libraries for use by others.

● **Exercise 5.3.8.** Short strings waste a lot of storage, because they only occupy a fraction of the char[MAXSIZE] array. Implement a more efficient scheme: Use a large character array buffer to store the actual strings. The read function, as well as the functions concat and substring with a String result, should append strings at the end of the buffer. Each string contains the starting index in the buffer, a single int.

```
class String
{ int start;      // start of string in buffer

  enum { STRINGBUFSIZE = 10000 };
  static char buffer[ STRINGBUFSIZE ];
  static int bufend;
public:
  // ...
};
```

Rewrite the member functions using this implementation.

● **Exercise 5.3.9.** Consider the bidiagonal matrices of Section 4.4. Design a class Bmat10 for 10 × 10 bidiagonal matrices. Define a member function elem returning a double&, as described in that section. Use a static member to implement the zero location.

5.4. CONSTRUCTORS

There is a problem with the Date class of the previous section: How can one set a date? The statement d.dy = 16 is illegal and, if the Julian representation is chosen internally, nonsensical. The access function d.day() can report a day but does not set it. We could provide a member function

```
void Date::set( int month, int day, int year; )
```

and use it to set dates:

```
Date d;
d.set( 6, 16, 59 );
```

C++ provides a better way. The class can define a *constructor* that sets the values as the variable is declared:

```
Date d( 6, 16, 59 );
```

A constructor is a special member function whose name is the same as the name of the structure or class:

```
class Date
{ int dy, mo, yr;
public:
  Date( int, int, int );
  // ...
};
```

```
Date::Date( int month, int day, int year )
{ dy = day;
  mo = month;
  yr = year;
}
```

Constructors are not real functions. They are called only when an object is created. Once an object exists, you cannot change its value by calling the constructor again. Constructors do not have a return type.

You can supply more than one constructor, and it is often convenient to do so:

```
class Date
{ // ...
  Date( int, int, int );
  Date( const char* );
  Date(); // initializes to today's date
  // ...
};
```

```
Date d( "June 16, 1959" );
Date t; // initialized to today's date
```

The correct constructor is called, depending on the type of the initializer. Constructors often have default arguments:

```
Date::Date( int month, int day, int year = 0 )
{ mo = month;
  dy = day;
  if( year == 0 )
    // set year to current year
  else
    y = year;
}
```

```
Date d( 6,16 ); // sets year to current year
```

Constructors can create temporary objects.

```
Date today;
// ...
age = today.diff( Date( 6, 16, 1959 )) / 365;
```

This code causes creation of an unnamed temporary variable, which is initialized and passed to Date::diff. It is equivalent to:

```
Date temp( 6, 16, 1959 );
age = today.diff( temp ) / 365;
```

Afterward, the temporary variable is forgotten.

Constructors are used to initialize data members of class type as well. Here is an Employee class that stores the birthday of the employee.

```
class Employee
{ char name[ 30 ];
  Date bday; // class type
  double salary;
public:
  Employee( const char n[], int m, int d, int y, double s );
  // ...
};
```

Every Employee object contains a bday subobject of type Date. Provided the Date class has at least one constructor, all Date objects are guaranteed to be initialized with one of its constructors. In particular, that holds for the bday objects. Now let us look at the Employee constructor.

```
Employee::Employee(
  const char n[], int m, int d, int y, double s )
{ strcpy( name, n );
  bday = Date( m, d, y ); // OK but inefficient
  salary = s;
}
```

This constructor will work properly, but it is inefficient. C++ guarantees that all member objects of a class are constructed before entering the { ... } block of a constructor. In particular, the bday member will already be constructed with the default constructor of the Date class. It is then overwritten with the desired date.

There is a better way. We can direct the Employee constructor to invoke the Date(int, int, int) constructor to initialize bday. The syntax is a bit peculiar.

```
Employee::Employee(
  const char n[], int m, int d, int y, double s )
: bday( m, d, y )
{ strcpy( name, n );
  salary = s;
}
```

Now bday is constructed with the desired data before the body of the constructor is executed. You can also initialize bday as a copy of an existing date.

```
Employee::Employee( const char n[], Date d, double s )
: bday( d )
{ strcpy( name, n );
  salary = s;
}
```

This places a copy of d into bday before the `Employee` constructor body starts executing. Constructing bday with a copy of d is faster than first constructing it with the default constructor and then overwriting it with d.

You can initialize the `salary` member with the same syntax.

```
Employee::Employee( const char n[], Date d, double s )
: bday( d ), salary( s )
{ strcpy( name, n );
}
```

However, since `salary` is of type `double`, and `double` is not a class type, the salary field is never constructed with a default constructor, so it makes no difference whether you initialize it with s before entering the constructor body or inside the body.

There is one case in which you *must* explicitly construct data members before entering the constructor body. If a member object belongs to a class with no default constructor, you must provide an explicit construction directive.

● **Exercise 5.4.1.** Write the `Date( int, int, int = 0 )`, `Date( const char* )`, and `Date()` constructors, using the dy, mo, yr representation.

● **Exercise 5.4.2.** Write the constructors of the previous exercise using the Julian representation.

● **Exercise 5.4.3.** Write constructors for the `String` class of Exercise 5.3.7.

```
String::String()
String::String( char* )
String::String( char )
```

that enable construction of

```
String s( "Harry" ), t( 'a' );
```

● **Exercise 5.4.4.** Write a constructor for the `Point` class of Exercise 5.2.3., making a `Point` from a pair of `double` s. Write constructors `Line( Point, Point )`, `Line( double slope, double yIntercept )`, and `Line( double xIntercept )`, the last-named for vertical lines. For the last two constructors, you have some freedom in choosing the points. Pick some with convenient values.

5.5. FRIENDS

The level of protection given by the `class` mechanism can be too restrictive. Suppose a type for vectors in 3-space has been defined as

```
class Vec3
{ double vcoord[ 3 ];
```

```
public:
  Vec3();
  double elem( int ) const;
  double sprod( const Vec3& ) const; // scalar product
  Vec3 xprod( const Vec3& ) const;   // cross product
};


Vec3::Vec3()
{ vcoord[ 0 ] = vcoord[ 1 ] = vcoord[ 2 ] = 0;
}


double Vec3::elem( int i ) const
{ if( 0 <= i && i < 3 )
    return vcoord[ i ];
  else error();
}


double Vec3::sprod( const Vec3& v ) const
{ double r = 0;
  for( int i = 0; i < 3; i++ )
    r += vcoord[ i ]*v.vcoord[ i ];
  return i;
}
```

and a matrix type similarly

```
class Mat3
{ double mcoord[ 3 ][ 3 ];
public:
  Mat3();
  double elem( int i, int j ) const;
  // ...
}
```

The elem access functions provide safe access to the entries; for example

```
Vec3 v;
double a = v.elem( 3 ); // ERROR
```

returns a default value of 0 because the vectors only have three coordinates, indexed as 0, 1, 2. Of course, this access checking takes time. The member function Vec3::sprod can dispense with it because the member function has access to the private part.

Consider the problem of writing a function that multiplies a matrix and a (column) vector, resulting in a vector. The function must be a member function of Vec3, because it needs to build the result, and the public elem function can only look up, not change, a value.

```
Vec3 Vec3::multiply( const Mat3& a ) const
   // multiplies a and *this
{ Vec3 r;
  for( int i = 0; i < 3; i++ )
  { double sum = 0;
    for( int j = 0; j < 3; j++ )
      sum += a.elem( i,j ) * vcoord[ j ];
                           // i.e., this->vcoord[ j ]
      r.vcoord[ i ] = sum;
  }
  return r;
}
```

This looks strange, because it reverses the order of the factors. It is also inefficient. Each call to a.elem checks the bounds before handing out the value. If multiply were a member function of Mat3, it could bypass elem and directly access a.mcoord[i][j] and v.vcoord[j], but a function cannot be a member function of two classes. This problem can be overcome by having Mat3 declare the function a friend:

```
class Mat3
{ // ...
   friend Vec3 Vec3::multiply( const Mat3& ) const;
};
```

Or the function could be rewritten as a nonmember,

```
Vec3 multiply( const Mat3& a, const Vec3& b )
   // multiplies a and b
{ Vec3 r;
  for( int i = 0; i < 3; i++ )
  { double sum = 0;
    for( int j = 0; j < 3; j++ )
      sum += a.mcoord[ i ][ j ] * b.vcoord[ j ];
    r.vcoord[ i ] = sum;
  }
  return r;
}
```

and declared a friend by both classes:

```
class Vec3
{ // ...
   friend Vec3 multiply( const Mat3&, const Vec3& );
};

class Mat3
{ // ...
   friend Vec3 multiply( const Mat3&, const Vec3& );
};
```

Actually, our example is a bit contrived, because it relies on hiding the implementation details of 3 × 3 matrices—something one might not bother with in practice. For large vectors and matrices, however, different representations are indeed appropriate. Sparse matrices (with many zero entries) can be represented in special ways, and changing, yet efficient implementations are very important.

● **Exercise 5.5.1.** Consider the bidiagonal matrix class of Exercise 5.3.9. Make a class Vec10 for vectors with 10 components. Code a fast function for computing the product of a Bmat10 and a Vec10. It should be a friend of both classes.

Sometimes friend functions are preferred for their syntax. For example, the String class of Exercise 5.3.7 has a concat member function: s.concat(t) returns the concatenation of s and t. It seems more natural to make concat a friend instead, to be called as concat(s, t).

Class definitions are not supposed to be edited by class users (and are best stored in a read-only file). Friend declarations are part of the class definition. A class user therefore cannot gain access to private parts of a class by declaring a function a friend. The initiative must come from the class designer.

A member function of one class can be a friend of another (like the Vec3::multiply function already seen). It is not uncommon that all member functions of one class are friends of another. There is a shorthand for this.

```
class Mat3
{ // ...
    friend class Vec3;
};
```

5.6. CLASS INTERFACES

By now, an important dichotomy has presented itself several times. On one side of the fence is the class designer, who has to worry about supplying enough functions (or *methods,* in the terminology of some object-oriented languages) to satisfy the legitimate needs of the class user, yet hide all details that might change when the data representation is modified. On the other side is the class user, who, depending on temperament, may be grateful not to be bothered with the details of the representation or may be infuriated by the inability to obtain access. Designing classes that are easy and efficient to use can be surprisingly hard.

What makes a good class?

▪ Something that you might need more than once (in the same or different projects)

▪ Something of which you might want to have more than one

In this section we look at some classes that are desirable from the point of view of the class user, ignoring the complexities of the implementation.

A safe integer array type, with bounds checking and arbitrary starting index, can be designed with the following interface:

```
class IntArray
{ // ...
public:
  IntArray( int lo, int hi );
  int& operator[]( int );
};
```

Once someone has taken the trouble to implement the class, it is easy to declare an array:

```
IntArray a( 10, 20 ); // like Pascal a:Array[10..20] of integer
```

Thanks to the overloading of the [] operator, an IntArray is used exactly like an ordinary array:

```
a[ 12 ] = 5;
cout << a[ 5 ]; // calls error function—index out of range
```

Operator overloading is discussed in Chapter 7.

Vector and matrix classes with arbitrary sizes can be defined and used with the standard mathematical operators, almost as if they were built-in types.

```
class Vector
{ // ...
public:
  Vector( int dim );
  friend Vector operator+( const Vector&, const Vector& );
  friend Vector operator-( const Vector&, const Vector& );
  friend double operator*( const Vector&, const Vector& );
    // dot product
  friend Vector operator*( double, const Vector& );
    // scalar multiplication
  friend Vector operator*( const Vector&, double );
    // scalar multiplication
  friend Vector operator*( const Matrix&, const Vector& );
    // matrix multiplication
  friend Vector operator*( const Vector&, const Matrix& );
  double length() const; // distance from origin
  double& operator[]; // access coordinates
  double operator[] const;
  friend ostream& operator<<( ostream&, const Vector& );
    // print
  friend istream& operator>>( istream&, Vector& ); // read
};

class Matrix
{ // ...
public:
  Matrix( int rows, int cols );
  friend Matrix operator+( const Matrix&, const Matrix& );
  friend Matrix operator-( const Matrix&, const Matrix& );
```

```
    friend double operator*( const Matrix&, const Matrix& );
      // dot product
    friend Matrix operator*( double, const Matrix& );
      // scalar multiplication
    friend Matrix operator*( const Matrix&, double );
      // scalar multiplication
    friend Vector operator*( const Matrix&, const Vector& );
      // matrix multiplication
    friend Vector operator*( const Vector&, const Matrix& );
    static Matrix identity( int n );
      // computes  n × n identity matrix
    Matrix& inv(); // invert and return *this
    double det() const; // determinant from origin
    Vector& operator[]( int ); // access row vector
    const vector& operator[]( int ) const
    friend ostream& operator<<( ostream&, const Matrix& );
      // print
    friend istream& operator>>( istream&, Matrix& ); // read
};
```

Here is how you use them:

```
Vector v( 4 ); // a vector with four components
v[ 0 ] = 1; v[ 2 ] = -1;
Vector w = 2 * v; // w = (2,0,-2,0);
Matrix a( 4, 4 ); // a 4 × 4 matrix
cin >> a;
cout << a * v + w;
a[ 1 ][ 1 ] = 0; // a[1] is a row vector, so second [] makes sense
Matrix b = a.inv();
cout << b.det();
Vector u = w*(a-Matrix::identity( 4 ));
```

Where does all the memory come from? The class did not know that we were going to do linear algebra in 4-space only. We could have asked for 10×8 matrices. Well, it isn't our problem, is it? Right now, we are just users of the class and can be blissfully ignorant about the details.

I hope that I have whetted your appetite in this section. Wouldn't you enjoy using some of these classes, especially if you knew that someone else was to implement them?

● **Exercise 5.6.1.** Design the class interface for a Set class implementing finite sets of integers. What operations are desirable on sets?

- Adding an element, taking the union or intersection of two sets
- Computing the set difference (all elements in *A* but not in *B*)
- Finding out whether a number is an element of a set
- Finding whether one set is equal to another, or a subset of another

Write the `class` definition only. Do not worry where the memory for potentially large sets comes from or how any of the operations might be implemented.

● **Exercise 5.6.2.** Full-fledged sets require dynamically allocated storage, which we have not covered yet. Let us consider sets containing numbers between 0 and 255 only. These can be easily implemented through bit vectors: sequences of 256 bits, with the ith bit 1 if i is an element of the set. Such vectors can be represented as arrays of 32 bytes. Union and intersection become bitwise | and &. Implement the class interface of Exercise 5.6.1 with bit vectors.

5.7. UNIONS

Unions are a space-saving device to use the same storage space for different items when there is no possibility that more than one of them applies for any given instance. Such situations are rare and inherently dangerous. In C++, many problems can be solved better with derived classes (Chapter 10) than with unions. After these words of warning, let us proceed to the classic example. A compiler symbol table stores names, types, and values of constants:

```
union Value
{ int ival;
  double dval;
  char* sval;
};

struct Constant
{ char* name;
  char type; // i for integer, d for double,
            // s for string
  Value val;
};

Constant c;

switch( c.type )
{ case 'i': cout << c.val.ival; break;
  case 'd': cout << c.val.dval; break;
  case 's': cout << c.val.sval; break;
}
```

It is entirely the programmer's responsibility to ensure that the type field and the branch of the union correspond. The compiler has no conception of the rules that dictate what value is currently stored in the union. There is no field to remember what, if anything, has been stored previously in a union. The following code is legal but almost certainly meaningless:

```
Value v;
v.ival = 10;
double x = v.dval; // unpredictable
```

It is very easy to write buggy code with unions. Yet the alternative—to have three fields ival, dval, sval in the struct, of which all but one are always zero—is also unattractive.

The notation c.val.dval is cumbersome, with val selecting the union and dval the item inside it. The union declaration can be placed inside the structure, with the union name omitted,

```
struct Constant
{ char *name;
  char type;
  union
  { int ival;
    double dval;
    char* sval;
  };
};
```

and the items inside the union can be accessed like c.dval. These constructs are called *anonymous unions.*

Unions can have member functions, constructors, and destructors. However, unions are rare, and unions with such full-fledged support even rarer.

To initialize a union safely a set of type-sensitive constructors can be used:

```
union Value
{ int ival;
  double dval;
  char* sval;
  Value( int i ) { ival = i; }
  Value( double d ) { dval = d; }
  Value( char* s ) { sval = s; }
};

Value v( 12 ); // Calls  Value( int ) constructor
```

Pascal Note

Unions in Pascal are called *variant records,* and they are safer because they contain a built-in variant selector.

C Note

As with enumerations and structures, the union name becomes a type name. Anonymous unions are new to C++.

● **Exercise 5.7.1.** Write a safe union type

```
class SafeValue
{ char type;
```

```
union
{ int ival;
   double dval;
   char* sval;
};
// ...
};
```

with constructors and access functions `ivalue()`, `dvalue()`, `svalue()` that generate an error message if a different item (or no item) was stored in the union.

● **Exercise 5.7.2.** The implementation of the `Line` class in Exercise 5.2.3 was wasteful. You do not *need* two points (4 `doubles`) to specify a line. Reimplement the `Line` class by storing line segments in the form `struct { double slope, yIntercept; }`, except that vertical lines are stored as `double xIntercept`. The `struct Line` should contain a union of those types and a field `int vertical` to describe the two situations. Write constructors

```
Line( double, double ) // not vertical
Line( double )         // vertical
Line( Point, Point )
```

and a function `equation` that prints the equation of the line. Do use classes, not structures, for points and lines, hiding the coordinate representation. (It will change in Exercise 5.7.5.)

● **Exercise 5.7.3.** Implement the `intersect` function of Exercise 5.2.6 using the data structure of Exercise 5.7.2. You may make `intersect` a member of `Line` or just an ordinary function; the choice is yours.

The remaining three exercises have nothing to do with unions, but they show that, in the case of lines, just a little mathematical sophistication can lead to a much more useful data representation.

● **Exercise 5.7.4.** The trouble with lines is that vertical lines are treated differently. Reimplement the `Line` class by storing $[a, b, c]$ if its equation can be written as $ax + by + c = 0$. Keep the constructors `Line( double, double )` and `Line( double )` as in Exercise 5.7.2, and write `isEqual` and `intersect` member functions. Two lines $a_1x + b_1y + c_1 = 0$ and $a_2x + b_2y + c_2 = 0$ are equal if the coordinates $[a_1, b_1, c_1]$ and $[a_2, b_2, c_2]$ differ by a constant factor. For example, $[1.5, -2, 4.2]$ and $[3, -4, 8.4]$ denote the same line.

● **Exercise 5.7.5.** The trouble with the `intersect` function is that parallel lines do not intersect. Represent points by projective coordinates $[x, y, z]$. The point (x, y) on the plane has projective coordinates $[x, y, 1]$. Two projective coordinates denote the same point if they differ by a constant factor, just as with line coordinates.

For example, $[5, -1.5, 2]$ and $[2.5, -0.75, 1]$ denote the same point. The point $[x, y, z]$ lies on the line $[a, b, c]$ if $ax + by + cz = 0$. This makes the onLine function of Exercise 5.2.5 quite simple.

z is nonzero if the point is a "real point". In that case, one can divide by the z-coordinate and get the regular x- and y-coordinates. For example, $[5, -1.5, 2]$ corresponds to the point $(2.5, -0.75)$ on the plane. Points with $z = 0$ are brand-new points, called "points at infinity".

Two parallel lines meet in such a point. For example, $2x - y - z = 0$ and $2x - y - 2z = 0$ meet in $[1, 2, 0]$. Therefore, *all lines have a common point of intersection.*

Using projective coordinates, write an intersect function. If the lines are identical, return an arbitrary point thereon.

● **Exercise 5.7.6.** Using projective coordinates, write a constructor Line(point, point) that computes the line joining two points. (If the two points are identical, return an arbitrary line.) *Hint:* You are using representations for points and lines that are identical (three double s, considered the same if they differ by a common factor). Joining two points is *very* closely related to intersecting two lines.

● 5.8. PITFALLS

5.8.1. Forgetting the ;

The most common error when using struct or class (or enum or union) is to forget the ; behind the closing brace. Some compilers produce *strange* error messages when this happens. It is, of course, a common error since functions do not have a terminating ;.

Here is a particularly unsettling example:

```
struct Date
{ int mo, dy, yr;
} // WRONG—no  semicolon

main()
{ // ...
}
```

In conformance with classic C, this is interpreted as defining main to be a function with return type Date!

5.8.2. Confusing . and ->

Beginners are often unsure when to use . and ->. It is actually very simple. . is used with actual struct values, -> with pointers to struct. For example,

```
void f( Date* pd )
{ Date d;

  d.yr = pd->yr; // d is a Date,  pd a Date*
  // ...
}
```

A Date& reference behaves just like a Date and the . is used (although internally it is represented as a Date*).

The same applies to class and union types.

5.8.3. When to Use () with Default Constructors

The following code does not allocate two Date objects.

```
int main()
{ Date bday( 6, 16, 1959 );
  Date today(); // NO!
  // ...
}
```

It appears as if bday was constructed with Date(int, int, int) and today was constructed with Date(). Unfortunately, that is not the case. It is legal (although not really useful) in C++ to declare functions in the scope of a block. The declaration

```
Date today();
```

declares today to be a *function* with no arguments and return type Date. When defining a named variable constructed with the default constructor, you *cannot* use (). The correct definition of a Date variable today is

```
Date today; // uses default constructor
```

However, when defining an unnamed temporary variable, you *must* use ():

```
n = bday.diff( Date() );
```

Omitting the parentheses (bday.diff(Date)) is a syntax error.

5.8.4. Construction as a Copy of an Existing Object

There are two ways of coding the construction of an object as a copy of another object.

```
Date today;
Date d = today;    // Syntax 1
Date e( today );   // Syntax 2
```

Both definitions do the same: allocate a variable that is constructed as a copy of today. When declaring a variable, you can use either syntax, although the first one, using the = sign, is much clearer. Note, by the way, that

```
Date d = today;
```

in not at all the same as

```
Date d;
d = today;
```

In one case d is constructed as a copy of today. In the other, d is constructed with the default constructor, and the value of d is then overwritten with today. When you know how you want to initialize a variable, you should do so as you define it, possibly moving its definition down from the beginning of the block.

The second syntax for copy construction is *required* when constructing a member object.

```
Employee::Employee( const char n[], Date d, double s )
: bday( d )
{ strcpy( name, n );
  salary = s;
}
```

The seemingly logical

```
Employee::Employee( const char n[], Date d, double s )
: bday = d // NO!
{ strcpy( name, n );
  salary = s;
}
```

is a syntax error.

Here is a final puzzle. What is the meaning of the following statements?

```
Date a( Date );
Date b( Date() );
```

Answer: The first line declares a function a that has a Date argument and returns a Date. The second line defines a variable b that is constructed as a copy of an anonymous object Date(), constructed with the default constructor.

5.8.5. Wasteful Default Construction

A constructor always initializes all class-type data members before entering the body of a constructor.

```
class Employee
{ String name;
  Date bday;
  double salary;
public:
  Employee( const char n[], int m, int d, int y, double s );
  // ...
};
```

```
Employee::Employee (
const char n[], int m, int d, int y, double s )
{ // name already constructed with String()
  // bday already constructed with Date()
```

```
   name = n;
   d = Date( m, d, y );
   salary = s;
}
```

It is wasteful first to construct a field with the default constructor and then to overwrite it. Instead, explicitly construct those data members that should not be constructed with the default constructor:

```
Employee::Employee(
   const char n[], int m, int d, int y, double s )
: name( n ), bday( m, d, y )
{ salary = s;
}
```

This is a concern only for data members of class type. Characters, numbers, and pointers have no default constructor. But for consistency, many programmers initialize nonclass types outside the constructor body as well. This often results in an empty constructor body:

```
Employee::Employee(
   const char n[], int m, int d, int y, double s )
: name( n ), bday( m, d, y ), salary( s )
{
}
```

5.8.6. Order of Member Construction

When data members are constructed before the body of the constructor begins, the initialization always follows the order of the members in the class definition, not the order in the constructor. For example, the following code is an error:

```
class Employee
{ String name;
  int age;
  Date bday;
  double salary;
public:
  Employee( const char n[], int m, int d, int y, double s );
  // ...
};

Employee::Employee(
   const char n[], int m, int d, int y, double s )
: name( n ),
  bday( m, d, y ),
  age( Date::today().diff( bday ) / 365 ), // NO
  salary( s )
{
}
```

Even though the construction of bday is specified before the construction of age, the age field is constructed first, since it is listed first in the class definition. There is a reason for this seemingly irrational behavior. In Section 9.2 we will encounter destructors: functions that automatically clean up objects, just as constructors automatically initialize them. C++ guarantees that destruction always occurs in reverse order of construction. Furthermore, a destructor automatically calls the destructors of all member objects, in the reverse order of their occurrence in the class definition. This cannot be changed by the programmer. For that reason, constructor order cannot be changed either.

CHAPTER 6

ADVANCED POINTER TOPICS

6.1. TWO-DIMENSIONAL ARRAYS

We have already seen that two-dimensional arrays are declared and accessed with two separate []s.

```
char month[ 12 ][ 10 ] = { "January", "February", "March",
    "April", "May", "June", "July", "August", "September",
    "October", "November", "December" };
```

This allocates an array of 120 consecutive characters. The second array bound is chosen to be 10 because the longest month name, September, has nine characters and one additional character is required for the zero terminator. The empty space after all other names is uninitialized.

J a n u a r y \0
F e b r u a r y \0
M a r c h \0
A p r i l \0
M a y \0
J u n e \0
J u l y \0
A u g u s t \0
S e p t e m b e r \0
O c t o b e r \0
N o v e m b e r \0
D e c e m b e r \0

month, the array name without any brackets, points to the beginning of the array. month[2] is also a pointer. It points to the third string (because the index starts at 0). month[2][3] is 'c'.

What is the type of month? Of month[2]? Of month + 2? There are unambiguous answers that are consequences of the array/pointer duality law. month[2] is a char[10]. It gets converted to a char* when used in any expression. For example, applying [3] to month[2] computes *(month[2] + 3). The expression month[2] + 3 has type char* and applying the * yields a character. Of course, month has type char[12][10]. To see the type of month + 2, imagine adding 1 to it. This moves it by 10 characters, which shows that month + 2 is a pointer to char[10].

Although month + 2 and month[2] have the same address value (both are 20 characters away from month), their types are very different. Adding 1 to month + 2 moves it by 10 characters. Adding 1 to month[2] moves it by one character. Note that month[2] is *(month + 2). In this situation, the * operator does not actually perform a memory lookup but changes the type of the pointer expression.

We have seen that month + 2 is a pointer to blocks of 10 characters. One might call it a char[10]*. Unfortunately, the C++ syntax requires a much more cumbersome description, because the * operator must come before the []. month + 2 is a constant pointer, always pointing to the same place. Imagine declaring a pointer variable m of the same type as month + 2. It is either

```
char *m[ 10 ];
```

or

```
char (*m)[ 10 ];
```

The operator precedence table tells us that [] has a higher precedence than *. That makes the first declaration an array of 10 char*. The second declaration is what we want: a pointer to char [10]s. The type of m, (and of month) can be obtained by removing the variable name from the declaration: They are char (*)[10].

Nothing charitable can be said about expressions like this. They are a consequence of declaring variables by placing type names and *s before variable names, [] behind. Languages like Pascal do not suffer from that problem, because array, pointer, and type specifiers all follow the variable name in a declaration.

You might find the following table helpful. Note the repeated application of the array-pointer duality law.

Expression	Type	Offset
month	char [12][10]	0
month + 2	char (*) [10]	20
*(month+2) = month [2]	char [10]	20
month [2]+3	char*	23
*(month[2]+3) = month [2][3]	char	

Note again that the first *, changing month + 2 to month[2], did not perform a memory lookup. It did affect the type, changing the pointer from a char (*) [10] to a char[10].

Advanced Pointer Topics **109**

● **Exercise 6.1.1.** Write a program that declares the month array and prints the integer values of the pointers month, month + 2, month[2], and so forth from the table and verify the offsets.

If a two-dimensional array is passed to a function, the first bound can be left open, but the second one must be specified:

```
dateprint( Date d, const char mnames[][ 10 ] )
{ cout << mnames[d.month - 1] << " " << d.day << ", " << d.year;
}
```

This is not surprising. For the address computation it is necessary to know by how many chars to move up to reach mnames + d.month - 1. This is also consistent with the discussion of Section 4.2. The empty [] behind an argument is identical to a * in front; that is, we could have equally well declared

```
dateprint( Date d, const char (*mnames)[ 10 ])
```

This is as it should be. When calling

```
dateprint( hiredate, month )
```

the value of the expression month is the array's starting address and of type char (*)[10]. It is copied into the local variable mnames. Again, mnames is not an array but merely a pointer variable. sizeof(mnames) is the same as the size of any pointer, certainly much smaller than sizeof(month) = 120. Only the array address has been transferred to dateprint.

In general, when a function receives a multidimensional array, all bounds but the first one must be specified:

```
void rubik( int cube[][ 3 ][ 3 ] );
```

● **Exercise 6.1.2.** Write a function

```
void matmul(
   const double a[ 3 ][ 3 ],
   const double b[ 3 ][ 3 ],
   double result[ 3 ][ 3 ])
```

that multiplies two 3 × 3 matrices.

● **Exercise 6.1.3.** Explain why the first 3 in the matmul declaration from the previous exercise can be omitted,

```
void matmul(
   const double a[][ 3 ],
   const double b[][ 3 ],
   double result[][ 3 ])
   // OK
```

but the second cannot:

```
void matmul( const double a[][],
  const double b[][],
  double result[][] )
  // WRONG
```

● **Exercise 6.1.4.** Because only the first array bound can be omitted, it is difficult to write a program that multiplies two square matrices of arbitrary size n. To do this, the function must receive double* s and do the address computation itself: a[i][j] becomes a[i * n + j]. Write a function

```
matmul( double* a, double* b, double* result, int n )
```

that performs this multiplication. To use the function, you must cast the argument types:

```
double a[ 4 ][ 4 ], b[ 4 ][ 4 ], c[ 4 ][ 4 ];
// ...
matmul( (double*)( a ), (double*)( b ), (double*)( c ), 4 );
```

● **Exercise 6.1.5.** What is wrong with this code?

```
double a[ 4 ][ 4 ], b[ 4 ][ 4 ];
// ...
double* result;
matmul( (double*)( a ), (double*)( b ), result, 4 );
```

● **Exercise 6.1.6.** Improve the matmul function to multiply two matrices of size m × n and n × k; the result is a m × k matrix.

6.2. ARRAYS OF POINTERS

Storing strings in a two-dimensional array is wasteful. The shorter strings do not need all the space allotted for them. It is better to store the characters somewhere and remember their locations in an array of pointers. The declaration is quite similar to a two-dimensional array

```
char* pmonth[ 12 ] = { "January", "February", "March",
      "April", "May", "June", "July", "August", "September",
      "October", "November", "December" };
```

but the memory layout is completely different:

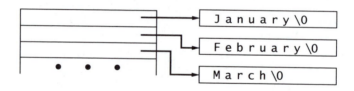

There is no guarantee that the month names are stored consecutively.

pmonth is an array of char*, containing the addresses of the individual strings. pmonth[i] is the ith address. Because pmonth points to an array of char*, its type is char**. Let us follow up on the computation of pmonth[2] [3].

Expression	Type	Offset
pmonth	char* [12]	0
pmonth+2	char**	$2 \times \text{sizeof}(\text{char*})$
*(pmonth+2) = pmonth[2]	char*	(outside pmonth)
pmonth [2] + 3	char*	(outside pmonth)
*(pmonth[2]+3) = pmonth[2][3]	char	

Although pmonth is an array of pointers, the magic of the array-pointer duality law makes it possible to access the jth element of the ith string as pmonth[i][j], giving the illusion of a two-dimensional array. Of course, it is not. There is no pmonth[2][9].

● **Exercise 6.2.1.** Write a program that declares the pmonth array and prints the integer values of the pointers pmonth, pmonth + 2, pmonth[2], and so forth from the table. Explain the output.

● **Exercise 6.2.2.** Write a function that can print a date in the format June 16, 1959. The prototype should be dateprint(Date d); use a static local array pmonth of pointers.

● **Exercise 6.2.3.** Given a type enum Language { ENGLISH, GERMAN, FRENCH } and three arrays of pointers to month names emonth, gmonth, fmonth, write a function

    dateprint(Date d, Language 1)

Inside the function, declare a

    static char** monthName[] = { emonth, gmonth, fmonth };

● **Exercise 6.2.4.** In Exercise 6.2.3, what is the type of monthName? What is sizeof (monthName)?

6.3. THE COMMAND LINE

Many operating systems interact with the user through a command line. Programs are executed when the program name is typed at a command prompt. The operating system locates the executable file and starts it. The program name can be followed by other items: options and redirection information. The operating system handles the redirection, connecting standard input and output to the specified files. The other command line arguments are passed to the program.

Consider a program called `count` that counts how often a word occurs in the input. The word to be searched for is specified on the command line. If desired, a `-i` option can be specified to make the comparison case-insensitive. A `-n` option counts all words except the one specified. It is a common convention that program options start with a `-`. Some programs require that the options appear in a certain order, but we will write `count` to accept the options and the word to match in any order. For example,

```
count dracula <input.txt -i
```

counts how often the word "dracula" occurs in the input text, ignoring the distinction between upper- and lowercase letters. The input could come from the keyboard, but in the call here it is redirected from a file. (In fact, without redirection this program is next to useless. When was the last time you felt inclined to type a bunch of words on the keyboard, just to be told how often you entered one of them?)

We need to know how our program can gain access to the command line. The strings on the command line are passed to `main`. The correct declaration for `main` is actually

```
int main( int argc, char *argv[] )
```

When `main` starts, it receives an argument count (including the program name but excluding redirection information—in the foregoing example, `argc` is 3) and an array of string pointers, as shown in the following figure:

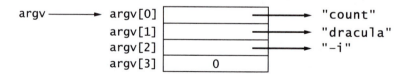

`argv[ 2 ]` is a pointer to the string `"-i"`, and `argv[ 2 ][ 0 ]` is the `'-'` character. `argv` is a pointer to an array of pointers. Note that the redirection information (`<input.txt`) is stripped off by the operating system and not included in `argv`.

● **Exercise 6.3.1.** What is `sizeof( argv )` ? The type of `argv` ?

Here is the program. Pay particular attention to the characteristic loop analyzing `argv`.

```
#include <stream.h>
#include <string.h>
#include <ctype.h>

void usage( char* progname )
{ cerr << "USAGE: " << progname << " word [-n] [-i]\n";
}
```

```
int stricmp( const char* s, const char* t )
// case-insensitive string compare
{ int d;
  while(( d = toupper( *s ) - toupper( *t )) == 0 && *s )
  { s++; t++; }
  return d;
}


int main( int argc, char* argv[] )
{ int countMatch = 1;
  int caseSens = 1;
  char* mw = 0;                    // the word to match
  int count = 0;

  for( int i = 1; i < argc; i++ )
    if( argv[ i ][ 0 ] == '-' )
      switch( argv[ i ][ 1 ] )
      { case 'n': countMatch = 0; break;
        case 'i': caseSens = 0; break;
        // more options can be added later
        default: usage( argv[ 0 ] ); return 1;
      }
      else
      { if( mw )
        { cerr << argv[ 0 ] <<
            ": Can count only one word.  \n";
          return 1;
        }
        else mw = argv[ i ]; // doesn't copy the word,
                             // just the address
      }

  char word[ 100 ];
  while( cin >> word ) // fails at end of file
  { int match = (caseSens ?
      strcmp( word, mw ) : stricmp( word, mw )) == 0;
    count += countMatch ^ !match;
  }
  if( !countMatch ) cout << "Not ";
  cout << mw << ": " << count << "\n"
  return 0;
}
```

Note that the program name (count) in argv[0] is passed to the usage function—after all, someone might have renamed the program file to ct, and the program might have been launched as ct dracula -i <input.txt. We programmed main to return an integer value, 1 for a command line error and 0

for successful completion. This return value can be tested by the operating system (through $? in Unix, IF ERRORLEVEL in DOS.) The convention is that a zero return value from main indicates success, a nonzero value failure. You can indicate what kind of failure by exiting with different error codes. Return values are optional. You could return a random value (by having no return statement in main), but the polite thing is to return 0.

The argv variable is an argument of main. Like all other array arguments, it is a pointer variable, initialized to point to the actual array. The strings are stored elsewhere. We can take advantage of that and rewrite the for loop:

```
for( char* progname = *argv; --argc; )
  if( **++argv == '-' )
    switch( *( *argv + 1 ))
    { case 'n': countMatch = 0; break;
      case 'i': caseSens = 0; break;
      default: usage( progname ); return 1;
    }
  else mw = *argv;
```

● **Exercise 6.3.2.** Explain the meaning of **++argv.

You will find code like this in some programs. I cannot find a convincing reason to advocate it. Sure, the pointer access and increment are marginally more efficient, and you can show off your mastery of pointers, but this is hardly a time-critical code. The run time saved over the lifetime of the program will be dwarfed by the time spent by future maintainers who have to decipher the code.

● **Exercise 6.3.3.** Enhance the count program to print the counts for a number of words, for example,

```
count  transylvania  station  <input.txt
```

● **Exercise 6.3.4.** Write a program that takes a string argument on the command line, reads in lines from standard input, and prints the lines containing that string to standard output. Call the program find. A sample call is

```
find  object  <chapter1.txt
```

● **Exercise 6.3.5.** Write a program that takes a number of strings on the command line, reads in lines from standard input, and prints the lines containing *all* those strings. For example,

```
find object oriented <chapter1.txt
```

● **Exercise 6.3.6.** Modify the program in Exercise 6.3.5 to support a -*n* option. If it is present (as any one of the strings, not necessarily the first or last one), all lines containing at least *n* of the keywords are printed. If not, all keywords must be present for the line to be printed. For example,

```
find object oriented programming -2 <chapter1.txt
```

You will need to convert the string "2 " into a number. Use

```
if( argv[ i ][ 0 ] == '-' ) n = atoi( argv[ i ] + 1 )
```

6.4. POINTERS TO FUNCTIONS

Consider the task of plotting the graph of a function f for x-values in an interval $[x_{min}, x_{max}]$. We will make use of the Grid class of Section 5.3, which encapsulates a screen grid of 24×80 characters. To fit the graph, we will scale the x-values so that x_{min} corresponds to column 0, x_{max} to column 79. Similarly, we will scale the y-values. Here is an outline of the program:

```
double f( double x ) // the function to be plotted
{ return( 2 - x + x * x * x );
}

void plot( double xmin = -10, double xmax = 10 )
{ Grid disp;
  disp.clear();

  double y[ Grid::XSIZE ];
  double ymin, ymax;
  for ( int i = 0; i < Grid::XSIZE; i++ )
  { double x = xmin + ( xmax - xmin ) * i / ( Grid::XSIZE - 1 );
    y[ i ] = f( x );
    if ( i == 0 ) ymin = ymax = y[ 0 ];
    else
    { if ( y[ i ] < ymin ) ymin = y[ i ];
      if ( y[ i ] > ymax ) ymax = y[ i ];
    }
  }

  int y0 = ( Grid::YSIZE - 1 ) * ymax / ( ymax - ymin );
  int x0 = ( Grid::XSIZE - 1 ) * xmin / ( xmin - xmax );
  disp.line( 0, y0, Grid::XSIZE - 1, y0 ); // x-axis
  disp.line( x0, 0, x0, Grid::YSIZE - 1 ); // y-axis
  for ( i = 0; i < Grid::XSIZE; i++ )
    disp.set( i, int(( Grid::YSIZE - 1 )
      * ( ymax - y[ i ]) / ( ymax - ymin )));
  disp.show();
}
```

Note how inflexible the plot function is. The x-bounds are passed as parameters, but the function f is hard-wired into the code. It would be desirable to supply the function as another parameter. For example,

```
plot( sin, 0, 3.15 );
```

In C++ this can be achieved by giving plot a *pointer* to a function, that is, the starting address of its code. The starting address of a function can be obtained by simply omitting the () from the function name, for example, sin. (This is entirely analogous to arrays, where the starting address is obtained by removing the [].)

We will modify plot to receive a pointer pf to a function. For example, in the given call pf will be initialized with sin, the starting address of the sine function. To see how pf must be declared, observe that pf is a pointer to a function; hence, *pf is a function, and the declaration is

```
double (*pf)( double )
```

The parentheses around *pf are necessary because the operator precedence table tells us that the function call () operator is stronger than *. Without the parentheses,

```
double *pf( double )
```

would declare a function (and not a variable) that eats a double and returns a double*. (The placement of spaces before or after an * is immaterial.) The function pointer is used inside plot as

```
y[ i ] = (*pf)( x );
```

because (*pf) is a function and capable of consuming x.

● **Exercise 6.4.1.** What is the size of a pointer to a function on your system? Probably the shortest program to determine this is: cout << sizeof(main). Of course, this tells only the size of the pointer to the starting address of the function, not the number of bytes in the function code.

● **Exercise 6.4.2.** Write a function that computes a numerical value for an integral $\int_a^b f(x)dx$. a, b, and f are passed as function arguments:

```
double integrate( double a, double b, double (*f)( double ));
```

To compute the integral, split the interval $[a, b]$ into n pieces (starting with $n = 16$) and add up the sizes of the rectangles with base $= (b - a)/n$ and height $= (*f)$ (midpoint of ith interval). This sum of rectangles approximates the integral. Then double the number of intervals n. Compute the sum again. Compare it to the previous sum. Keep on going until two consecutive results differ by less than, say, 10^{-6}, or n becomes too large.

Try not to recompute all function values in each iteration, but reuse values from the previous one.

Test your function with the following integrals:

```
#include <math.h>

double f( double x ) { return ( x*x*x - x + 1 ); }
```

```
cout << integrate( 0, 3.14159, sin );
cout << integrate( 0, 1, exp );
cout << integrate( -1, 1, f );
```

A common application for pointers to functions is sorting. Algorithms to sort an array a typically consist of some way of selecting elements a[i], a[j] to compare them and then swapping them if they are out of order. Merely by modifying what it means to be "out of order", we can implement different sorting behaviors. For example, strings can be sorted lexicographically, or without regard to case, or taking into account sort orders of European alphabets (such as aäbc . . . in German), or by length first, or numerous other ways.

Here is such a flexible string sort function. To keep the code at a minimum, we are merely using the (inefficient) bubblesort algorithm.

```
void sort( char* a[], int n,
    int (*comp)( char*, char* ) =strcmp )
{ // bubblesort
  for( int i = n - 1; i > 0; i-- )
    for( int j = 0; j < i; j++ )
    if( (*comp)( a[ j ], a[ j + 1 ]) > 0 )
    { // lines not in order—swap them
      char* temp = a[ j ];
      a[ j ] = a[ j + 1 ];
      a[ j + 1 ] = temp;
    }
}
```

The argument comp is a pointer to a function returning a positive number if the strings are out of order. The default comparison is to use the standard strcmp. By calling

```
sort( a, sizeof( a ) / sizeof( *a ), stricmp )
```

the strings are sorted without regard to case. (See Exercise 6.3.1 for the stricmp function.)

● **Exercise 6.4.3.** Improve the sort function by implementing the quicksort algorithm.

● **Exercise 6.4.4.** Write a comparison function that can be used to sort strings by increasing length, with strings of the same length sorted lexicographically.

Pointers to functions are extremely useful. Whenever you need to communicate to a function some behavior that is too complicated to put into a number, consider writing a small function and passing a pointer to it. If you have a bunch of those, it can be handy to pack them into an array. Consider, for example, a stack-based calculator program receiving commands

+	Pop two numbers off the stack, add them, and push the result
-	Same, but subtract the first number popped from the second
*	Same, but multiply the two numbers popped
/	Same, but divide the second number popped by the first
xchg	Exchange the top two stack elements
print	Pop and print the top of stack
dup	Duplicate the top of stack (for example, dup print is a nondestructive print)

For example, 4 dup dup * xchg 2 / - computes $4^2 - 4/2$.

To execute a command, we can keep an array of commands and a parallel array of function pointers:

```
char* name[ 7 ]
    = { "+", "-", "*", "/", "xchg", "print", "dup" };
void (*action[ 7 ])()
    = { add, sub, mul, div, xchg, print, dup };
```

This says, "action is an array of seven things whose * are functions with no arguments and returning void." In the next section we will see how to clarify declarations like this. Each of the elements of action is the address of an actual function, which must be supplied; for example,

```
void sub() { double b = pop(); push( pop() - b ); }
```

The following function finds and executes a command:

```
void exec( char* cmd )
{ for( int i = 0; i < sizeof( name ) / sizeof( char* ); i++ )
    if( strcmp( cmd, name[ i ] ) == 0 )
    { (*action[ i ])();
      return;
    }
}
```

● **Exercise 6.4.5.** Implement the stack calculator using this technique. Read in the commands from the command line:

```
for( int i = 1; i < argc; i++ )
  if ( argv[ i ]   is a number )
    push( atof( argv[ i ]);
  else
    exec( argv[ i ]);
```

The commands can then be entered as follows:

```
calc 4 dup dup * xchg 2 / - print
```

● **Exercise 6.4.6.** Enhance the calculator with commands for sqrt, sin, cos, exp, and log.

● **Exercise 6.4.7.** Combine the plot function and the calculator to plot an arbitrary function that can be specified on the command line. For example,

```
plot  dup 2 xchg - xchg dup dup * * +
```

pushes numbers x between -10 and 10 onto the stack, applies the commands dup 2 xchg - xchg dup dup * * + (which compute $2 - x + x^3$), pops the result, and plots it. *Hint*: Write a function double execcmds(double x) that pushes x on the stack, executes all commands in argv, and returns pop(). Pass its address to plot. (Under Unix you need to escape the * character in the command line — use *.)

● **Exercise 6.4.8.** Add a constructor Set(int (*f)(int)) to the Set class of Exercise 5.6.2 that constructs the set of all x, $0 \le x < 256$ for which the function returns a true (nonzero) value. For example, if int isprime(int n) tests whether n is a prime number, then Set(isprime) returns the set of primes < 256.

6.5. TYPE DEFINITIONS

To clear up complicated type declarations such as arrays of function pointers, the typedef construct can be used. typedef introduces new names for types. The general rule for its use is:

- Pick a name for the desired type.
- Write a declaration defining the name as a variable of the desired type.
- Precede the declaration by typedef.

For example, to make String a synonym for char*, first think how you would declare a single String as a char* variable:

```
char* String;
```

Now introduce typedef :

```
typedef char* String;
```

The type String can be used like any other type:

```
String s,t;

int main( int argc, String argv[] );
```

These type synonyms are smart. In the foregoing example, both s and t are char*, whereas in the declaration

```
char* s, t; // maybe WRONG
```

s is a char* but t is a char, because the * really binds with the s.

To untangle the declaration of function pointers, it is quite common to declare types

```
typedef int (*Stringfun)( String, String );
```

making `Stringfun` a pointer to an integer function eating two strings. Thereafter, such function pointers can be declared as

    Stringfun comp;

and arrays of them as

    Stringfun sortfuns[3] = { strcmp, stricmp, numcmp; };

This is a big improvement over int (*sortfuns[3])(char*, char*).

Pascal Note

typedef is not quite the same as the Pascal **type**. It merely introduces synonyms for the same type. For example, String and char* variables can be freely assigned to each other. The Pascal **type** introduces new types, incompatible with the defining **type**.

● **Exercise 6.5.1.** Write a type definition Mat3 for a 3 × 3 matrix. For example,

    Mat3 a,b;

should declare two such matrices, and the matmul function of Exercise 6.1.2 could have the prototype

    matmul(Mat3 a, Mat3 b, Mat3 result)

● **Exercise 6.5.2.** Using the Mat3 type of the previous exercise, why can't we write a function

    Mat3 matmul(Mat3 a, Mat3 b)
    { Mat3 r;
        // compute r as the matrix product of a and b
        return r;
    }

    c = matmul(a, b);

● **Exercise 6.5.3.** Declare a function f receiving an int and returning a pointer to a procedure without arguments. Do this without, then with, typedef.

● **Exercise 6.5.4.** As we have seen, the C++ style pointer syntax can lead to declarations that some might find hard to read. In this exercise we consider a logical alternative. We choose ∧ as pointer dereferencing operator and make it postfix. We separate type and variable names. The following examples should speak for themselves.

```
int x;            x: int;
char* c;          c: ∧char;          Pointer to char
double a[ 10 ];   a: [ 10 ]double;   10 doubles
char *p, *q       p,q: ∧char;
```

`char (*a)[ 10 ];`	`a: ^[ 10 ]char;`	Pointer to 10 char
`c = (*a)[ k ];`	`c = a^[ k ];`	
`char *b[ 10 ];`	`b: [ 10 ]^char;`	10 pointers to char
`c = *b[ k ];`	`c= b[ k ]^;`	
`char **c;`	`c: ^^char;`	Pointer to pointer to char
`int (*f)(int);`	`f: ^(int)int;`	Pointer to `int` -> `int` function
`n = (*f)( x );`	`n = f^( x );`	
`int (*g[ 10 ])( int );`	`g: [ 10 ]^(int)int;`	10 pointers to `int` -> `int` function
`n = (*g[ k ])( x );`	`n = g[ k ]^( x );`	
`char *p = "Hi";`	`p: ^char = "Hi";`	Cannot initialize two variables
`Employee* e[ 100 ]`	`e: [ 100 ]^Employee;`	
`e[ i ] -> age`	`e[ i ]^.age`	

Look, ma, no parentheses! Let us refer to this as the D-style syntax. Write a program `encrypt` that reads a D-style type declaration such as p: `^[ 10 ] int;` and translates it into the C++ equivalent `int (*p)[ 10 ]`.

● **Exercise 6.5.5.** Write a program `explain` that translates C++ style type declarations into D-style. (*Hint*: Use recursive-descent parsing.)

6.6. ERROR HANDLING

Consider a stack class

```
class Stack
{ int stack[ STACKSIZE ];
  int sptr;
public:
  void push( int );
  int pop();
  // ...
};
```

How should errors (underflow, overflow) be handled? In general, there are four different possibilities:

- Return an error code
- Set a global variable
- Abort the program with an error message
- Throw an exception (see Section 12.4)

None of these is ideal. If a function already returns a value (such as pop), it is not feasible to return an error code because there is no way of distinguishing it from an integer return value. (Functions returning a pointer are luckier; they can send a 0 pointer as an error code). Setting a global variable is ugly and error-prone. (Someone else might reset it.) It also requires constant monitoring of the variable.

Terminating the current program works fine for debugging. Then we can use the `assert` macro to test for error conditions. This macro, defined in assert.h, tests a condition and aborts the program with an error message when the condition is not true. Here is a typical example.

```
int Stack::pop()
{ assert( sptr > 0 );
   return s [ --sptr ];
}
```

Of course, abandoning the program is not a good idea for most commercial software. Users do not enjoy losing their work on account of an internal error in a word processor or spreadsheet. The `assert` macro can be redefined to do nothing, simply by compiling with the preprocessor variable NDEBUG defined. But then no error checking occurs at all, which is also dangerous. *Throwing an exception,* as we will see in section 12.4, can be problematic too, because an uncaught exception terminates the program.

The most flexible and least distasteful method is to use a user-modifiable error function. (This then leaves the class user the choice between the four options.) We demonstrate this method with the stack class:

```
void error( const char* s ) // default error handler
{ cout << "Stack error: " << s << ".\n" ;
   exit( 1 ); // exit with an error code
}

typedef void (*ErrorFun)( const char* );
ErrorFun stackError = error;

int Stack::push( int n )
{ if( sptr < STACKSIZE ) return s[ sptr++ ] = n;
   else { (*stackError)( "Overflow" ); return n; }
}

int Stack::pop()
{ if( sptr > 0 )return( s[ --sptr ] );
   else { (*stackError)( "Underflow" ); return 0; }
}
```

Once the code has been fully debugged and is ready to ship, the error function could be replaced with

```
void ignore( const char* s ) {}
```

This replacement can be performed with a function that provides access to the stackError variable:

```
ErrorFun setStackError( ErrorFun f )
{ ErrorFun r = stackError;
  stackError = f;
  return r;
}
```

To install the new error handler, call **setStackError(ignore)**. The function returns the old error handler, making it possible to install **ignore** temporarily and later restore the old handler.

It would be desirable to package the error-handler variable more closely into the stack class. The function pointer could be a data member, giving each instance of the stack class its own personal error handler. For stacks this might be quite reasonable, because any program will only have a few of them. On the other hand, in a matrix class it makes no sense to store an individual function pointer with each matrix. If a thousand matrices are allocated, there would be that many copies of an identical pointer. Or worse, if different matrices have different error handlers, which one should be chosen in an operation involving two matrices? The answer is to make **ErrorFun error** a **static** data member inside the stack class, shared by all instances (see Section 5.3).

```
class Stack
{ int s[ STACKSIZE ];
  int sptr;
  static ErrorFun error;
  static void defaultError ( const char* );
public:
  Stack();
  static ErrorFun setError( ErrorFun );
  //  ...
};

void Stack::defaultError( const char* s )
{ cout << "Stack error: " << s << ".\n" )
  exit( 1 ); // exit with an error code
}

ErrorFun Stack::error = Stack::defaultError;
Stack::Stack()
{ sptr = 0;
}

ErrorFun Stack::setError( ErrorFun f )
{ ErrorFun r = error;
  error = f;
  return r;
}
```

```
int Stack::push( int n )
{ if( sptr < STACKSIZE )
    return s[ sptr++ ] = n;
  else
    { (*error)( "Overflow" ); return n; }
}
```

Note that calling the error function does note necessarily mean exiting the function or the program. We must take care to keep going with reasonable defaults in case the error function merely records the problem and returns.

To set the error function, the client calls the static member function

```
Stack::setError( ignore );
```

This changes the error function for all stacks. (Recall that a static member function has no implicit this argument and can act on the static data members only.)

● **Exercise 6.6.1.** Exercise 5.3.7 discusses a string class with fixed storage for each string. Add an error handler to the class. Possible errors are overflow during concatenation and access of nonexistent substrings.

● 6.7. PITFALLS

6.7.1. Using Commas when Accessing Two-Dimensional Arrays

Elements of a two-dimensional array should be accessed with two separate [], for example, a[i][j]. Surprisingly, though, the Pascal-style a[i, j] is not a syntax error. The comma in i, j is a comma operator, evaluating and discarding its first argument i and then returning the value of the second operand j. a[i, j] is therefore identical to a[j], a pointer to the *j*th row of the array. Usually, this use does lead to a syntax error. If a is a double array of char, then

```
char ch = a[ i, j ]; // WRONG
```

is illegal—a char* cannot be placed into a char without conversion. But in some contexts, both a char and char* can be acceptable:

```
cout << a[ i, j ]; // Syntax OK, will print a[ j ]
```

6.7.2. Forgetting Parentheses when Evaluating a Pointer to a Function

If a function receives a pointer pf to another function, it must be called as (*pf)() or pf(), not simply as pf.

```
void exec( void (*pf)() )
{ // ...
  pf; // WRONG
}
```

The statement pf; simply accesses the value of pf (the starting address of some function) and does nothing with it.

C H A P T E R   7

OVERLOADING

7.1. FUNCTION OVERLOADING

Certain function names are meaningful for a wide range of types. It makes sense to compute the length of a string, of a linked list, of a vector, and it is tedious to have to come up with unique names stringLength, listLength, vectorLength. There is the temptation to come up with cryptic abbreviations, strlen, lstlen, veclen. (The standard C library is certainly guilty of that. What do you think strrchr does?) And it is all so unnecessary. The compiler could just look inside the (...) and call the appropriate function, depending on whether it finds a string, list, or vector.

C++ does precisely that: The compiler watches the argument(s) of the calls and picks the right functions.

```
int length( char* s )
{ char* t = s;
  while( *t ) t++;
  return t - s;
}

double length( double vec[], int n )
{ for( double r = 0; --n >= 0; r += vec[ n ] * vec[ n ] )
    ;
  return sqrt( r );
}

int n = length( "Harry" ); // calls int length( char* )
double l, x[ 3 ] = { 1, 0, -2 };
l = length( x, 3 ); // calls double length( double*, int )
```

● **Exercise 7.1.1.** Write two functions power that compute a^b. One of them,

```
double power( double a, int b )
```

should compute $a \times a \times \cdots \times a$ (*b* times) (or $-b$ times the reciprocal if $b < 0$), the other

```
double power( double a, double b )
```

should compute $e^{b \cdot \log(a)}$ (if a > 0). Write a short program to check that power (2, 0.5) and power(-2, -2) get computed correctly.

Type conversions, such as int to double, are added if necessary to make the values in the call conform to the arguments in the function. The compiler goes through the following steps to find a matching function:

- If an exact match of the argument type is found, use it.
- If there is a unique function that matches after the *promotions* char, unsigned char, short → int; unsigned short → int (if sizeof(short) < sizeof(int)) or unsigned (otherwise); float → double, use that function.
- If there is a unique function that matches after other standard type conversions, use that function.
- If there is a unique user-defined conversion (Section 7.4) achieving a match, use that function.

0 is an exact match for an int and can be converted to a pointer or double by a standard conversion. char and short are not considered exact matches for int. Standard conversions that might lead to information loss (such as int to char, double to int) are considered for matching. Use casts char(ch), int(x) if necessary.

If there is more than one argument, then the foregoing matching is applied to all arguments. Only if a unique function can be found that achieves a better match in one argument and at least as good a match in all others will it be taken.

The rules are complex. You should attempt not to create situations in which the rules do not obviously yield intuitive results.

One can think of member functions as overloaded as well. There can be a List::length(), Queue::length(), Vec3::length(). In compiling x.length(), one of them is selected, depending on the class to which x belongs. No type conversion is applied.

● **Exercise 7.1.2.** Write overloaded print functions to print an array of integers, an Employee record, and an array of Employee records.

● **Exercise 7.1.3.** Overload the min function to find

- The minimum of two integers
- The minimum of two doubles
- The minimum of an array of integers
- The minimum of an array of doubles

7.2. OPERATOR OVERLOADING

By defining special functions, the built-in operators can be defined to act on structured data types. Suppose a function

```
String operator+( const String&, const String& );
```

is defined, returning the result of concatenating the two argument strings. The addition

```
String a;
String b("Harry"), c(" Hacker");

a = b + c; // concatenate strings
```

is translated into a function call a = operator+(b, c). Of course, if you like typing, you can legally code the explicit call as well.

The following operators can be overloaded:

```
+  -  *  /  %  ^  &  |  ~  !  ,
=  <  >  << >> <= >= == && ||
++ -- += -= *= /= %= ^= &= |=
!= <<= >>=  -> [] () new  delete
```

The last four are subscript, function call, free store allocation, and recycling. You can attach `operator` functions only to existing operators. You cannot design new operators, tempting as it may be (:=, <>, |x| for absolute values...). You cannot change the precedence, prefix/postfix application, or the *arity*: no postfix !, binary ~, or unary ^ are possible. `operator->` takes no argument and must return a pointer to a structure.

Operator functions must take at least one `struct` (or `class`) argument. Thus, it is not possible to define

```
char* operator+( char*, char* ); // WRONG
```

to concatenate strings given as `char*`. Operator functions can be either global functions or member functions of a class:

```
class Vec3
{ // ...
public:
  double operator*( const Vec3& ) const;
  // ...
};
```

or

```
class Vec3
{ // ...
public:
  friend double operator*( const Vec3&, const Vec3& );
  // ...
};
```

Depending on which is used, the expression v * w is translated to either v.operator*(w) or operator*(v, w). Similarly, a unary minus can be supplied either as a member Vec3 Vec3::operator-() or as a nonmember Vec3 operator-(Vec3). Depending on the choice, -v is either v.operator-() or operator-(v). The choice usually depends on whether a type conversion should be permitted on the first argument (see Section 7.3). Exceptions are operator=, operator[], operator(), and operator->, which must be member functions.

No special meaning is attached to any of the operators. It is entirely possible to redefine + to denote vector subtraction—an exercise of dubious value. In particular, nothing dictates that an operator= must be assignment or that operator+= makes a += b the same as a = a + b. It is easy to go overboard. Is += really a good choice for stack pushing? Or () for traversing through a linked list? It seems wise to restrict oneself to time-honored mathematical notation, possibly augmented by an occasional cuteness such as using || for testing whether lines are parallel.

As you have undoubtedly realized by now, the "get from" cin >> x and "put to" cout << x operators are overloaded shifts << and >>. Details are given in Chapter 8.

Four operators, namely + - * and &, can be overloaded as unary or binary operators. For example, -f invokes the unary operator-(Fraction), whereas f - g invokes the binary operator-(Fraction, Fraction).

There is a minor complication with the ++ and -- operators. These operators have both prefix and postfix versions. Both are unary, and hence the number of arguments cannot be used to differentiate between them. Rather than inventing yet another bit of syntax, the following arbitrary rule was imposed: The prefix operation ++f invokes the function operator++(Fraction), and the postfix operation f++ invokes the function operator++(Fraction, int). The second integer argument is just a dummy that is inserted to distinguish the two functions.

For the remainder of this section we will analyze some examples of overloading. We are not quite ready to tackle concatenation in the string class, because of the memory management issue (where to put the concatenated string?), so we start with complex numbers, which use a fixed amount of memory. Complex numbers are sums

$$a + b\mathbf{i}$$

where a, b are real numbers (the real and imaginary parts) and $\mathbf{i}$, the imaginary unit, has the property that $\mathbf{i}^2 = -1$. This uniquely defines addition, subtraction, multiplication, and division:

$$(a + b\mathbf{i}) \pm (c + d\mathbf{i}) = a \pm c + (b \pm d)\mathbf{i}$$
$$(a + b\mathbf{i}) \cdot (c + d\mathbf{i}) = ac - bd + (ac \pm bd)\mathbf{i}$$
$$1/(a + b\mathbf{i}) = (a - b\mathbf{i})/(a^2 + b^2) \qquad \text{unless both } a \text{ and } b \text{ are } 0$$
$$(a + b\mathbf{i})/(c + d\mathbf{i}) = (a + b\mathbf{i}) \cdot 1/(c + d\mathbf{i})$$

Here is the Complex class:

```
class Complex
{ double re, im;
public:
  Complex( double r = 0, double i = 0 ) { re = r; im = i; }
  double real() const { return re; }
  double imag() const { return im; }
  Complex inv() const;
  Complex operator-() const { return Complex( -re, -im ); }
  friend Complex operator+(const Complex& x, const Complex& y);
  friend Complex operator-(const Complex& x, const Complex& y);
  friend Complex operator*(const Complex& x, const Complex& y);
  friend Complex operator/(const Complex& x, const Complex& y);
  Complex& operator+=( const Complex& y );
  Complex& operator-=( const Complex& y );
  Complex& operator*=( const Complex& y )
  { return *this = *this * y; }
  Complex& operator/=( const Complex& y )
  { return *this = *this * y.inv(); }
  friend int operator==( const Complex& x, const Complex& y );
  friend int operator!=( const Complex& x, const Complex& y );
};

Complex Complex::inv() const
{ double norm = re * re + im * im;
  if( norm == 0 ) return *this; // ( 0, 0 ) has no inverse
  return Complex( re / norm, -im / norm );
}

Complex operator+( const Complex& x, const Complex& y )
{ return Complex( x.re + y.re, x.im + y.im );
}

inline Complex operator-( const Complex& x, const Complex& y )
{ return x + ( -y );
}

Complex operator*( const Complex& x, const Complex& y )
{ return Complex( x.re * y.re - x.im * y.im,
  x.im * y.re + x.re * y.im );
}

Complex operator/( const Complex& x, const Complex& y )
{ return x * y.inv();
}
```

```
Complex& Complex::operator+=( const Complex& y )
{ re += y.re;
  im += y.im;
  return *this;
}
```

We have not opted for maximum consistency or speed in these examples but rather show a variety of possibilities. In practice, all functions would be coded simply by combining the proper re and im rather than calling other functions. This is boring but speedy.

The constructor Complex has default arguments:

```
Complex i( 0, 1 ); // 0 + 1i
Complex a( 2 );    // 2 + 0i
Complex z;         // 0 + 0i
```

It is instructive to see what happens in memory when

```
c = a * b;
```

is executed:

- Copies of a and b are made and placed in the local variables x and y of operator*.
- A temporary variable is created on the stack of operator* and initialized with re = x.re*y.re - x.im*y.im, im = x.im*y.re + x.re*y.im.
- The contents of that temporary variable are copied to another temporary variable on the stack frame of the caller, and the function exits.
- The result is copied from the second temporary variable into c.

The first copying can be avoided by defining

```
Complex operator*( const Complex&, const Complex& )
```

instead. The other copies cannot easily be prevented.

● **Exercise 7.2.1.** Write a program that makes a very approximate plot of the *Mandelbrot set*. Consider complex numbers $z_0 = x + yi, -2 \le x \le 1, -1 \le y \le 1$. If the sequence $z_{n+1} = z_n^2 + z_0$ does not diverge, then z_0 is in the Mandelbrot set. It can be shown that the series diverges if $|z_n| \ge 4$ for some n. You only need to check up to $n = 64$. Use the Grid class to show the points in the Mandelbrot set.

● **Exercise 7.2.2.** Implement the += -= *= /= functions as nonmembers

```
Complex& operator+=( Complex&, Complex )
```

Why must the first argument be a reference argument? Why is this actually not desirable? (*Hint*: What is the effect of x += z if x is a double?)

● **Exercise 7.2.3.** Why wasn't operator== defined as a member function in the foregoing class definition?

● **Exercise 7.2.4.** Consider the string class of Exercise 5.3.7. Define `operator+` (concatenation) and all relational operators (`== != < > <= >=`). Should these be members or nonmembers? (*Hint:* `if( "Harry" < s )...`).

It is worth noting that most operators can be coded as friend functions, receiving arguments of either type `Complex` or `const Complex&`. The latter is more efficient, because it passes only the address of the complex number to the function rather than two `double`s. Either the `+= -= *= /=` and (if desired) `++ --` must be member functions, which allow modification of the first argument, or the first argument must be a non-const reference.

For a realistic example involving overloading of function call `()`, consider a `Polynomial` class. To avoid memory issues, we restrict ourselves to polynomials of degree ≤ 10 and store the coefficients $a_0, \ldots, a_{10}$ of a polynomial

$$a_0 + a_1 x + a_2 x^2 + \cdots + a_{10} x^{10}$$

in an array `coeff`:

```
class Polynomial
{ double coeff[ MAXDEGREE + 1 ];
public:
  Polynomial();
  // ...
  void set( int n, double c ) { coeff[ n ] = c; }
  double operator()( double ) const;
};

Polynomial::Polynomial()
{ for( int i = 0; i <= MAXDEGREE; i++ ) coeff[ i ] = 0;
}
```

We want `()` to denote evaluation, for example

```
Polynomial p;
p.set( 0, 2 ); p.set( 1, -1 ); p.set( 3, 1 ); // p = x³ − x + 2
cout << p( 3 );                                 // Plug in 3 for x:
                                                // 27 − 3 + 2 = 26
```

We use Horner's method:

```
double Polynomial::operator()( double x ) const
{ double r = 0;
  for( int i = MAXDEGREE; i >= 0; i-- )
    r = r * x + coeff[ i ];
  return r;
}
```

● **Exercise 7.2.5.** Write operator functions to add, subtract, and multiply polynomials (truncate degrees > 10).

● **Exercise 7.2.6.** Write a member function Polynomial::plot so that f. plot (a, b) plots f between a and b. Write a member function deriv that computes the derivative.

● **Exercise 7.2.7.** Build a stack-based polynomial calculator. x enters the linear polynomial x; a number enters a constant polynomial on the stack. All other polynomials are obtained from them by reverse Polish notation:

```
2 x * 1 - x * 0.5 + x * 4 +
```

creates $2x^3 - x^2 + 0.5x + 4$. ' computes the derivative, ? prints the top of the stack, and Q quits.

● **Exercise 7.2.8.** Overload +, -, * for Vec3 objects. Define a unary - and use it for the binary - : a - b is a + (-b). Be sure to include scalar multiplication double * Vec3, Vec3 * double, dot product Vec3 * Vec3, and cross product Vec3 % Vec3. (Unfortunately, you cannot use x for cross product.)

● **Exercise 7.2.9.** Overload * for the Mat3 * Mat3 and Mat3 * Vec3 (Vec3s are column vectors.)

● **Exercise 7.2.10.** Consider the Point and Line classes of Exercises 5.2.4 and 5.4.4. Implement - to join two points to a line, + to intersect two lines in a point, and || to test whether two lines are parallel as well as to compute the line passing through a given point parallel to a given line.

7.3. OVERLOADED operator[]

In the IntArray class of Section 5.6, we already advertised an overloaded []. Here is the code:

```
class IntArray
{ int value[ MAXSIZE ];
  int lower, upper;
public:
  // ...
  int& operator[]( int );
};

int& IntArray::operator[]( int n )
{ if( n < lower || n > upper )
    error( "Index out of bounds" );
  return value[ n - lower ];
}
```

Because the function return type is int&, a[n] actually returns a pointer to a.value[n] and can be used on the left side of an assignment:

```
a[ 2 ] = 5;
```

means

```
* (pointer to a.value[ 2 - lower ]) = 5;
```

Another common application of overloaded [] is an *associative array*. This is a data structure that associates certain keys, typically strings, with other values. For example, .

```
AssocArray a;
a[ "Harry" ] = 5.3;
cout << a[ "Harry" ];
```

A typical implementation consists of an array of strings and a parallel array of double. We use a simple hashing scheme for the strings. If a hash collision is found, the next available entry in the string array is used.

```
class AssocArray
{ char* key[ MAXENTRY ];
  double val[ MAXENTRY ];
  char buffer[ BUFSIZE ]; // stores actual strings
  int bufend;

  int locate( const char* ) const; // find hash location
                                    // of a string
public:
  // ...
  double& operator[]( char* );
};

int AssocArray::locate( const char* s ) const
{ int h = hash( s ) % MAXENTRY;
  int i = h;
  do
  { if( key[ i ] == 0 || strcmp( s, key[ i ]) == 0 )
      return i;
    if( ++i >= MAXENTRY ) i = 0;
  }
  while( i != h )
  return( -1 );
}

double& AssocArray::operator[]( char* s )
{ int i;
  if( key[ i = locate( s )] == 0 ) // new string
  { key[ i ] = buffer + bufend;
    strcpy( buffer + bufend, s );
    bufend += strlen( s ) + 1;
  }
  return val[ i ];
}
```

● **Exercise 7.3.1.** Add error handling to the AssocArray class. The hash table or the string buffer might overflow. (In the former case, return a reference to a zero location, as in Section 4.4.)

The operator[] for the AssocArray class has one disadvantage: It cannot be applied to a constant object of type AssocArray.

```
void print( const AssocArray& a, const char s[] )
{ cout << s << " ";
  cout << a[ s ]; // ERROR
  // ...
}
```

Because a is a constant object, the nonconstant operator[] cannot be applied, even if only to do a lookup, not change the array. The solution is to supply a *second* version of operator[] that can be applied to constant objects:

```
double AssocArray::operator[]( const char s[] ) const
{ int i = locate( s );
  if( i == 0 ) return 0; // no matching string
  return val[ i ];
}
```

This version of [] does not add another string into the associative array. Nor does it return a reference, because we do not allow modification of the associated value either. It is very common to have two operator[] functions: one for variable and one for constant objects.

There is no operator[][] for double subscripts in C++. As we have seen in Section 6.1, multiple subscripts are really successive applications of single subscripts. With some care, this can be achieved for user-defined types as well. Consider, for example, the Grid class of Section 5.3. This class abstracts a terminal display, and we would like to implement [] to allow the following operations:

```
Grid d;
d[ y ][ x ] = '#';    // modify a value, instead of set( r, c, '#' )
if( d[ y ][ x ] == ' ' )    // test a value
  // ...
```

We must define a Grid::operator[] returning a value to which another [] can be applied.

```
class Grid
{ char g[ GRID_YSIZE ][ GRID_XSIZE + 1 ];
public:
  // ...
  char* operator[]( int y ) { return g[ y ]; }
};
```

In the expression d[y], the function returns d.g[y], a char* pointing to the yth row of d.g. A second [] can be applied to that pointer: d[y][x] is

(d[y] + x) or d.g[y][x]. Note that because d[y] is a char,
d[y][x] can appear on the left side of an assignment.

Alternatively, one can overload the () operator so that g(y, x) returns
a reference. Unfortunately, this means having parentheses instead of brackets.

● **Exercise 7.3.2.** Write operator[] for the Vec3 and Mat3 classes.

7.4. TYPE CONVERSIONS

The use of type conversions is essential for effective operator overloading. If an
automatic type conversion double → Complex were not available, one would
either have to write Complex(2) * z instead of 2 * z or supply a special
complex operator*(double, Complex) (and all the other possible operations
with double as first or second arguments). That would be unbearably dull.

A type conversion from type X to type Y can be achieved simply by
supplying a constructor for Y with argument X (or X&). Typical examples are

```
Complex( double )
String( char* )
Fraction( int )
```

This device cannot be used to convert back to a built-in type, because built-in
types are not classes and cannot have constructors. It also cannot always be
used to effect a conversion to an existing class—we might not be permitted to
add the constructor into the class definition.

To circumvent these restrictions, there is an alternate way of providing
a type conversion from type X to type Y, by supplying a member function
X::operator Y().

```
class Fraction
{ int num, den;
public:
  // ...
  operator double() const;
};

Fraction::operator double() const
{ return double( num )/double( den );
}
```

The istream class has a conversion istream::operator void*() that returns
the 0 pointer at end of file or in case of trouble, or a nonzero pointer otherwise.
This is invoked in statements such as

```
while( cin >> x )
  // ...
```

which means while(operator >> (cin, x).operator void*()) because
cin >> x returns cin, and the while loop breaks when the result of converting
the structure cin into a void* yields a 0 pointer.

It should be pointed out that the translator does not do more than one level of user-defined type conversion when trying to match an overloaded function. For example,

```
Fraction f( 1, 2 );   // f = 1/2
Complex z( 2, -1 );   // z = 2 - i
Complex w = f * z;
```

will not work, because the conversion Fraction → double → Complex is too complex. We have to either help the compiler along

```
Complex w = double( f ) * z;
```

or supply a type conversion Fraction → Complex, either as a constructor Complex(Fraction) or a Fraction::operator Complex().

● **Exercise 7.4.1.** Add type conversions int → String and String → int to the string class of Exercise 5.3.7. For example, the integer 10 should be converted into the string String("10"), and conversely, a string starting with digits (and maybe a leading '+' or '-') should be converted to the corresponding integer. All other strings should be converted to 0.

● **Exercise 7.4.2.** Construct a type conversion double → Polynomial, creating a constant polynomial. Test with

```
Polynomial x; x.set( 1, 1 );
Polynomial f = 1 + 3*x - 2*x*x;
```

● **Exercise 7.4.3.** A Point structure contains the x- and y-coordinates of a point. A Rectangle class is defined by two opposing corner points, a Polygon class by an array of its corner points. Write a type conversion Rectangle → Polygon

▪ As a member function of Polygon
▪ As a member function of Rectangle

Write a nonmember function perimeter of Polygon and test that it can be used to compute the perimeter of a Rectangle. What if perimeter is a member function of Polygon?

● **Exercise 7.4.4.** (Hard) Write a conversion double → Fraction converting a floating-point number into the fraction most closely representing it.

● 7.5. PITFALLS

7.5.1. Type Conversions and Reference Arguments

Consider a function

```
void swap( double& a, double& b )
{ double temp = a;
  a = b;
  b = temp;
}
```

to swap two doubles. Suppose one of the arguments is a Fraction:

```
double x = 3.0;
Fraction f( 1, 2 );
```

```
swap( x, f );   // f is not changed
```

A type conversion Fraction → double is performed, the result is stored in a temporary variable, a reference to that temporary variable is passed to swap, and its contents are swapped with x. Afterward, the temporary variable is forgotten. f is unaffected.

7.5.2. Unintended Type Conversion

C++ automatically uses constructors with a single argument as type converters. This can lead to quite surprising results. Here is an example:

```
class Point
{ double _x, _y;
public:
  Point( double x = 0, double y = 0 );
  // ...
};

int main()
{ double a, r, x, y;
  // ...
  Point p = ( x + r * cos( a ), y + r * sin( a ));
  // ...
  return 0;
}
```

Of course, the programmer had intended to write

```
Point p( x + r * cos( a ), y + r * sin( a ));
```

but the = had somehow crept in. Surprisingly, the code compiles and runs. Here is why. The expression

```
( x + r * cos( a ), y + r * sin( a ))
```

uses the *comma* operator. The first subexpression is computed and discarded. The second subexpression becomes the value of the entire expression. It is of type double. It becomes the first argument of the Point constructor, and the second argument defaults to 0. We have made a

```
Point( y + r * sin( a ), 0)
```

There is a moral here: Default arguments can lead to unintended calls. In our case the construction Point(double) is not reasonable, but the constructions Point(double, double) and Point() are. In this situation it is better to supply two separate constructors rather than relying on default arguments.

Here is another, very common example. Suppose a `String` class has two constructors:

```
class String
{ char s[ 256 ];
public:
  String( const char* );
  String( int n ); // makes a string with n spaces
  char& operator[]( int );
  // ...
};
```

Now consider the following code:

```
String a( 4 );
a[ 0 ] = 'A'; a = 'd'; a[ 2 ] = 'a'; a[ 3 ] = 'm';
```

There is a typo—it should have been a[1] = 'd'. But again the code will compile and run! The compiler will carry out a series of type conversions, creating an entirely unintended interpretation. The character 'd' is converted to its integer equivalent (100 in the ASCII encoding scheme). The assignment a = 100 is interpreted as a = String(100). That constructs a new string filled with 100 spaces, which replaces a. Upon completion, a is the string " . . . am ".

7.5.3. Precedence of Overloaded Operators

It would appear to make sense to overload the ∧ operator to raise a fraction to an integer power.

```
Fraction operator∧( const Fraction& f, int n );

Fraction a, b;
b = a ∧ 3;
```

However, introducing this operator creates a pitfall. The statement

```
b = a ∧ 3 + 1;
```

does *not* compute $a^3 + 1$. Because + has a higher precedence than ∧, the expression a ∧ 3 + 1 is interpreted as a ∧ (3 + 1), computing a^4.

This makes the ∧ operator inappropriate for carrying out the operation of raising a quantity to a power. The ∧ operator, when used for this purpose, is likely to cause quite a few programming errors that are hard to detect by the untrained eye. Remember that the only point of overloading an operator is to help the human reader understand the code. The compiler just translates overloaded operators to function calls.

INPUT AND OUTPUT

This is a short chapter collecting information about the C++ stream input and output operations. This is not an exhaustive coverage of the I/O packages. For more details, refer to [Stroustrup], [Lippman], or [Teale] in the Bibliography at the end of this book.

8.1. THE >> AND << OPERATORS

As you have undoubtedly noticed by now, the "get from" cin >> and "put to" cout << operators are simply overloaded << and >>, applied to members cin, cout of some classes. These classes are in fact istream and ostream, defined in iostream.h. If we want to read from another file, we have to initialize another istream object, say ifile, suitably and then use ifile >> ....

Let us have a closer look at the << >> operators. Why can they chain together, as in

```
cout << "Salary: " << e.salary;
```

According to the operator precedence table, << binds left to right, and the expression is fully parenthesized as

```
( cout << "Salary: " ) << e.salary;
```

Each << has a return value that is identical to its first argument. That is, cout << "Salary: " returns cout, and the second << is simply cout << e.salary. Actually, ostreams are fairly sizable objects, and the operator<< functions take an ostream& and return it. The following are defined inside the ostream class:

```
ostream& operator<<( ostream&, char* );
ostream& operator<<( ostream&, int );
```

To define a << function for a user-defined type, an operator<< must be declared in the class definition, and it must be a friend, because the first argument is an `ostream` and not an object of the user-defined class. Of course, the `ostream` class is not ours to touch, and further `operator<<` member functions cannot be added to it. Here is an output operator for fractions:

```
class Fraction
{ int num, den;
public:
  // ...
  friend ostream& operator<<( ostream&, constFraction& );
};

ostream& operator<<( ostream& s, const Fraction& f )
{ return s << f.num << "/" << f.den;
}
```

An input operator can be written similarly:

```
istream& operator>>( istream& s, Fraction& f )
{ s >> f.num;
  char ch;
  s >> ch;
  if( ch != '/' ) error( "/ expected" );
  s >> f.den;
  return s;
}
```

The input operator must have a `Fraction&` as second argument because it modifies the fraction. The output operator has a `const Fraction&` for efficiency, passing a reference rather than the actual structure.

● **Exercise 8.1.1.** Supply << and >> operators to read and write `Employee` records.

● **Exercise 8.1.2.** Supply << and >> operators to read and write complex numbers. Use a pleasant format, like this:

2.5 + 3.1 i	General
3.1 i	No real part
2.5	No imaginary part
2.5 - 3.1 i	Negative imaginary part
1 + i	Imaginary coefficient 1

Why were << >> chosen as input/output operators? Originally, = was considered, but it binds the wrong way (cout = "Salary" = e.salary parenthesizes to cout = ("Salary" = e.salary)), and most people preferred different operators for input and output. < and > were tried, but they were too frequently confused with their original meanings. << and >> are sufficiently rare in regular C code to stand out.

● **Exercise 8.1.3.** A logical choice might have been <<= >>=. Yes, they bind the wrong way, but we could place the stream argument *to the right:*

```
e.salary >>= cout;
```

That operator would still return cout for further chaining. Because the first argument is now a class object, they even can be declared as member functions:

```
ostream& Fraction::operator>>=( ostream& )
```

What is wrong with this idea?

8.2. INPUT AND OUTPUT OF CHARACTERS AND STRINGS

There is an ostream::put(char) function that puts a single character to the output stream, such as cout.put(ch). For character-based input, cin.get (ch) can be used instead of cin >> ch. The difference is that get reads a white space character rather than skipping over it. A character can be put back onto the input stream with cin.putback(ch). cin.peek() returns the next character without extracting it.

● **Exercise 8.2.1.** Write a program that reads in a file from standard input, expands tabs to spaces, and writes the resulting file to standard output. Default tab stops are every 8 columns; other values can be given on the command line (e.g., tab 3 < test.c > test.out).

For line-based input, there are two functions

```
istream& istream::getline( char* buffer, int bufsize,
    char terminator ='\n' );
istream& istream::get( char* buffer, int bufsize, char
    terminator = '\n' );
```

cin.getline(line, 80) reads a line. cin.get(word, 20, ' ') reads in a word, because the termination character has been changed to ' '. The termination character is left as the next character on the input stream when calling get, whereas getline extracts the termination character and throws it away. Both functions place a zero terminator into the buffer. Both functions stop reading when the buffer is full. Calling istream::gcount() immediately afterwards returns the number of characters transferred into the buffer, excluding the terminating zero.

C Note

The C programmer will encounter some familiar concepts. The member functions get, getline, put , and putback are the equivalents of fgetc, fgets, fputc, and ungetc. C++ can afford prettier names because of function overloading. Calls to the C f... functions and the C++ stream functions do not mix, because each library includes its own buffering.

8.3. FORMATTED INPUT AND OUTPUT

The stream library actually performs two unrelated tasks: formatting and buffering. Formatting is the act of translating between binary data and their character representations. It is done by the class `ios`, the base class for both `istream` and `ostream`. The `ios` class keeps a *format state* that governs formatting. The format state specifies

- Field width
- Fill character
- Field alignment
- Integer base (decimal, hex, or octal)
- Floating-point format (fixed, scientific, or general)
- Whether to show a + sign, trailing decimal point and zeros thereafter, or the integer base
- Whether to use upper- or lowercase letters for E, 0X, and the hex digits A ... F

For each setting there are two ways to change it: with an `ios` member function and with a *manipulator*. For example, to set the fill character to `*` and the width to 10, say for printing checks, you call either

```
cout.fill( '*' );
cout.width( 10 );
```

or

```
cout << setfill( '*' ) << setw( 10 );
```

Then

```
cout << 1370.25
```

prints `***1370.25`.

The `fill` and `width` functions are just ordinary member functions of the `ios` class. The `setfill` and `setw` manipulators generate special objects that are sent to the stream. When the stream receives those objects, it will carry out the requested format change. The effect is the same, but the manipulators are a bit more convenient, because they can be combined with other << operations in the same statement. On the other hand, the member functions return the old fill character and field width values—a handy feature if you need to restore them. (In this book we discuss only how to use manipulators, not how to implement them. The implementation technique is a bit involved; see [Teale] for details.)

For output, the field width denotes the minimum number of characters printed for a field. For input, the width is meaningful only when reading a string. It denotes the maximum number of characters to place into the string:

```
char text[ SIZE ];
cin >> setw( SIZE ) >> text;
```

The other portions of the format state are implemented as bits or groups of bits. Bits can be turned on with the member function `ios::setf` or a manipulator called—you guessed it—`setiosflags`. To turn a bit off, use `ios::unsetf` or the manipulator called (I am not making this up) `resetiosflags`. For example, to show a + sign for positive numbers, you use

```
cout.setf( ios::showpos );
```

or

```
cout << setiosflags( ios::showpos );
```

To turn the flag off again, that is, to suppress the + for positive numbers, you use

```
cout.unsetf( ios::showpos );
```

or

```
cout << resetiosflags( ios::showpos );
```

To complicate matters, some options are not binary, but ternary. For example, there are three choices for integer base: decimal, hexadecimal, and octal. We cannot simply make a selection by turning on a single bit, but must instead make a selection within a field group. The field group becomes the second argument to setf/unsetf/setiosflags/resetiosflags. For example,

```
cout.setf( ios::hex, ios::basefield )
```

selects hexadecimal output of integers.

The following table contains a complete list of the available flags.

ios flag	Field group	Meaning
left	adjustfield	Left alignment
right	adjustfield	Right alignment
internal	adjustfield	Sign left, remainder
dec	basefield	Decimal base
hex	basefield	Hex base
oct	basefield	Octal base
showbase		Show integer base
showpos		Show + sign
uppercase		Uppercase E, X, and A ... F
fixed	floatfield	Fixed floating-point
scientific	floatfield	Scientific floating-point
showpoint		Show trailing decimal point

For example, to have a string left aligned in a field with width 20 and fill character *, use either

```
cout.setf( ios::left, ios::adjustfield );
cout.fill( '*' );
cout.width( 20 );
cout << "Hello, World!";
```

or

```
cout << setiosflags( ios::left, ios::adjustfield )
  << setfill( '*' ) << setw( 20 )
  << "Hello, World!";
```

Either way, the output is

```
Hello,World!*******
```

By default, floating-point numbers are printed in general format, in which scientific notation is used when necessary to show the significant digits (6 by default), fixed-point format otherwise. For example,

```
cout << 123.456789 << ' ' << 123456789;
```

prints 123.457 1.23457e+007. (You can get an uppercase E by setting ios::uppercase.) You can explicitly choose either scientific or fixed format with the ios flags scientific or fixed.

```
cout << setiosflags( ios::fixed, ios::floatfield );
cout.setf( ios::scientific, ios::floatfield );
```

To reset to general format, there isn't a flag ios::general. Instead, you must use

```
cout << resetiosflags( ios::floatfield );
```

or

```
cout.unsetf( ios::floatfield );
```

To see a + sign for positive numbers, use ios::showpos. (This also works for integers.) To see trailing zeros, use ios::showpoint. For example,

```
cout.setf( ios::fixed, ios::floatfield );
cout.setf( ios::showpoint | ios::showpos );
cout << 123.456;
```

prints +123.456000.

You can change the precision from the default value of 6 digits:

```
cout << setprecision( 10 ) << 123.45678
```

or

```
cout.precision( 10 );
cout << 123.45678
```

prints 123.45678. In general format the precision denotes the number of *significant* digits; in fixed and scientific formats the precision denotes the number of digits *after the decimal point*.

● **Exercise 8.3.1.** Write a program that reads in a list of employees, raises their salaries by 3 percent, and then prints out a table of all employees. Of course, the columns for name, age, salary, and social security number should line up. The names should be left-aligned, and the age and salary fields should be right aligned. Show salaries with two digits after the decimal point.

● **Exercise 8.3.2.** Write a function to print a matrix so that the columns line up at the decimal points. For example,

```
12.3
 0.001
8100.
```

Integers can be formatted in decimal, hexadecimal, or octal.

```
int n = 12;
cout << hex << n << ' ';
cout << oct << n << ' ';
cout << dec << n << endl;
```

prints c 14 12. To show the base and print the letters in uppercase, use

```
cout.setf( ios::showbase | ios::uppercase );
```

Now the same numbers print as 0XC 014 12. Instead of the manipulators, you can also use ios flags dec, oct, and hex:

```
cout.setf( ios::hex, ios::basefield );
```

As a final twist, all format state settings persist until they are set to a different value, *except* for field width. Field width reverts to 0 (that is, read or print as many characters as necessary) after each input or output operation requiring a width.

The following table summarizes the available manipulators and corresponding ios functions.

Manipulator	ios member function
setfill	fill
setw	width
setprecision	precision
setiosflags	setf
resetiosflags	unsetf
hex	
oct	
dec	

C Note

C programmers will find the formatting interface of the stream library unbelievably cumbersome. To print a plus sign and leading zeroes in a decimal number using `printf`, write `"%+06d"`. The iostream equivalent is

```
cout << setiosflags( ios::internal, ios::adjustfield )
    << setiosflags( ios::showpos )
    << setiosflags( ios::dec, ios::basefield )
    << setfill( '0' ) << setw( 6 );
```

Admittedly, that is probably the worst case, but it cannot be denied that the stream-formatting commands are overly verbose and inconsistent. On the positive side, a very common C error, namely the mismatch between the format string and the data type, is completely avoided in the C++ stream library. For example,

```
int x;
printf( "%10f", x );
```

has unpredictable results. In C++ you can't get it wrong:

```
int x;
cout << setw( 10 ) << x;
```

prints x as an integer with field width 10.

● **Exercise 8.3.3.** According to [Kernighan & Ritchie], p. 243, the format string of the `printf` function in the standard C library consists of flags (in any order), a number specifying the field width, a period followed by the precision (for floating-point numbers only), and a type. Flags and types are

-	Left justification
+	Show + sign
0	Show leading zeroes
#	Use "alternate" format—leading 0 or 0x/0x for octal or hexadecimal numbers, show decimal point and trailing zeroes for floating-point numbers
space	If the first character is not a sign, prefix a space
d	Decimal
o	Octal
x, X	Hexadecimal; X uses uppercase letters
f	Fixed floating-point
e, E	Scientific floating-point, E uses uppercase E
g, G	General floating-point, G uses uppercase E

For example, `printf( "%+10.2f", x )` prints a floating-point number with field width 10, 2 digits after the decimal point, and a + for positive numbers. The stream equivalent is `cout << setw( 10 ) << setprecision( 2 ) << setiosflags( ios::showpos ) << x`.

Write a function `setformat( ostream& os, const char f[] )` that scans a format string in the C `printf` format and sets the stream state of os accordingly. (If you are ambitious, consult [Teale] to find out how to make `setformat` into a manipulator.)

● **Exercise 8.3.4.** Write an `operator<< ( ostream&, const Fraction& )` that prints fractions, respecting the format state. Pay attention to field width, fill character, a leading + sign, and alignment. For example,

```
cout << setfill( '*' ) << setw( 10 )
   << setiosflags( ios::showpoint ) << Fraction( 1, 2 );
```

should print `******+1/2`. Use the `ios::flags()` function to read the format state flags.

8.4. USING FILES FOR INPUT AND OUTPUT

To link streams to files, the header file fstream.h must be included. To open a stream attached to a file for input, use

```
ifstream is( "input.txt", ios::in );
ofstream os( "output.dat", ios::out );
```

The classes `ifstream` and `ofstream` are derived from `istream` and `ostream` (see Chapter 10). An `ifstream` object is an `istream` object with added capabilities. In particular, all `istream` functions (get, putback, >>) can be used.

Here is an example, a program counting the number of lines in a file. It does that simply by counting the number of `'\n'` characters. The filename is given on the command line.

```
int main( int argc, char* argv[] )
{ int count = 0;
  char ch;

  if( argc == 1 )
  { cerr << "No filename given.\n"; return 1; }
  ifstream is( argv[ 1 ], ios::in );
  if( !is )
  { cerr << "Can't open input file: " << argv[ 1 ] << "\n";
    return 2;
  }
  while( is ) // becomes false at end of file
  { is.get( ch );
    if( is ) count += ch == '\n';     // add 0 or 1 to count
  }
  cout << count << " lines.\n";
  return 0;
}
```

Note the use of the standard `cerr` stream, which sends output to the screen even if `cout` has been redirected to a file. The return value of `main` is 0 if no error is found, 1 if no file was specified on the command line, and 2 if the input file cannot be opened.

● **Exercise 8.4.1.** Modify the counting program of Section 6.3 to take a source file optionally. A filename can be specified on the command line by either -f*filename* or -f *filename*.

8.5. ERROR STATES

All streams (both input and output) have a *state*, one of the following:

- Good
- End of file
- Fail
- Bad

There is a difference between "bad" and "fail." The "fail" state occurs because of a logical error, for example trying to read an integer when the next character is a letter. "Bad" occurs because of a physical error, such as hardware failure or memory exhaustion. A stream can easily become not good: Just calling `cin >> n` (n an `int`) when the next string on the input stream is not an integer makes the state "fail".

There are four access functions to report the stream state: `good()`, `eof()`, `bad()`, and `fail()`. `fail()` is true if the stream is in either state, "fail" or "bad". `eof()` returns 1 if the end of file is reached *and the stream is not in a failed state*, 0 otherwise.

The states can be tested with the `rdstate` member function

```
if( s.rdstate() & ios::failbit) ...
```

A stream can be set to be good with

```
s.clear();
```

or set to be fail with

```
s.clear( ios::failbit | s.rdstate() );
```

Clearing the state is necessary if you want to continue reading after the state has been set to "bad" or "fail", for example, by a failed `cin >> n`. In a user-defined `operator>>` you can set the state to "fail" if you find the wrong characters in the input stream.

● **Exercise 8.5.1.** Enhance the `operator>>( istream&, Employee& e )` function of Exercise 8.1.2 to set the stream to "fail" if it could not successfully read an employee record. Take care not to change e unless input succeeds.

An automatic type conversion istream → void* returns 0 if the state is "fail", a nonzero pointer otherwise. It is automatically invoked if the return value of >> is used in a condition such as

```
while( cin >> ch )
  // ...
```

This loop reads characters until >> fails, most likely at the end of the file.

● **Exercise 8.5.2.** Write an object-oriented front end to the C f... library. Define

```
class File
{ int mode; // store whether read/write/both
  FILE* fp;
public:
  FILE* handle() { return fp }
          // to allow for fprintf( f.handle(), ... )
  File( const char*, const char* ); // calls fopen
  ~File(); // calls fclose
  File& operator>>( int ); // calls fprintf( "%d", ... );
  // ...
  File& operator<<( int& ); // calls fscanf( "%d", ... );
  // ...
  File& get( char& );
  File& get( char*, int, char );
  File& unget( char );
  File& put( char );
  File& read( void*, unsigned, unsigned );
  File& write( void*, unsigned, unsigned );
  void seek( long );
  long tell() const;
  int eof() const;
  operator void*() const; // returns this if file OK,
                          // 0 otherwise
};
```

The mode field serves for testing that read/write operations are performed only on files opened with the correct permission. Provide File equivalents for stdin and stdout. A usage example follows:

```
char word[ 20 ];
File f( "input.txt", "r" );
File g( 0, "w" ); // stdout
while( !f.eof() )
{ char ch;
  do
  { f.get( ch );
  } while( isspace( ch ));
  f.unget( ch );
```

```
    f.get( word, 20, ' ' );
    g << word << "\n";
}
// f automatically closed by destructor when it leaves
// scope (Section 9.2)
```

8.6. ATTACHING STREAMS TO STRINGS

Often input data is line-based, with some variable number of items per input line. Then it is necessary to read in a line (with getline) at a time, break it up into fields, and convert each field into a value. The last-named operation can be greatly simplified by tying a stream to the buffer holding the input line.

In the string stream package, this is achieved as follows:

```
#include <strstream.h>
const int BUFLEN = 100;
char buf[ BUFLEN ];
istrstream si( buf, sizeof( buf ));
```

We can now read in and analyze an input line at a time. Suppose, for example, that each input line contains a string field and a floating-point number, followed by a comment of arbitrary length. For example,

```
DE   1944.50  Depreciation for copying machine
```

The following loop can be used to process a file with such records:

```
const int ALEN = 10;
char acct[ ALEN ];
double amt;
while( cin.getline( buf, sizeof( buf ))
{ si >> acct >> amt;        // comment field is ignored
  si.seekg( ios::beg );     // reset to start
}
```

Similarly, an output stream can be attached to a string if the output data needs to be massaged before we actually send it.

The constructor requires a third argument: ios::out if output is to start at the beginning of the string, ios::app if output is to be appended at the first '\0' in the string. For example,

```
#include <strstream.h>

ostrstream so( buf, sizeof( buf ), ios::out );
```

The stream can be reset with so.seekp(ios::beg).

● **Exercise 8.6.1.** Modify the operator>> that reads an employee record. Read the input line into a character array, then attach a string stream and use it to extract the age, salary, and ID number, as

```
si >> e.age >> e.salary >> e.ssNum;
```

● 8.7. PITFALLS

8.7.1. ?: Has Lower Precedence than << >>

For example,

```
cout << im > 0 ? "+" : "-"; // WRONG
```

does not print what one would expect. It prints the value of im > 0 (which is 0 or 1) and evaluates to "+" if the state of cin is not "bad" or "fail", to "-" otherwise. That value is discarded. The ?: expression must be enclosed in parentheses:

```
cout << ( im > 0 ? "+" : "-" ); // OK
```

The relational, logical, Boolean, and assignment operations also have precedence lower than << >>, as has the comma operator.

8.7.2. get Leaves the Terminator on the Input Stream

The following code will lead to an infinite loop:

```
while( cin.get( buffer, sizeof( buffer )))
    cout << buffer;
```

because the terminating '\n' stays on the input stream. The first line is read in full, subsequent calls to cin.get report blank lines. Remedy: use getline.

8.7.3. Improper End-of-File Detection

It can be difficult to locate the end of input when using the stream functions. For example, the following code does not work:

```
int n;

while( !cin.eof() ) // WRONG
{ cin >> n;
    cout << n << "\n";
}
```

After the last number is read, the state is not yet "eof", and the loop is entered once more. When attempting to read the next number, the end of file is reached, the cin >> n read request fails, and cin falls into state "fail" or "bad", staying in the while loop forever. The following is also incorrect:

```
while (( cin >> n ).good() )
    cout << n << "\n";
```

If an end of file has been encountered immediately after the last integer, the stream state may be set to "eof", which is not good, and the last number is not printed.

A correct loop is

```
while( cin >> n )
    cout << n << "\n";
```

8.7.4. Improper End-of-Word Detection

The following code will not read a word at a time:

```
char word[ SIZE ];
while ( cin.get( word, SIZE, ' ' ))...
```

The termination character ' ' matches only an exact space character, not any white space. For example, if two words are separated by a newline or a tab, they will be read as one word with an embedded newline or tab character. Instead, use

```
while ( cin >> word ) // ...
```

or better

```
while ( cin >> setw( SIZE ) >> word ) //...
```

This will treat any white space as a word separator.

8.7.5. Streams as Truth Values

The type conversion istream → void* is supplied to make is easy to check whether a stream is still happy:

```
if ( cin ) // ...
```

is equivalent to

```
if ( !cin.fail() ) // ...
```

You may well ask why there isn't a conversion istream → int instead. Using a void* target type seems unnecessarily complex. But it is never a good idea to use a conversion to int, because it can easily lead to unintended interpretations. Suppose that there were such a type conversion. Consider the condition

```
if ( cin << n ) // ...
```

This is actually an error—it should be cin >> n—but the compiler would find a spurious meaning: shift the result of the integer conversion of cin by n bits to the left. Since cin cannot actually be converted to an int, only to a void*, and bitwise shift on pointers is undefined, the compiler can detect this typing error.

However, there is a different typing error that the compiler cannot detect. If you accidentally write

```
char word[ SIZE ];
if ( cin > word ) // ...
```

the compiler will silently find an unintended interpretation: It will convert cin to a void* and compare that pointer against the starting address of word.

MEMORY MANAGEMENT

9.1. DYNAMIC ALLOCATION

Often it is difficult or impossible to estimate beforehand how many items of a data structure are required in a program run. In such cases dynamic allocation of storage is required.

There are four areas of storage in every program:

- *Code.* This area contains the machine instructions for all functions. Pointers to functions point here.
- *Static data.* This area contains all global data and all local and member data declared `static`. It is allocated and initialized before `main` starts.
- *Stack.* This area contains all local, non-`static` data, including function arguments. When a block is entered, all variables in it are allocated on the stack; on exit, they are forgotten.
- *Free store or heap.* This area is available on request for data that grows or shrinks as a program executes.

Free store memory is obtained through the `new` operator. `new` is followed by a type name and causes a block of memory, sufficient to hold one instance of the type, to be allocated on the free store. Its value is the address of the allocated block.

```
Date* d;
d = new Date;
```

If the type has a constructor with no argument, `new` calls it. We can supply arguments to a constructor:

```
Complex* pz;
pz = new Complex( 1.5, -2 * x );
```

An array can be allocated as well:

```
char* p = new char[ n ];
    // allocates an array with n characters
```

If an array of a type with constructors is allocated, the constructor without arguments is called on all elements:

```
Complex *az = new Complex[ 10 ];
    // calls Complex() on all az[ i ]
```

There is no way to pass arguments into the constructor. It is an error to allocate an array of a type with constructors but lacking a constructor without arguments.

new is an *operator*, not a function. It causes two function calls: one to the free store allocator and one to the appropriate constructor.

The delete operator recycles a pointer obtained through new:

```
delete d;
```

The allocated storage is returned to the free store for reuse by a subsequent call to new. If there is a destructor (Section 9.2), it is called. To recycle an array, you must use

```
delete[] pz;
```

since the destructor needs to be called on all array elements. The array allocation/deallocation syntax is asymmetric. Because its argument is a type, the new operator has the [] after the type name: new char[10]. The argument of delete is an expression, and to delete an array the [] must appear before the pointer variable: delete [] p1. Both new and delete are operators, not functions. They handle free-store management and automatic construction/destruction.

Pascal Note

new and delete are exactly like **new** and **dispose** in Pascal, except that they can allocate arrays of objects and they can perform construction and destruction.

C Note

Do not confuse new and delete with malloc and free : new X is the equivalent of malloc(sizeof(X)) plus constructor calls. delete p is the equivalent of destructor calls plus free(p). C++ programs should rarely use malloc and free.

Here is a stack class that allocates the stack on the free store. The class itself contains merely a pointer variable, and a constructor allocates the actual storage by calling new. If the stack overflows in a push operation, it is moved and copied to a larger location.

```
const int SDEFSIZE = 10;

class Stack
{ int* s;
  int stackPointer;
  int size;
```

```
public:
  Stack( int = SDEFSIZE );
  ~Stack();
  int push( int );
  int pop();
  int isEmpty() const;
};

Stack::Stack( int initialSize )
{ size = initialSize;
  s = new int[ size ];
  stackPointer = 0;
}

Stack::~Stack()
{ delete[] s;
}

int Stack::push( int n )
{ const int SGROW = 10;

  if ( stackPointer >= size ) // out of space
  { int* snew = new int[ size + SGROW ]; // get larger block

    for ( int i = 0; i < size; i++) // transfer contents
      snew[ i ] = s[ i ];
    size += SGROW;
    delete[] s;        // recycle smaller block
    s = snew;
  }
  return s[ stackPointer++ ] = n;
}

int Stack::pop()
{ assert( stackPointer > 0 );
  return s[ --stackPointer ];
}

int Stack::isEmpty() const
{ return stackPointer == 0;
}
```

● **Exercise 9.1.1.** Use this stack in the stack-based calculator and verify its dynamic growth capability.

● **Exercise 9.1.2.** Rewrite the pop function to shrink the stack back if it is less than half full. Shrink it to 50% of its size + 10.

A general vector class is another typical example: An instance of type Vector contains a pointer variable that is initialized by the constructor to an address on the free store:

```
class Vector
{ double* co; // coordinates
  int dim;
public:
  Vector( int );
  ~Vector() { delete[] co; }
  double& operator[]( int );
  // ...
};

Vector::Vector( int d )
{ dim = d; co = new double[ d ];
}

double& Vector::operator[]( int n )
{ if( 0 <= n && n < dim )
    return co[ n ];
  else ...
}
```

The declaration

```
Vector v( 3 );
```

causes the constructor Vector to be called and to initialize v.co with a new double[3]. Vectors of completely arbitrary size can be allocated, for example, Vector w(100).

● **Exercise 9.1.3.** Restructure the Polynomial class of Section 7.2 to allow for polynomials of arbitrary degree. Supply operator+ and operator* functions. (For now, do not supply a destructor; the reason will become apparent in Section 9.3.)

● **Exercise 9.1.4.** Design an integer array class in which the storage grows on demand. (The set function can grow the array, but [] cannot.)

```
class DynArray
{ int* mem;
  int lo,hi;
public:
  DynArray( int, int );
  int lowerBound() const { return lo; }
    // current lower bound
```

```
int upperBound() const { return hi; }
  // current upper bound
int operator[] ( int ) const;
void set ( int, int );
  // never fails—increases array if necessary
};
```

● **Exercise 9.1.5.** Unfortunately, you cannot write an operator[] function that automatically grows the DynArray when the index is outside the current array range. Explain the problem that can be caused by the following naïve implementation of operator[]:

```
int& DynArray::operator[]( int n )
//DANGER—possible memory corruption
{ if ( n < lo || n > hi )
  { int newlo = min ( lo, n );
    int newhi = max ( hi, n );

    int* newmem = new int [ newhi - newlo + 1 ];
    for ( int i = newlo; i < lo; i++ ) newmem[ i - newlo ] = 0;
    for ( ; i <= hi; i++ ) newmem[ i - newlo ] = mem[ i - lo ];
    for ( ; i <= newhi; i++ ) newmem[ i - newlo ] = 0;
    delete[] mem;
    mem = newmem;
    lo = newlo;
    hi = newhi;
  }
  return mem[ n - lo ];
}
```

Hint: Consider an expression that passes two array values to function arguments of type int&.

If frequent insertions or deletions occur in the middle of a sequence, then arrays, even dynamically growing ones, are not the appropriate data structure. In this case, we turn to linked lists. A linked list is a sequence of cells, each of which contains an information field and a pointer to the next cell.

We will distinguish between *cells*, the actual containers of the information, and *lists*, which contain pointers to the first container in a chain and to one currently selected container. The following declaration shows a list of integers:

```
class Cell
{ int info;
  Cell* next;
  friend class List;
};

class List
{ Cell* head;
  Cell* cur;  // current position
  Cell* pre;  // predecessor of current position
public:

  List();
  ~List();
  void insert( int n );  // insert before current position
  void remove();         // remove current position
  int info() const;      // info of current element
  void advance();        // advance current position
  void reset();
  int atEnd() const { return cur == 0; }
};

List::List()
{ head = cur = pre = 0;
}

int List::info() const
{ return cur ? cur->info : 0;
}

void List::advance()
{ if( cur )
  { pre = cur;
    cur = cur->next;
  }
}

void List::reset()
{ cur = head;
  pre = 0;
}
```

Cell has no public access, but all member functions of List have been declared friends with the friend class List statement. This loop walks through a list 1 :

```
for( l.reset(); !l.atEnd(); l.advance() )
  do something with l.info();
```

When inserting a new element, new storage space is allocated:

```
void List::insert( int n )
{ Cell* p = new Cell;
  p->info = n;
  p->next = cur;
  if( pre ) pre->next = p; else head = p;
  pre = p;
}
```

For removing a cell, the storage is recycled:

```
void List::remove()
{ if ( ! cur ) return;
  if( pre ) pre->next = cur->next; else head = cur->next;
  Cell* p = cur;
  cur = cur->next;
  delete p;
}
```

The destructor removes all cells of a list. The next section explains when it is called.

```
List::~List()
{ Cell* p = head;

  while( p != 0 )
  { Cell* q = p;
    p = p->next;
    delete q;
  }
}
```

● **Exercise 9.1.6.** Implement the list package. Write a program that reads numbers from standard input and inserts them in the list. Then print all numbers in the list.

● **Exercise 9.1.7.** Modify the previous exercise to insert all numbers in reverse order. To insert all even numbers before all odd numbers. To insert all numbers and then delete the odd ones.

● **Exercise 9.1.8.** Write a constructor List::List(int n) that initializes a list with a single cell containing n.

● **Exercise 9.1.9.** Write a member function void List::append(const List& b) that appends all entries of b to the end of a list.

● **Exercise 9.1.10.** Write a `Polynomial` class that implements polynomials as linked lists storing the degree and the coefficient of each nonzero term. Supply `operator[]` and `operator+` functions. `p[i]` should be the coefficient of x^i. Can `operator[]` return a `double&`? (For now, do not supply a destructor. The reason will become apparent in Section 9.3.)

9.2. CONSTRUCTION AND DESTRUCTION

Classes can have constructor and destructor members. A *constructor* is a member function with the same name as the class and no return type. (We introduced constructors in Section 5.4.) A *destructor* is a member function with name *~class-name*, no arguments, and no return type. A class can have many constructors but at most one destructor. These are not actually functions. You cannot call them. You can only cause them to get called.

Construction deals with initialization of storage that has already been obtained in some way (as static data, on the stack, or on the free store). Destruction deals with cleanup that should occur before that storage is given up (when the program ends, when a stack-based variable goes out of scope, or just before an object is recycled onto the free store).

Not all classes have constructors. An instance of a class without constructors is initialized with a random value or an exact (memberwise) copy of another object. Many classes, even classes with constructors, do not have destructors. Instances of such classes are just forgotten when they go out of scope, their storage space on the stack later reused. Constructors are very common because they are useful for initialization and type conversion. Destructors are necessary only for classes that need some kind of cleanup, most commonly recycling of data allocated on the free store. Destructor actions are not limited to freeing memory. Other tasks, such as decrementing a reference counter or closing a file, are commonly found in destructors.

A constructor for a class X is called in the following circumstances:

- A `static` local or a global variable of class X is declared. The constructor is called before `main` starts, or when the program enters its scope for the first time.

- An automatic variable of class X is declared within a block and the location of its declaration is reached.

- A function is called with argument X. A function call causes all its argument variables to be allocated and initialized.

- An unnamed temporary variable is created to hold the return value of a function returning X.

- An instance is obtained from the free store with `new X`.

- A variable is being initialized that has a member of type X.

- A variable is being initialized that is derived from X (Section 10.1).

    The destructor ~X is called:

- After the end of `main` to destroy all `static` local or global instances of X.

- At the end of each block containing an automatic variable of type X.
- At the end of each function containing an argument of type X.
- To destroy any unnamed temporaries of type X after their use.
- When an instance of X is `deleted`.
- When a variable with a member of type X is destroyed.
- When a variable derived from X is destroyed.

For example, if a `List` is declared within a block, the destructor `~List()` is called after the end of the block to recycle all cells contained in the list:

```
{   List l;

    //...

}// l.~List() called here
```

If `List` had no destructor, l, which contains the starting address of the chain of cells on the free store, would be forgotten, and the cells would be orphaned on the free store, never to be recycled. Clearly this situation must be avoided, or the free store, a finite resource, will eventually be exhausted. All classes with data members pointing to the free store need destructors or the programmer must actively perform deallocation. The latter is not an option if the class is to be used by a client who may not be aware how the class stores its information.

When initializing an object through a declaration, initializers can be specified in parentheses:

```
Date d( 6, 16, 1959 );
```

or

```
Date* pd = new Date( 6, 16, 1959 );
```

A class can have many constructors with different argument types. Two constructors are special:

- The constructor with no arguments X()
- The *copy constructor* X(const X&)

When an array is initialized, either as X x[n] or as px = new X[n], the constructor with no arguments is called on each array element. It is not possible to supply arguments for array initialization. If a class has constructors, but none of them without arguments, it is an error to allocate an array.

The copy constructor is called whenever a copy of an object needs to be made. This happens when a function argument is initialized with the value in the call, when a return value is copied out of the function into an unnamed temporary, or when a variable is declared with an initializer of the same type:

```
List l = tasklist;
```

This is *not* the same as

```
List l;
l = tasklist;
```

Initialization is not assignment. In the first case, l is initialized with tasklist through a call to List(const List&) (if it exists). In the second case, l is initialized with List() and tasklist is copied into it with List::operator= (if that exists). If X(const X&) or X::operator= do not exist, they default to memberwise copying. We will see in the next section why that is undesirable for classes that keep information on the free store and how suitable copy constructors and assignment operators can be defined.

When a function is called, the function arguments are variables that are allocated on the stack and initialized with a copy of the values in the call. For example, if the function

```
Date add( Date d, int n )
{ Date r;
  // ...
  return r;
}
```

is called with

```
b = add( bday, 10 );
```

then two local variables d and n are allocated and initialized, d with a copy of bday and n with 10. The return value is copied from r into an unnamed temporary variable. The sequence of events on return is:

- Copy r to temp in the scope of the caller (using the copy constructor if it exists).

- If a destructor exists, destroy r.

- Return to caller.

- b = temp ;

- If a destructor exists, destroy temp.

More than one temporary variable may be involved in an expression. For example, if a, b, c, d are complex numbers, the expression

```
cout << a*b + c*d
```

is equivalent to

```
Complex temp1 = a * b;
Complex temp2 = c * d;
Complex temp3 = temp1 + temp2;
cout << temp3;
```

Each temporary gets initialized with the return value of an operator function.

When a class with members of another class is constructed, the constructors of the member classes are called. It may be necessary to pass arguments to those constructors. Consider this example. A text-formatting program keeps tables storing the page numbers for each section, each footnote, and each figure. Such tables are arrays of

```
class Item
{ int number;        // sequence number
  char* description;
          // section heading, figure caption, footnote text
  int page;           // page on which item occurs
  friend class Chapter;
};
```

Because the number of such items can vary greatly, the arrays are allocated on the free store:

```
class Table
{ int tablesize;
  Item* table;
  Table() { tablesize = 0; table = 0; }
  Table( int size )
    { table = new Item[ tablesize = size ]; }
  ~Table() { delete[] table; }
  friend class Chapter;
};
```

We store information separately for each chapter:

```
class Chapter
{ Table sections;
  Table figures;
  Table footnotes;
  // ...
public:
  Chapter( int secsize = 20 );
};
```

The `Chapter` constructor must call the constructor for the three `Table` objects. However, the programmer cannot explicitly call a constructor to initialize an existing object. To cause the constructor for the member objects to be called, the following syntax must be used:

```
Chapter::Chapter( int secsize = 20 ) :
  sections( secsize ),
  footnotes( 10 )
{
  // other initializations...
}
```

This causes initialization of sections through Table(secsize), figures through Table(), and footnotes through Table(10). The constructors for the members are called before the code of the object constructor is executed. Member constructors are executed in the order in which they are declared. If a member that is a class object is not specified after the : in the constructor header, it is initialized with a call to the constructor without arguments of that class. This occurs with figures, which is initialized to an empty table. It is an error if that class has some constructor but not one without arguments.

When Chapter is destroyed, destruction occurs in reverse order: first ~Chapter() is executed, then ~Table() is executed for each of the tables. This does not mean that the Chapter is actually recycled or forgotten before the Tables are destroyed, merely that the code in the Chapter destructor is called before the code in the Table destructor is executed for each table. Only after the execution of that code is the storage given up.

Because construction and destruction happen so frequently and at times unexpectedly, we will supply one more set of examples to illustrate each case (except for the case of derived classes, which will be introduced in Chapter 11).

STATIC DATA

```
Complex i( 0,1 );   // a global variable
Fraction a[ 10 ];   // a global array
```

i and a are allocated in the static data area. i is initialized through the Complex(double, double) constructor before main starts. a is initialized with 10 calls to Fraction(), and all are initialized to the default value (num = 0, den = 1). There is no ~Complex or ~Fraction destructor, so no cleanup occurs.

LOCAL VARIABLES

```
int count( List l, int n )
{ List p = l;
   . . .
}
```

p is allocated on the stack and initialized with a copy of l, either through a call to List(const List&) if it exists, or as a memberwise copy. At the end of the function, it is destroyed with ~List(), recycling all cells.

FUNCTION ARGUMENTS

```
i = count( tasklist, 0 );
```

When count starts, two local variables l and n are allocated on the stack. l is initialized with a copy of tasklist (either through a call to List(const List&) if it exists, or as a memberwise copy). n is initialized with 0. At the end of the function, the destructor call l.~List() is executed and the contents of the storage locations l and n are forgotten.

UNNAMED TEMPORARIES

```
Fraction z, w;
// ...
cout << z * w;

Fraction operator*( Fraction a, Fraction b )
{ Fraction r;
  // ...
  return r;
}
```

In the call to operator*(z, w), the result is computed in r. An unnamed temporary variable, allocated before the call in the scope of the caller, is then initialized with a copy of r, either through a call to List(const List&) if it exists, or as a memberwise copy. The temporary variable is then given to operator<< and subsequently forgotten. If a constructor is called explicitly, it also allocates an unnamed temporary:

```
cout << Fraction( 1,2 )
```

If there was a destructor ~Fraction(), it would be called before the unnamed temporary is forgotten.

FREE-STORE DATA

```
File* f = new File( "input.dat" );
// ...
delete f;
```

A File structure is allocated on the free store, and the File(char*) constructor initializes it (by opening the file whose name is given in the constructor). When the File storage is recycled, first the destructor ~File() is called (which closes the file), and then the storage is given back to the free store:

```
List* a = new List[ 10 ];
// ...
delete[] a;
```

An array of 10 lists is allocated on the free store. Each element is initialized to an empty list by a call to List(). When the array is deleted, the destructor ~List() is called 10 times, once on each array element (in reverse order, starting with the last element of the array).

MEMBER DATA

```
struct WordRef
{ char* word;
  List pages; // the pages on which the word occurs
  WordRef( char* w, int firstPage );
  ~WordRef();
};
```

```
WordRef::WordRef( char* w, int firstPage )
  : pages ( firstPage )
{ word = new char[ strlen( w ) + 1 ];
  strcpy( word, w );
}

WordRef::~WordRef()
{ delete[] word;
}
```

When a WordRef object is declared, say WordRef r("Hello", 2), then the constructor WordRef(char*, int) initializes the storage set aside for r. Before its code is executed, the constructor List(int) fills the storage area reserved for r.pages with a pointer to a list of one cell containing n. Then the body of the WordRef constructor initializes r.word with a pointer to a new block of memory and fills that block with a copy of the string w.

When r goes out of scope, the destructor ~WordRef() first recycles the string storage space. Then the destructor ~List() is called, freeing all cells of the list. Then the storage space for r is given up.

The following two situations do *not* involve constructor/destructor calls.

ASSIGNMENT

```
List a,b;
// ...
a = b;
```

The old value of a is replaced with the value b, either through a call to List::operator=(const List &), if it exists, or as a memberwise copy otherwise. The cells in the list to which a previously pointed are not automatically recycled unless the operator= has been programmed to take care of that. Assignment is not initialization, and no constructor/destructor activity takes place.

POINTER OR REFERENCE ARGUMENTS

```
int count( const List& l, int n )
{
    ...
}

i = count( tasklist, -1 );
```

The List& argument is initialized with the pointer &tasklist. Because List& and List* are not classes, no constructors or destructors can be attached to them.

● **Exercise 9.2.1.** To observe constructors and destructors in action, one can simply place debugging messages into the code. Do this in the Complex class:

```
Complex::Complex( ... )
{ ...
  cout << "\nConstructing " << long( this )
     << ",re:" << re << ",im:" << im;
}

Complex::~Complex() { cout << "\nDestructing " << long( this );}
```

Follow through the construction/destruction sequence in the following cases:

- Construction of a local variable (inside main)
- Construction of a global static variable (verify its construction before main)
- Construction of a local static variable in a function other than main
- Passing of a Complex to a function
- Returning a Complex from a function
- Creation of temporary variables in arithmetic expressions
- Obtaining an array from new and recycling it through delete
- Construction of another class with a Complex member

Also verify that assignment and Complex*/Complex& transfers do not invoke constructors.

9.3. COPYING DYNAMICALLY ALLOCATED OBJECTS

The default copy of one structure to another makes an exact copy of all members. This is desirable when copying complex numbers:

```
z = w;
```

should be the same as

```
z.re = w.re; z.im = w.im;
```

It is usually *not* desirable if one of the members is a pointer to the free store. For example, if a and b are linked lists,

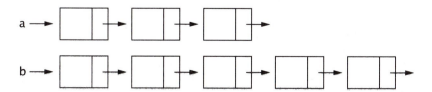

the effect of the assignment

    a = b

is

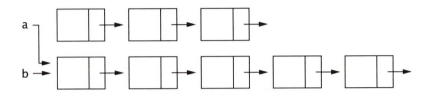

because a.head simply is set to the same address stored in b.head. The old cells of a are not recycled. If b goes out of scope before a does, the destructor b.~List() returns all cells in b (which are now also cells in a !) to the free store, making a.head point to a memory location that it doesn't own:

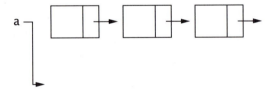

Clearly, memberwise copying is not appropriate in this situation. The intended meaning of the expression a = b is to make a a copy of the entire list pointed to by b, not just of the control structure. Redefining operator= solves that problem. We define two new member functions:

```
void List::free()
{ Cell* p = head;

  while( p != 0 )
  { Cell* q = p;
    p = p->next;
    delete q;
  }
}

void List::copy( const List& b )
{ head = pre = cur = 0;
  Cell* q = 0;
  for( Cell* p = b.head; p != 0; p = p->next )
```

```
{ Cell* n = new Cell;        // create fresh cell
  n->info = p->info;          // copy info
  if( q != 0 ) q->next = n; else head = n;
  q = n;
  if( p == b.pre ) pre = n;
  if( p == b.cur ) cur = n;
}
if ( q ! = 0 ) q->next = 0;
}
```

free is identical to ~List() and recycles all cells in a list, but it is a real function that can be called as a.free(), whereas the destructor cannot be called explicitly by the programmer. copy makes a copy of a list, using fresh cells. The second list is passed as a List& to avoid copying *it* into the function or invoking a destructor on it. Now we can write operator= :

```
List& List::operator=( const List& b )
{ if( this != &b ) // otherwise  b = b would lead to
                    // trouble
  { free();         // i.e., this->free
    copy( b );      // i.e., this->copy( b )
  }
  return *this;
}
```

The function receives references to avoid actual copying or destructor invocation. It returns what it assigns to enable multiple assignments:

```
a = b = c;
```

parenthesizes as

```
a = (b = c);
```

and is translated into the call

```
a.operator=( b.operator=( c ));
```

assigning the return value of the function call b.operator=(c) to a. Taking over the assignment operation solves the problems of memberwise copying completely, because both old cells are recycled and fresh copies of new cells are made.

However, copying can occur without involving operator=. When a new variable is created and initialized with a copy of another one, operator= is not called. This can happen in three situations:

- Declaration with initialization, List a = b
- Initialization of function arguments
- Transfer of a function return value to an unnamed temporary

In these cases, a constructor List(const List&) (in general referred to as *copy constructor* or X(const X&)) is invoked. It is a constructor that simply builds a fresh copy:

```
List::List( const List& b )
{ copy( b ); // i.e., this->copy( b )
}
```

For example, in a function call

```
int count( List l, int n )
{
    . . .
}

i = count( tasklist, -1 );
```

the local variable l of the function is initialized as l.List(tasklist), which makes a fresh copy of each cell in tasklist. When l goes out of scope at the end of the function, those fresh cells are deleted with l.~List(), and the original cells in tasklist are unaffected.

● **Exercise 9.3.1.** Implement these memory management tools. Add a message to the constructor and the copy and free functions printing the addresses of new and deleted cells. Verify that passing a list to a function and assigning a list to another makes a fresh copy of each cell.

Making a fresh copy of each cell is clearly inefficient when passing a list to a function that does not modify it. In that case, a reference should be used:

```
int count( const List& l, int n ) { ... }
n = count( tasklist, n );
```

When called as shown, the address of tasklist is transferred into a reference variable l. No construction or destruction takes place.

● **Exercise 9.3.2.** In fact, there still is a problem with the preceding solution. How can count look at the list? Only by resetting the list cursor with l.reset() and traversing the list. The function therefore has the side effect of modifying the list cursor.

To enable lists to be passed as const List& and yet be inspected, design another class Iterator that is a friend of List and Cell. The class provides a constructor resetting a cursor to the beginning of the list and functions advance, atEnd, and info compatible with the regular list functions. The following code traverses through a list l.

```
for( Iterator iter( l ); !iter.atEnd(); iter.advance() )
    // do something with iter.info()
```

(You will find iterators in [Stroustrup], but he uses operator() for the advance operation: iter() advances the iterator. There is no use arguing about taste, but we would suggest that you consider overloading ++ instead if you find advance too long.)

Any class X that stores data on the free store will need a full set of memory management operators:

```
X() (sets pointer to 0)
X( const X& )
~X()
X& X::operator=( const X& )
```

Because operator= typically deletes the old value of its first argument and then copies its second argument but cannot call the destructor and constructor explicitly, it is very common to have member functions X::free() and X::copy (const X&) that are shared:

```
X( const X& b ) { copy( b ); }
~X() { free(); }
X& operator=( const X& b )
{ if( this != &b ) { free(); copy( b ); }
  return *this;
}
```

As another example, we present a simple string class that stores the strings on the free store.

```
class String
{ char* sp;   // string pointer—points to string in free store
  void free() { delete [] sp; }
  void copy( const String& b );
public:
  String() { sp = 0; }
  String( const String& b ) { copy( b ); }
  ~String() { free(); }
  String& operator=( const String& b );
  int length () const { return sp ? strlen ( sp ) : 0 ; }
  String( const char* ); // type conversion "..." →  String
  friend ostream& operator<<( ostream&, const String& );
  friend String operator+( const String&,
    const String& ); // concatenation
};

String& String::operator=( const String& b )
{ if( this != &b )
  { free();
    copy( b );
  }
  return *this;
}
```

In the copy function we must take care to handle the case sp = 0 separately.

```
void String::copy( const String& b )
{ if( b.sp )
    { sp = new char[ strlen( b.sp )+1 ];
      strcpy( sp, b.sp );
    }
    else sp = 0;
}
```

To make a String out of a regular string (zero-terminated char*), the string must be copied into the free store:

```
String::String( char* s )
{ strcpy( sp = new char[ strlen( s )+1 ], s );
}
```

Now Strings can be declared as String a("Harry"), and a type conversion char* → String occurs automatically:

```
cout << a + " Hacker";
```

calls

```
operator+( a, String( " Hacker" ));
```

To print a string, we supply

```
ostream& operator<<( ostream& s, const String& a )
{ if ( a.sp ) s << a.sp;
    return s;
}
```

which calls operator<<(ostream&, char*) and returns the same ostream&. To concatenate two strings, memory must be allocated to hold the result:

```
String operator+( const String& a, const String& b )
{ String r;
    int len = a.length() + b.length();
    if ( len == 0 )
      r.sp = 0;
    else
    { r.sp = new char[ len + 1 ];
      if ( a.sp ) strcpy( r.sp, a.sp );
      if ( b.sp ) strcpy( r.sp + a.length(), b.sp );
    }
    return r;
}
```

● **Exercise 9.3.3.** List *all* constructor, destructor, and operator= calls that are executed during the run of the following program:

```
int main()
{ String a( "Harry" );
  String b( "Hacker" );
  String c = a + " " + b;
  cout << c;
  return 0;
}
```

Verify this by inserting test messages into those functions and running the program.

● **Exercise 9.3.4.** Add the full complement of memory-management operations to the flexible array class of Exercise 9.1.4.

● **Exercise 9.3.5.** Improve the `List::operator=` function. It is wasteful to delete all cells first and then create new ones. Reuse as many existing cells as possible, and delete only those that are not needed.

9.4. MEMBERWISE COPYING

As we have seen, structure objects can be copied during initialization (including function call and return) and through assignment. If no special copy semantics are specified through the copy constructors (`X( const X& )`) or `operator=`, a default method is used. Care must be taken, because some structure members might be objects that *do* have special copy semantics. The following recursive copy rule applies:

- If the object has a copy initializer/`operator=`, it is called.
- If the object is a built-in type or a pointer, a bitwise copy is made.
- Otherwise, memberwise assignment is applied recursively to each subobject.

In old versions of C++ this rule was not laid down. Instead, the default copy was just a bitwise copy of all members. That can become a problem when we don't expect it. Consider, for example, the description of a line in 3-space by a point on it and a direction vector.

```
class Vector // in 3-space
{ double x,y,z;
  // ...
};

class Line
{ Vector point;
  Vector direction;
  // ...
};
```

No copy constructor or `operator=` is present. Assignment of one line to another is made by bitwise copying; so far that is not a problem. However, suppose that later the `Vector` class is changed to handle vectors of arbitrary dimension:

```
class Vector
{ int dim;
  double* co; // points to coordinates on the free store
public:
  Vector( int ) { dim = d; co = new double[ d ]; }
  Vector( const Vector& );
  Vector& operator=( const Vector& );
  ~Vector() { delete co; }
  // ...
};
```

Without memberwise copying, this modification breaks the Line code. Suppose one Line is initialized with another,

```
Line m = 1;
```

and Vector fields are still copied bitwise. When either one goes out of scope, the destructor ~Vector is called, leaving dangling references in the other. The change of the Vector code would force a change in the Line code. A copy constructor would have to be added:

```
Line::Line( const Line& 1 ) : point( 1.point ),
  direction ( 1.direction )
{}
```

This is against the principle that code should continue to work if internals of a class representation have changed. For that reason, C++ replaced the concept of bitwise copying with that of memberwise copying.

Frequent copying of objects with free-store components is inefficient. Copying *into* a function can usually be avoided by replacing an argument of type X with const X&. Then the address of the object (rather than a copy of the object itself) is passed to the function. Implicit arguments of member functions are passed by reference as well; their address is copied into this. However, it is difficult to avoid the copy of the result *out of* a function. Consider addition in a vector class:

```
class Vector
{ int dim;
  double *co; // points to coordinates on the free store
public:
  Vector( int ); // creates a vector and fills it with 0
  Vector operator+( const Vector& ) const;
  // ...
};

Vector::Vector( int d )
{ dim = d;
  co = new double[ d ];
  for( int i = 0; i < d; i++ ) co[ i ] = 0;
}
```

```
Vector Vector::operator+( const Vector& b ) const
{ if( dim != b.dim ) error( "Dimensions do not match" );
  Vector r( dim );
  for( int i = 0; i < dim; i++ )
    r.co[ i ] = co[ i ] + b.co[ i ];
  return r;
}

Vector a( 3 ), b( 3 ), c( 3 );
// ...
c = a + b;
```

The operator+ function receives a pointer (this) to a because it is a member function. It receives a pointer to b because we used a reference argument. Copying vectors into the function was avoided. The return value r is computed and returned, that is, copied to an unnamed temporary. Then r is destroyed. The contents of the unnamed temporary are copied into c. The unnamed temporary must receive a distinct copy of the result, because the contents of r are destroyed before the result can be copied into c.

The problem could be avoided entirely if the compiler could change the semantics of operator+ to

```
void operator+( const Vector& a, const Vector& b,
  Vector& result );
```

and replace calls c = a + b with operator+(a,b,c). But it does not.

Can the copying be avoided by *returning a reference*? A reference to what?

```
Vector& Vector::operator+( const Vector& b ) const
{ Vector r( dim );
  // ...
  return r; // WRONG
}
```

This returns a pointer to r, a structure containing a dim and a co field located on the stack. When the function exits, that location is no longer reserved and will soon be overwritten. A reference to such a location is clearly worthless. (In addition, r continues to get destroyed.) Or, we could allocate the structure itself (and not just storage for the numbers in the vector) on the free store:

```
Vector& Vector::operator+( const Vector& b ) const
{ Vector* r = new Vector( dim );
  // ...
  return *r; // OK, but...
}
```

This is fine. The returned reference points to a persistent object on the free store. But how will that object ever get deallocated when it is no longer needed? Destructors cannot be attached to Vector&, and because the return value is stored in an unnamed temporary, it is totally beyond the programmer's control.

The problem is that destructors get called too often (returning `Vector`) or not often enough (returning `Vector&`). Should we *not* supply a destructor? We could supply the class user with public `free` and `copy` member functions, caution against assigning one `Vector` to another, recommend passing arguments by reference, and let the user worry about when to `copy` and when to `free`. That seems distasteful and error-prone.

● **Exercise 9.4.1.** Jon Shapiro of AT&T suggests the following strategy to overcome the problem of needless copying of structure return values. This trick makes use of the fact that constructors can be overloaded and that they initialize preallocated memory space without copying. Define a dummy class for each operator with no members; these only serve as selectors for constructors.

```
class dummyAdd
   { dummyAdd() {} /* do-nothing constructor */ };
class dummySub
   { dummySub() {} /* do-nothing constructor */ };
```

Then define a separate constructor for each operator:

```
Vector::Vector( const Vector& x, const Vector& y,
   dummyAdd d )
{ dim = x.dim;
  co = new double [ dim ];
   // ...
}
Vector::Vector( const Vector& x, const Vector& y,
   dummySub d )
{ dim = x.dim;
  co = new double [ dim ];
   // ...
}
```

and translate each operator into the appropriate constructor call:

```
inline Vector Vector::operator+( const Vector& b ) const
{ return Complex( *this, b, dummyAdd() );
}
inline Vector Vector::operator-( const Vector& b ) const
{ return Complex( *this, b, dummySub() );
}
```

Now the statement

```
a = b + c;
```

is translated into

```
Vector temp( b, c, dummyAdd() ); // initialization, not function call
a = temp; // still one copy
```

Try this out on your system. Compare code size and run time of both methods. Although we can see its advantages, we do not like this trick. If this mechanism is so wonderful, why isn't it built into the translator?

A different approach to memory management is used in languages such as Lisp, Smalltalk, and Eiffel. Objects are not actively deallocated, but when memory gets low, a garbage-collection process marks all free-store objects that are no longer pointed to and recycles them. The garbage collector must be tightly integrated into the language, because it must be able to recognize when a bit pattern in memory is a pointer to the free store. C++ provides no such capability.

9.5. REFERENCE COUNTING

The technique of *reference counting* is a solution to the problem of slow copies. Rather than constantly allocating and freeing copies of a storage block, a counter is attached to the block that keeps track of how many pointers reference it. When that count drops down to 0, the block is deallocated.

Let us apply that idea to the Vector class. We will make a Vector a pointer to a class VecStor, which contains the actual information of a vector and a reference count of the number of Vectors pointing to it:

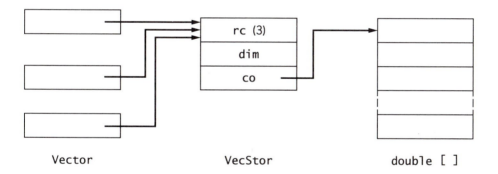

Vector   VecStor   double [ ]

Both the VecStor and the actual doubles are stored on the free store. Several Vectors can point to a single VecStor. Once that count is decremented to 0, the VecStor and the associated array of doubles are recycled:

```
class VecStor
{ friend class Vector;  // all Vector members are friends
                        // of VecStor
    int rc;
    int dim;
    double* co;  // points to coordinates on the free store
};
```

This class has no public access. Only member functions of Vector can access it. It has no constructor or destructor. Instances of VecStor are created only in conjunction with Vectors and are initialized and destroyed by the Vector constructors and destructors.

```
class Vector
{ VecStor* stor;
  void copy( const Vector& );
  void free();
public:
  Vector( int ); // creates a vector and fills it with 0
  Vector( const Vector& b ) { copy( b ); }
  ~Vector() { free(); }
  Vector& operator=( const Vector& b );
  Vector operator+( const Vector& );
  // ...
};

Vector::Vector( int d )
{ stor = new VecStor;
  stor->rc = 1;
  stor->dim = d;
  stor->co = new double[ d ];
  for( int i = 0; i < d; i++ ) stor->co[ i ] = 0;
}

Vector& Vector::operator=( const Vector& b )
{ if( this != &b )
  { free();
    copy( b );
  }
  return *this;
}
```

The Vector(const Vector&), ~Vector(), and operator= refer to copy and free functions as in the previous section. copy simply copies the pointer to the VecStor and increments the reference count. free decrements the reference count and, if it becomes 0, deallocates the VecStor.

```
void Vector::copy( const Vector& b )
{ stor = b.stor;
  stor->rc++;
}

void Vector::free()
{ stor->rc--;
  if( stor->rc == 0 )
```

```
        { delete[] stor->co;
          delete stor;
        }
    }
```

The operator+ function is as before:

```
Vector Vector::operator+( const Vector& b )
{ if( stor->dim != b.stor->dim )
    error( "Dimensions do not match" );
  Vector r( stor->dim );
  for( int i = 0; i < stor->dim; i++ )
    r.stor->co[ i ] = stor->co[ i ] + b.stor->co[ i ];
  return r;
}
```

We need no longer be afraid to copy out the result. r is created with reference count 1. When copying r to the unnamed temporary, the reference count is incremented to 2. When r is destroyed, the reference count drops to 1. If the unnamed temporary is destroyed (for example, after completion of cout << a + b), the reference count drops to 0 and the storage is recycled.

● **Exercise 9.5.1.** Draw storage diagrams for the following situation:

```
Vector a( 4 ), b( 4 ), c( 4 );
// a, b, c get filled with values
Vector d = c; // calls Vector( const Vector& )
```

Pay special attention to the reference counts. Then list *all* constructor, destructor, and operator= activity during the execution of

```
d = a + b;
```

Don't forget the unnamed temporary.

● **Exercise 9.5.2.** Recode the String class from the previous section using reference counts. The String class should have only a single pointer, stor, to a StrStor that contains a reference count 1 and a pointer to the free store. To conserve storage, denote an empty string with stor = 0 pointer (rather than stor = a pointer to a structure with reference count and a pointer to a 0 byte).

Reference counts have one serious problem. If an object whose reference count is > 1 is modified, an *on-the-fly copy* must be performed to avoid changing the meaning of the other references. In our vector class this can occur with the [] operator. Suppose

```
v = u;
v[ 0 ] = -2.5;
```

is executed, we do not want u to change with v. The operator[] code must check for multiple references and make an on-the-fly copy if necessary.

```
double& Vector::operator[]( int n )
{ if( n < 0 || n >= stor->dim )
    error( "Index out of bounds" );

  if( stor->rc > 1 )
  { stor->rc--;
    VecStor* old = stor;
    stor = new VecStor;
    stor->rc = 1;
    stor->dim = old->dim;
    stor->co = new double[ stor->dim ];
    for( int i = 0; i < stor->dim; i++ )
      stor->co[ i ] = old->co[ i ];
  }
  return stor->co[ n ];
}
```

This makes the [] operator far less attractive. Just looking at a cooordinate
(cout << v[i]) can force duplication! The operator[] function has no way
of testing whether v[i] occurred on the left side of an = or on the right side.
Of course, we could provide a separate operator for looking up a coordinate
only. It would not need to make a copy.

● **Exercise 9.5.3.** Provide an operator[] for the String class that is "safe": if
the index is larger than the string length, it should give an error message. For
example,

```
String s( "Harry" );
s[ 6 ] = 'H';
// error  message
```

● **Exercise 9.5.4.** Implement a list in which each Cell has a reference count.
When the list is copied, the first reference count is incremented. When the list
goes out of scope, the first cell's reference count is decremented, deallocating
the cell and thereby decrementing the reference count of the second cell, and so
forth. *Implementation hints:* Each Cell contains a reference count, a pointer to the
next cell, and actual information. A List contains a pointer to the head. Rather
than implementing traversal operations, supply a function int head() with
the info of the head and List tail() that returns a list starting at the second
cell (whose reference count is then incremented). The code for list traversal
becomes

```
for( List t = 1; !t.isEmpty(); t = t.tail() )
    // do something with t.head()
```

This is a much more "Lisplike" list: head/tail are similar to **car/cdr**.

Reference counting is not ideal, but in the absence of garbage collection it is just about the only game in town that does automatic deallocation without frequent copying.

● **Exercise 9.5.5.** Reference counts have a major limitation: They fail for circular references. Illustrate this phenomenon by considering the creation of a circular linked list in which each cell has a reference count. When the pointer to the circular list is destroyed, the list is not reclaimed, because each cell still has a positive reference count. Discuss strategies for circumventing this problem.

9.6. TAKING OVER STORAGE ALLOCATION

There are times when we want to take storage allocation and deallocation into our own hands rather than leaving it up to new and delete. This is especially true for dynamic allocation of constant-size objects, such as cells of linked lists or trees.

We will demonstrate a customized storage allocator for Cells of lists. We are not concerned with the structure of the Cell type. Because all cells have the same size (sizeof(Cell)), they can be recycled simply by putting them onto a *free list* and allocated by removing the first cell in the free list and using it to fulfill the request. Here are the functions:

```
union FreeCell
{ Cell   c;
  FreeCell* next;
};

static FreeCell* freelist = 0; // a global variable
const NCELL = 100; // 10 in the picture
```

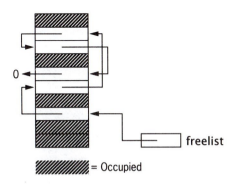

= Occupied

```
void recycle( FreeCell* f )
{ f->next = freelist;
  freelist = (FreeCell*)f;
}
```

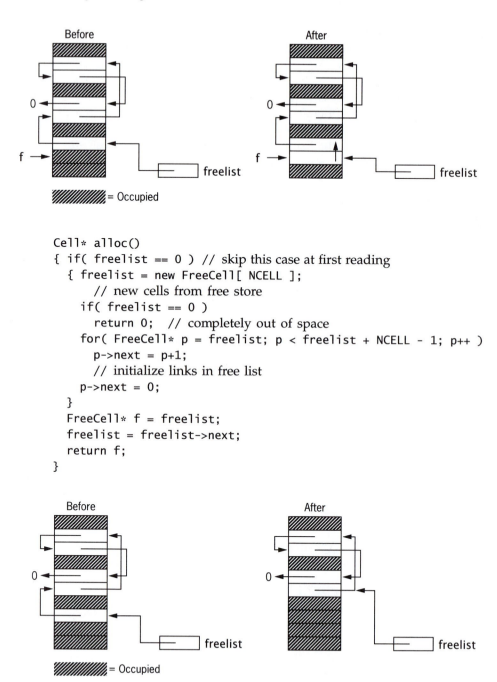

```
Cell* alloc()
{ if( freelist == 0 ) // skip this case at first reading
  { freelist = new FreeCell[ NCELL ];
      // new cells from free store
    if( freelist == 0 )
      return 0;   // completely out of space
    for( FreeCell* p = freelist; p < freelist + NCELL - 1; p++ )
      p->next = p+1;
      // initialize links in free list
    p->next = 0;
  }
  FreeCell* f = freelist;
  freelist = freelist->next;
  return f;
}
```

● **Exercise 9.6.1.** Work through the code and draw pictures illustrating the next six calls to alloc (with NCELL = 10).

This allocation is far more efficient than the general purpose new/delete allocator, which must pay attention to the sizes of the memory blocks. Cell overloads operator new and operator delete:

```
void* Cell::operator new( size_t bytes )
{ if( bytes != sizeof( Cell ))
  { error( "Wrong size" ); return 0; }
  return alloc();
}

void Cell::operator delete( void* p )
{ recycle( (FreeCell*) p );
}
```

The size_t type is declared in stddef.h to be sufficient to hold sizes of data blocks, that is, typically unsigned or unsigned long.

Note the peculiarities of these operations. operator new receives a byte count. This is necessary if it is used to allocate storage for a *derived-class* object (see Chapter 11), which might be bigger. It returns a void* rather than a Cell*. operator new and operator delete are static member functions. They may not refer to the this pointer or to any class members. For this reason, operator delete requires an explicit (void*) pointer to the object to be deleted.

● **Exercise 9.6.2.** Use the fixed-size allocation technique to manage the cells in the list representation of the Polynomial class (Exercises 7.2.7 and 9.1.0). Implement the stack calculator and measure the difference in performance between new/delete and custom memory management under some large computations.

● 9.7. PITFALLS

9.7.1. Deleting Unallocated Blocks

Passing a pointer to delete that was not obtained through new is a certain recipe for disaster.

```
char buffer[ 10 ];
char *p = buffer;

// ...
if( n >= 10 )
{ p = new char[ 20 ];
  strcpy( p, buffer );
}
// ...
delete p; // WRONG
```

The free-store manager expects to find information, such as the block size, just below the recycled address. Some implementations are sophisticated, checking whether the returned pointer is within a reasonable range; others are not and simply incorporate the block for later reallocation. It is also an error to delete the same block twice "just to be sure." However, deleting a 0 pointer is safe—it simply does nothing.

9.7.2. Deleting Too Early

When a block is deleted, the free-store manager may overwrite some of the storage. For example,

```
for( p = head; p != 0; p = p->next )
  delete p; // WRONG
```

When the block with address p is deleted, its next field may be overwritten and the p = p->next instruction may fetch a corrupted value. The correct method is

```
for( p = head; p != 0; )
{ Cell* q = p;
  p = p->next;
  delete q; // OK
}
```

9.7.3. Memberwise Copying of Objects with a Destructor

This error is most common with classes that have a destructor but no copy constructor and operator=. Consider such a class:

```
class File
{ FILE* fp;        // a C-style file pointer
public:
  File() { fp = 0; }
  File( char* name, char* mode )
  { fp = fopen( name, mode ); }
  ~File() { fclose( fp ); }
  fptr() { return fp };
};

Employee read( File f )  // no  File( const File& ),
                         // f = memberwise copy
{ Employee r;
  fread( r, sizeof( Employee ), 1, f.fptr() );
}    // f destroyed,  fclose called
```

The remedy is to pass a File& or File*, because constructors and destructors are attached only to actual classes, not to references or pointers.

INHERITANCE

10.1. DERIVED CLASSES

We will consider some elements of a chart-drawing package. We wish to display bar charts and other chart types. Unfortunately, we cannot draw on a common graphics standard that is available to all readers. To cater to the lowest common denominator in available output devices, we use text-based screen output. Lines are formed with * characters and stored in a double array that is displayed on the screen at appropriate times. A Grid class for this purpose was developed in Sections 5.3 and 7.3:

```
class Grid
{
public:
  enum { XSIZE = 79, YSIZE = 24 };
  Grid();
  void clear(); // fill with ' '
  void show() const; // display current picture
  void set( int x, int y, char ch ='*' );
  void line( int xstart, int ystart, int xend, int yend );

private:
  char g[ YSIZE ][ XSIZE + 1 ];
};
```

We start the chart package with a box class (as for a bar chart).

```
class Box
{ int xleft, xright, ytop, ybottom;
public:
  Box( int x1, int y1, int x2, int y2 );
  int xsize() const;
  int ysize() const;
  int xcenter() const;
  int ycenter() const;
  void plot( Grid& ) const;
};
```

```
Box::Box( int x1, int y1, int x2, int y2 )
{ xleft = x1, ytop = y1, xright = x2; ybottom = y2;
}

int Box::xsize() const
{ return xright - xleft + 1;
}

int Box::ysize() const
{ return ybottom - ytop + 1;
}

int Box::xcenter() const
{ return ( xleft + xright ) / 2;
}

int Box::ycenter() const
{ return ( ytop + ybottom ) / 2;
}

void Box::plot( Grid& g ) const
{ g.line( xleft, ytop, xright, ytop );
  g.line( xright, ytop, xright, ybottom );
  g.line( xright, ybottom, xleft, ybottom );
  g.line( xleft, ybottom, xleft, ytop );
}
```

It can be used like this:

```
Grid g;
Box b( 10,15, 15,20 );
b.plot( g );
g.show();
```

● **Exercise 10.1.1.** Improve the constructor so that it sorts the corner coordinates and achieves xleft < xright, ytop < ybottom even if the box was specified by other corners.

The next step is to design a type TextBox, a box filled with text:

Soybean
production

This is a box plus a string. Its `plot` function plots the box, then the string inside. Because a `TextBox` *is* a box, and all operations that make sense for a box automatically make sense for a `TextBox`, we will make use of a new language construct: We will *derive* `TextBox` from `Box`.

```
class TextBox : public Box
{ char text[ TEXTSIZE ];
public:
   TextBox( int, int, int, int, const char* );
   void plot( Grid& g ) const;
};
```

The class definition specifies that a `TextBox` is a `Box` with an additional data item, `text`, and with its own constructor and `plot` function. All other functions (`xsize`, `xcenter`,...) are *inherited* from `Box`. The new data elements are added to the `Box` data. A pointer to a `TextBox` is a pointer to a `Box`! (It just ignores the new data.)

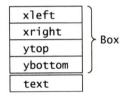

Let us write the `plot` function. If the string is to fit into the box, it must be broken up into substrings. We will ignore this need for now and assume that the string fits in one line, in which we will center it.

```
void TextBox::plot( Grid& g ) const
{ Box::plot( g );   // draw the box outline

   int y = ycenter();
   int len = strlen( text );
   int x = xcenter() - ( len - 1 ) / 2;
   for( int i = 0; i < len; i++ )
       g.set( x, y, text[ i ]);
}
```

Note the use of the `::` scope resolution operator to call the `plot` function of the base class. The `xcenter` function is a member function of `TextBox` that was inherited from `Box`.

When deriving, we need to specify only

- The member data added to the base class
- The member functions added to the base class
- The member functions that replace base class functions with the same name

We still need to supply a constructor for `TextBox`:

```
TextBox::TextBox(int x1, int y1, int x2, int y2, const char* t)
{ xleft = x1; xright = x2; ytop = y1; ybottom = y2; // WRONG
  strncpy( text, t, sizeof( text ));
  text[ sizeof( text ) - 1 ] = 0;
}
```

What should be wrong with that? If `TextBox` is a `Box`, it has an `xleft` field. Why can't it be accessed? `xleft` is a private member of `Box`, and *nobody* can access it without the explicit permission of the `Box` class. `Box` was not asked whether it wanted to be derived from. This may seem paranoid, but it is the only reasonable way of keeping a protection mechanism. If a derived class could access the private members of a base class, anyone could access private members of any class simply by deriving another class from it with the sole intention of peeking inside the base class. Of course, `TextBox` can use the public members such as `xcenter` of `Box`.

How then can the `Box` portion of `TextBox` be constructed? Only through the public members. There is a public constructor. But constructors are not functions that the programmer can call at will. The syntax for performing the construction is similar to invoking a member constructor (Section 9.2). The base class name is used instead of a member name:

```
TextBox::TextBox(int x1, int y1, int x2, int y2, const char* t)
: Box( x1, y1, x2, y2 )
{ strncpy( text, t, sizeof( text ));
  text[ sizeof( text ) - 1 ] = 0;
}
```

Section 10.3 contains the details about construction and visibility rules.

● **Exercise 10.1.2.** Implement `Box` and `TextBox`. Verify that a `TextBox` *is* a box: All box member functions can be applied to it. If `t` is a `TextBox`, compare the results of `t.plot()` and `t.Box::plot()`. Which `plot` routine does the code `Box* pb = &t; pb->plot();` execute?

● **Exercise 10.1.3.** Improve `TextBox::plot` to break up the character string into multiple lines, each at most `xsize()` - 2 characters long. Try to break at white space. If there are more than `ysize()` - 2 lines, ignore the remaining ones. For example, `TextBox( 10, 10, 23, 17, "Soybean production" ).plot( g );` `g.show();` should result in the display shown at the beginning of this chapter.

● **Exercise 10.1.4.** Implement a `Point` class storing row and column coordinates of a point. Redefine the `Box` class to store two corner points and rewrite the `Box` and `TextBox` constructors.

Now that we have rushed to embrace this new language concept, let us consider a more traditional alternative. `TextBox` could have made `Box` a member rather than deriving from it:

```
class TBox
{ Box b;
  char text[ TEXTSIZE ];
// ...
};
```

The memory layout looks just the same:

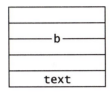

The members of b cannot be accessed directly, but neither could the base class members. There are indeed only two differences:

- A pointer to a TBox is not automatically a Box*.
- A public member function of Box cannot be applied to a TBox.

If t is a TBox then t.xcenter() is not correct. The function applies only to a box. If t.xcenter() is desired, it must be coded to call t.b.xcenter(). Here is a complete TBox type. Note in particular the member constructor call and the need to redefine the box measurement functions.

```
class TBox : public Box
{ Box b;
  char text[ TEXTSIZE ];
public:
  TBox( int x1, int y1, int x2, int y2, const char* );
  int xsize() const { return b.xsize(); }
  int ysize() const { return b.ysize(); }
  int xcenter() const { return b.xcenter(); }
  int ycenter() const { return b.ycenter(); }
  void plot( Grid& g ) const;
};

void TBox::plot( Grid& g ) const
{ b.plot( g ); // draw the box outline

  int y = ycenter(); // same as before
  int len = strlen( text );
  int x = xcenter() - ( len - 1 ) / 2;
  for ( int i = 0; i < len; i++ )
    g.set( x + i, y, text[ i ]);
}
```

Although eminently workable, this solution lacks the elegance of simply inheriting the box measurement functions. There is also a second disadvantage that will become clear in the next section: Class member data items do not support virtual functions.

This section introduced the first use of inheritance. Inheritance can be a *convenience feature*. You can take an existing, working class, add a few new data or function members, and replace only the functions that need to be modified. However, inheritance is a multifaceted concept, and other applications of it are described in subsequent sections.

● **Exercise 10.1.5.** Consider the `Vector` class developed in Section 9.5. *Derive* a safe array of `double` class from it. The `Array` constructor receives the low and high bounds of the array. Add as data a lower bound `lo` and modify `operator[]` to return `Vector::operator[]( i - lo )` or print an error message if `i` is out of range. Pay special attention to the copy constructor and assignment operator.

10.2. VIRTUAL FUNCTIONS

In the last section we noted that a pointer to a derived class automatically points to the base class. We can put `Box` pointers in an array or linked list, some of which are pointers to plain boxes and others to TextBoxes. Of course, we cannot put the actual plain or `Text` boxes into an array or linked list because they differ in size, whereas all pointers have the same size. Here is a box list type:

```
class BoxList
{ // ...
public:
  BoxList();
  ~BoxList();
  void insert( Box* n );
  void reset();
  void advance();
  Box* info() const;

  int atEnd() const;
};
```

Now we can insert both plain and text boxes:

```
BoxList bl;

bl.insert( new Box( 0, 5, 10, 15 ));
bl.insert( new TextBox( 10, 13, 20, 23, "Soybean production" ));
```

The value of new `TextBox(...)` is a `TextBox*`, which is in particular a `Box*`, and it can be inserted in the list without type conversion. But what is the use? When walking through the list and retrieving `Box*` pointers,

```
for( bl.reset(); !bl.atEnd(); bl.advance() )
   // do something with p = bl.info();
```

there is no way of telling whether a particular pointer p points to a plain box or a text box.

When calling p->plot(), it will merely call Box::plot(). One could add a *type field* into the box that has different values for plain boxes, text boxes, boxes with drop shadows, pie chart segments, and whatever other items we might come up with in the chart program. By inspecting p->type one could switch to the correct plot function:

```
switch( p->type )
{ case 0:
     p->plot(); break;
  case 1:
     ( (TextBox*) p )->plot(); // cast operator is weaker
                               // than ->
     break;
}
```

This is certainly a time-honored programming strategy, and there is nothing wrong with it for a program that never changes. However, we want to keep our program flexible for further enhancement. It would be desirable to free future generations of coders from the error-prone task of searching through the entire body of existing code for all occurrences of ->type (in switch (t->type) or a function pointer table ((*fp[t->type])()) whenever a new plottable item is introduced.

A truly marvelous concept, a *virtual function*, solves that problem. Making the plot function virtual in the base class,

```
class Box
{ // ...
   virtual void plot( Grid& g ) const;
};
```

alerts the compiler automatically to make a type field that distinguishes a plain Box and all its derived classes and to translate each call

```
p->plot(); // p a Box*
```

into a run-time selection of the correct plot. Think of plot as *run-time overloaded*. Each item is plotted according to its type:

```
BoxList bl;

bl.insert( new Box( 0, 5, 10, 15 ) );
bl.insert( new TextBox( 10, 13, 20, 23, "Soybean production" ) );

for( bl.reset(); !bl.atEnd(); bl.advance() )
   bl.info()->plot(); // uses Box::plot or TextBox::plot
```

To enable this feature, each function to be run-time selectable must be declared virtual in the base class. Only member functions can be virtual.

● **Exercise 10.2.1.** Write a program that can read plain and text boxes in and test the run-time selection of the virtual plot function. A fancy solution is to provide an operator>>(istream&, Box*&). Where does the decision whether to get a new Box or a new TextBox take place?

To add a print function that lists specific box information for debugging purposes, the base and derived classes must be enhanced as follows:

```
class Box
{ // ...
   virtual void print() const;
};

void Box::print() const
{ cout << xleft << " " << ytop << " "
       << xright << " " << ybottom;
}

class TextBox : public Box
{ // ...
   void print() const;
}

void TextBox::print() const;
{  Box::print();
   cout << " " << text;
}
```

The following code lists the box-specific information for each box in a list:

```
for( l.reset(); !l.atEnd(); l.advance() )
   l->print(); // uses Box::print or TextBox::print
```

The selection of the correct function occurs at run time.

● **Exercise 10.2.2.** Add the print function and test it.

How does this programming method differ from the switch solution? Adding another plottable item is localized. For example, to add a box with shading,

we provide

```
class ShadedBox : public Box
{ char shade; // the character used inside the box
public:
    // ...
    void plot( Grid& g ) const;
    void print() const;
};
```

and code for the plot and print functions. *No existing code needs to be modified.*

● **Exercise 10.2.3.** Add a ShadedBox to your code. Verify that the list traversal code did not change.

The implementation of the virtual function feature is left to the discretion of the compiler, and some authors feel that such details should be of no concern to the reader. I provide an explanation of the mechanism used by the standard C++→ C translator to show that virtual functions can be implemented with a surprisingly low space and time overhead.

A class that has at least one virtual member function allocates an additional data member: a pointer to a function table. You can think of this data member as a type field. An instance of a derived class is built on the base class structure, so it automatically inherits the pointer field, but it contains a different value: a pointer to a table with different function entries:

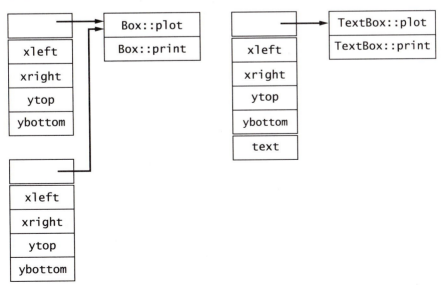

Recall that the function name `Box::plot` without the `()` refers to the *starting address* of the function. A pointer to an unknown object can still execute a virtual function as long as it knows the position of the function in the table:

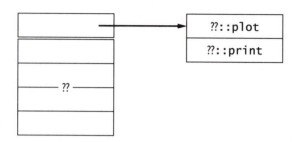

Think of the table of function pointers as an instruction manual. Each object comes with its own instruction manual, and all object manufacturers agree that the instructions for `plot` are on page 0, those for `print` are on page 1, and so on. All one has to do when asked to perform a task with an object of unknown type is to get the instruction manual from the glove compartment, open it on the agreed page, and execute the instructions. The call

```
p->print()
```

is translated into a call to

*(p->*function table* + *offset of* `print`)

The operations are

- Taking the table address from the structure
- Looking up the function address at a constant offset in that table
- Calling that function

The space overhead is equally modest. For each class, a small table is allocated with the starting addresses of virtual functions. Each *instance* of a class (base or derived) has a single additional pointer field. This is a problem only if there are a great many instances of the same class and a pointer cannot be tolerated in each of them.

Who enters the table pointer and when? The compiler generates code *function table* = *table address* in the constructors that get executed when a new object is allocated, either statically (`Box b`) or dynamically (`p = new TextBox`).

Clearly this mechanism is very efficient—much more efficient than a typical hand-coded `switch` statement.

● **Exercise 10.2.4.** This exercise gives an indication of the implementation of a multiple "undo" command in a word processor. For simplicity, we will just implement a (useless) line processor, editing a single line of text. Commands are

(any character key)	Enter the character at the cursor location
[Ctrl-L]	Move cursor left
[Ctrl-R]	Move cursor right
[Ctrl-B]	Move cursor to the beginning of the line
[Ctrl-E]	Move cursor to the end of the line
[Bksp]	Delete character before the cursor
[Ctrl-U]	Undo the previous command
[Ctrl-D]	Redo the previous command
[Ctrl-Q]	Quit

Any number of "Undo" commands should be supported, back to the starting state of a completely blank line.

Design a base class Command. Derive from it commands to move the cursor, to insert a character, to delete a character. Keep an array of pairs of Command*. Every time a new command is entered (except undo/redo), enter both the command and its inverse onto that array. Undo goes backward in the array, executing the inverses, and redo goes forward, reexecuting the previously entered commands.

Find out how you can get unbuffered input on your system and how you can move the cursor and insert or delete characters in a line. Encapsulate those system-dependent details.

● **Exercise 10.2.5.** Add commands to the program of the previous exercise:

[Ctrl-I]	Toggles the "insert mode" from insert to overtype
[Ctrl-A]	Deletes all characters after the cursor
[Ctrl-X]	Deletes the character under the cursor

10.3. VISIBILITY AND CONSTRUCTION

Which members of a base class are visible to a derived class? To the outside world when contained in a derived class? We saw in the last section that private members of a base class cannot be accessed in a derived class. Public members of the base class are accessible to member functions of the derived class. But to make them *public* members of the derived class, the keyword public must be inserted after the : derivation symbol. This sounds confusing, and it is. Consider the example from the last section, with the word public removed from the derivation:

```
class Box
{ int xleft, xright, ytop, ybottom;
public:
    Box( int x1, int y1, int x2, int y2 );
    int xsize() const;
    int ysize() const;
```

```
    int xcenter() const;
    int ycenter() const;
    void plot( Grid& ) const;
};

class TextBox : Box
{ char text[ TEXTSIZE ];
public:
    TextBox( int x1, int y1, int x2, int y2, const char* );
    void plot( Grid& g ) const;
};
```

If t is a TextBox, then

- t.xleft is an error. Private members of the base class cannot be accessed from the derived class.

- t.xsize() is OK inside a member function of TextBox but not inside any other function. Public members of a non-public base class become private members of the derived class.

- A cast (Box*) t is not legal outside a member function, because it could be used to circumvent the previous restriction.

All this is usually undesirable. Why shouldn't other functions be able to measure t.xsize()? Why indeed? To make public members of the base class public in the derived class, the base class must be declared public:

```
class TextBox : public Box
{ // ...
};
```

Public base classes are far more common than their more secretive cousins, and it is too bad that their declaration is longer. However, it is understandable from the close analogy between a base class and a class member. If Box had been a class member

```
class TBox
{ Box b;
    // ...
}
```

it would have been impossible as well to refer to t.b.xsize().

Consider a base class such as Box. Some members such as xsize() should be public members of any of its derived classes. For efficiency, it would be desirable to make xleft and so forth accessible to derived classes, but only as private members. The mechanism discussed so far does not offer this choice. Either all public members of a base class are public members of the derived class (class TextBox : public Box) or none are (class TextBox : Box). For this reason, there is another level, called protected. A protected member of the base class is visible to all member functions of all classes derived from it, but not to any other functions. The following setup is common:

```
class Box
{
protected:
    int xleft, xright, ytop, ybottom;
public:
    int xsize() const;
    // ...
};

class TextBox : public Box
{ char text[ TEXTSIZE ];
public:
    // ...
};
```

- t.xleft is OK inside a member function of TextBox but not inside any nonmember function. Protected members of the base class become protected members of the derived class.

- t.xsize() is OK everywhere. Public members of a public base class stay public in the derived class.

When designing a class that you expect others to use as a base for derivations, follow these rules:

- Place items about which *nobody* needs to know in the private section.

- Place items that might be useful for members of derived classes in the protected section.

- Place items that the derived class might want to make public into the public section. It still is up to the derived class whether to go ahead and make these items public (Derived : public Base) or not (Derived : Base).

A constructor for a derived class usually needs to initialize the base class members. Because it rarely has access to all of them, the base class constructor needs to perform this task. Because constructors are not functions, the derived class constructor cannot simply call the base class constructor. To cause the constructor to be called, its arguments are placed before the body of the derived-class constructor.

```
TextBox::TextBox(int x1, int y1, int x2, int y2, const char* t)
: Box( x1, y1, x2, y2 )
{ strncpy( text, t, sizeof( text ));
    text[ sizeof( text ) - 1 ] = 0;
}
```

This syntax is very similar to a member constructor call:

```
TBox::TBox( int x1, int y1, int x2, int y2, const char* t )
: b( x1, y1, x2, y2 )
{ strncpy( text, t, sizeof( text ));
    text[ sizeof( text ) - 1 ] = 0;
}
```

In fact, both kinds of constructor invocations may be present if a derived class also has class members.

```
class TextBox : public Box
{ String s;
public:
  TextBox( int, int, int, int, const char* );
  // ...
};
```

```
TextBox::TextBox(
    int x1, int y1, int x2, int y2, const char* str )
: Box( x1, y1, x2, y2 ), s( str )
{}
```

Note the difference between base class constructor invocation (with the type name) and member constructor invocation (with the member name). It is instructive to visualize the entire sequence of events. Keep in mind that constructors never actually obtain storage; they just serve to fill preallocated memory:

- First, storage for the object is allocated (on the static data area, stack, or heap).
- Then, the base class constructor initializes the base area.
- Then, the member class constructor(s) are launched on their areas.
- Then, the body of the constructor is executed.

Destructors run in the opposite order. The destructor does not actually destroy the object in question. It contains code that must run before the object is forgotten or recycled.

Here is the sequence of destructor events:

- First, the class destructor code is executed.
- Then, the destructor of each member is executed.
- Then, the destructor for the base class is executed.
- Then, the object is forgotten or recycled.

● **Exercise 10.3.1.** Write a set of functions that recursively evaluate nested arithmetic expressions. Allowable expressions are

Number	Any int
Sum	sum(e_1, e_2,..., e_n)
Product	prod(e_1, e_2,..., e_n)
Difference	diff(e_1, e_2)
Quotient	quot(e_1, e_2)

For example:

```
sum( 2, prod( 3, 4, -2 ), diff( 3, quot( 8, 2 )), 10 )
```

Design a base class `Expr` with virtual functions `eval` and `print`. Derive classes `Number` (containing `double`), `Sum`, and `Product` (containing an array of `Expr*` pointers), `Difference`, and `Quotient` (containing two `Expr*` pointers). Your program should read in an expression from standard input, print it back out, and print its value.

● **Exercise 10.3.2.** Change the `print` functions in Example 10.3.1 to print expressions in standard algebraic notation, such as

```
2 + 3*4*(-2) + (3-8/2) + 10
```

The challenge is not to print unnecessary `()`.

● **Exercise 10.3.3.** Change the `print` function once more to print quotients as fractions!

```
        10 - 2
   1 + ------
          3
   ----------
     2 * 12
```

Hint: Buffer the output in a 2-dimensional grid. Implement a virtual function `size` returning a structure containing the number of rows and columns needed for an expression. (For example, the vertical size of a fraction equals the vertical size of the numerator plus 1 (for the fraction bar) plus the vertical size of the denominator. The vertical size of a sum equals the maximum of vertical sizes of the summands.)

● **Exercise 10.3.4.** Add a square root operator and display it as in

```
      +--
   a + \| b
   --------
     2 * c
```

If you have an IBM PC or another system with special math characters, display

```
   a + √b
   ----------
     2 · c
```

instead.

10.4. INHERITANCE HIERARCHIES AND MULTIPLE INHERITANCE

It is quite common to have an entire hierarchy of derivation, with some classes twice or more removed from a base class. In our chart package we may well have shapes that are not boxlike, such as diamonds:

The plot function should therefore be based in a type Shape, from which both Box and Diamond are derived.

TextBox

ShadedBox

Diamond

Box

Shape

(Arrows point to base class)

```
class Shape
{
public:
  virtual void plot( Grid& ) const;
};

void Shape::plot( Grid& ) const
{ error( "This can't happen." );
}

class Box : public Shape
{
protected:
  // ...
public:
  void plot( Grid& ) const;
};

class TextBox : public Box
{ // ...
};
```

The Shape class has no data items. It merely holds the other classes together by providing a common virtual plot function. No actual instance of a plain Shape will ever be created, because it has no conceivable use. Such a class is called an *abstract base class*. If an instance is created accidentally and plotted, the default version of plot() generates an error.

A virtual function can be explicitly declared as abstract. For example,

```
class Shape
{
public:
  virtual void plot( Grid& ) const = 0;
};
```

A class with at least one abstract virtual function becomes an abstract class, and the compiler will not permit creation of any instances of the class itself. Of course, pointers to the class, pointing to (nonabstract) derived-class instances, are permitted.

● **Exercise 10.4.1.** Discuss the memory layout of a TextBox in this hierarchy. Where is the pointer to the virtual function table located?

● **Exercise 10.4.2.** Restructure the inheritance tree by basing it on a Shape and including a Diamond class.

In the examples that we have seen so far the inheritance graph is always a tree, because a derived class had only a single base class. That is not always desirable. Suppose that we wish to make use of an existing class,

```
class Text
{ char text[ TEXTSIZE ];
public:
  Text( const char t[], int margin = 0 );
  void breakLines( int margin );
  int nlines() const;
  void line( int i, int& from, int& to ) const;
  char get( int ) const;
};
```

that can change text to uppercase and break text into multiple lines. Now a text box

```
┌─────────────┐
│             │
│             │
│   Soybean   │
│  production │
│             │
└─────────────┘
```

could make good use of the services provided by both the Box and the Text classes.

```
class TextBox : public Box, public Text
{
public:

    // ...
    void plot( Grid& g ) const;
};
```

The inheritance graph now looks like

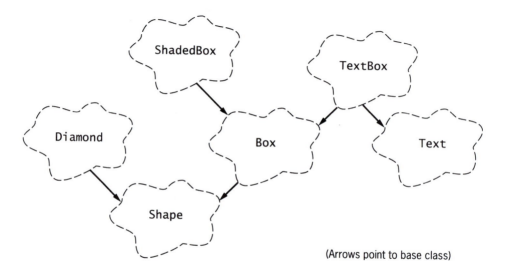

(Arrows point to base class)

It is no longer a tree, because TextBox has *two* base classes. If one thinks of the edges as having a direction (arrows pointing from the derived class to the base class), the inheritance graph is a *directed acyclic graph* (DAG). There can be no cycles, because no class can be its own direct or indirect derived class.

Couldn't we just define a TextBox as

```
class TextBox : public Box // using single inheritance
{ Text t;
public:
    // ...
    void plot( Grid& g ) const;
};
```

This looks almost the same as the foregoing code. But now a TextBox is no longer a Text. It cannot be placed onto a list of Text objects. The benefit of inheritance is not merely access to data; class members are adequate for that.

More important is the ability to select the correct member function at run-time when the object is grouped together with other objects sharing a common base class.

The syntax for multiple inheritance is a straightforward extension. The attribute `public` must be separately listed for each base class:

```
class TextBox : public Box, public Text
```

Any number of base classes can be specified. A constructor that calls base class constructors must explicitly name the base classes:

```
TextBox::TextBox(int x1, int y1, int x2, int y2, const char t[])
: Box( x1, y1, x2, y2 ), Text( t, x2 - x1 - 1 )
{}
```

All public members from any of the base classes can be accessed. If two of them happen to have the same name, the scope resolution operator must be used, for example, `Box::print()` and `Text::print()` can distinguish between two inherited `print()` functions.

Multiple inheritance poses several technical problems, which explain its omission in early versions of the C++ language. The most obvious is that a pointer to a derived class no longer automatically points to the base class. Consider the `TextBox` derived from two base classes:

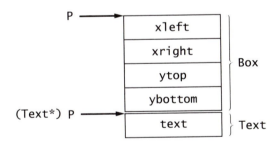

If the memory layout is as shown here (and there is no guarantee for that), a pointer `TextBox* p` points automatically to the `Box` portion but not the `Text` portion. Yet often we want it to point there. For example, `p->breakLines(...)` should receive the starting address of the `Text` portion as `this`.

The translator handles this automatically. When a pointer to a derived class is converted to a pointer to one of the base classes (either by an explicit cast or by a base member function call), the appropriate offset is added. The programmer must be more careful than ever about explicit type conversions. Casually placing a `TextBox*` into a `void*` and subsequently casting it as a `Text*` will not work at all.

● **Exercise 10.4.3.** Design a Text class. Then design the TextBox class by inheriting from Text and Box and test it.

Multiple inheritance is particularly useful if a class can be combined from several preexisting classes. For example, one might want to have a ShadedTextBox :

The most natural solution is to make a ShadedTextBox an object that is both a ShadedBox and a TextBox:

```
class ShadedTextBox : public ShadedBox, public TextBox
{ // ...

};
```

Here is the inheritance graph:

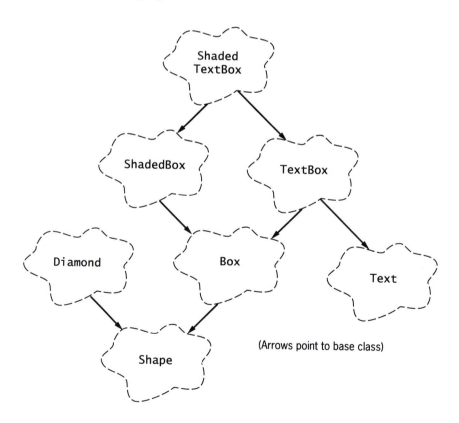

(Arrows point to base class)

This is much better than defining a ShadedTextBox as a TextBox with a shade data member. The shading function can be inherited, and a ShadedTextBox is *both* a TextBox and a ShadedBox .

However, there is a serious problem. Both parent classes derive from Box, and there are two different boxes in each instance of ShadedTextBox:

xleft
xright
ytop
ybottom
text
xleft
xright
ytop
ybottom
shade

If s is a ShadedTextBox, what is s.xcenter()? It is ambiguous and must be made explicit through scope resolution: s.ShadedBox::xcenter() or s.TextBox::xcenter(). After all, there *might* be different boxes stored in both parts, even though that is not our intention in this example. Wasting the space for both boxes is undesirable, as is the concern to keep the information in both of them identical. *Virtual base classes* are designed to overcome this problem.

If TextBox and ShadedBox both declare Box to be virtual,

```
class TextBox : virtual public Box { ... };
class ShadedBox : public virtual Box { ... };
// keyword order not significant
```

then a class inheriting from both gets only a single instance of Box. The declaration of ShadedTextBox is unchanged,

```
class ShadedTextBox : public TextBox, public ShadedBox
{ ... };
```

and the common virtual classes are coalesced to a single copy. No matter how often a virtual base class occurs in a derivation, only one common instance is created. The memory layout is as follows:

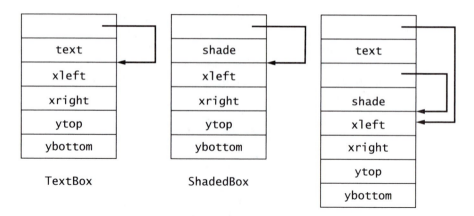

ShadedTextBox

The virtual base class is stored separately from the derived classes. The doubly derived class has two copies of the pointer to the common virtual base class. This is necessary to have a pointer to a ShadedTextBox convertible to a pointer to TextBox or ShadedBox.

Because a single copy of the virtual base class is shared, there is a restriction on virtual base class construction: A virtual base class may be initialized only from the *most* derived class or with a constructor that requires no arguments. Why is this necessary? If both TextBox and ShadedBox initialize Box with explicit arguments, which of the two should initialize the Box portion of a ShadedTextBox? The only safe strategy is to deny it to both. But ShadedTextBox is more derived than either and can initialize Box:

```
ShadedTextBox(...) : Box(...), ShadedBox(...), TextBox(...)
{};
```

This initializes the shared instance of Box.

The order of construction is as follows:

- Virtual base classes
- Base classes, in order of declaration
- Member classes, in order of declaration
- Derived class

Destruction proceeds in reverse order.

● **Exercise 10.4.4.** Implement the ShadedTextBox with virtual base classes. In the plot function, first shade, and then let the text overwrite over the shading.

10.5 RECOGNIZING INHERITANCE

Now that we have seen how the inheritance mechanism works, it is a good idea to reflect on the question of when it is appropriate to use inheritance in our programs.

Inheritance is a classification mechanism. We use it to describe the fact that objects have certain properties in common, even though they differ in other properties. For example, all shapes have something in common: They can be plotted and printed. We can take advantage of that in a graphics program. A graphic image consists of a collection of shapes. The function to draw the image on the screen doesn't need to know the exact nature of each shape. It simply calls the virtual plot function for each shape object. Similarly, the function that saves the image to disk simply calls the print function for each shape. Any data type whose objects can be plotted and printed can derive from the Shape class.

It is sometimes surprisingly difficult to find a good inheritance hierarchy. Consider this example, which was used in the tutorial manual of a popular C++ compiler vendor. The tutorial introduces a class Point with member functions move and plot. The move function moves the position of the point:

```
class Point
{ int x, y;
public
   Point( int, int );
   Virtual void move( int by_x, int by_y );
   Virtual void plot( Grid& g );
};

void Point::move( int by_x, int by_y )
{ x += by_x;
  y += by_y;
}
```

Then the authors derive a class Circle:

```
class Circle : public Point
{ int radius;
public:
   Circle( Point, int );
   virtual void plot( Grid& g );
};
```

Note that the move function can be inherited, since Point::move moves the center of the circle, and moving a circle doesn't change the radius. This seems like a splendid example for code reuse through inheritance. However, the inheritance becomes awkward with the next geometric construction.

```
class Rectangle : public Point
{ Point other;
public:
   Rectangle( Point, Point );
   virtual void move( int by_x, int by_y );
   virtual void plot( Grid& g );
};
```

One of the corner points is stored in the base, one as an explicit data member. There is no benefit from inheritance. The move function must be supplied, and it looks strangely asymmetric:

```
void Rectangle::move( int by_x, int by_y )
{ Point::move( by_x, by_y );
  other.move( by_x, by_y );
}
```

The polymorphic part of the program also looks weird:

```
Point* figure[ NPoint ];
figure[ 0 ] = new Rectangle(...);
```

The conversion Rectangle*→Point* is technically correct, but it is not intuitive.

In our examples we have avoided these problems by using a base class Shape. It seems much more believable to convert a Rectangle* into a Shape*, because a rectangle is a kind of shape.

There is a test to check if inheritance is appropriate. It is called the "is-a" test. You should ask yourself, "Is every rectangle a point?" The answer is no. Rectangles and points are similar, but a rectangle isn't a special case of a point. But if you ask "Is every rectangle a shape?" then the answer is yes, provided we understand a shape to be an object that can be moved and plotted. We use inheritance to express the "is-a" relationship.

The alternative to "is-a" is "has-a". A rectangle has a point. In fact, it has two corner points. Use data members to model "has-a".

```
class Rectangle
{ Point corner1, corner 2;
public:
  Rectangle( Point, Point );
  virtual void move( int by_x, int by_y );
  virtual void plot ( Grid& g );
};
```

A common reason to abuse inheritance is laziness. Suppose we have a nicely working linked-list class, and now we are asked to write an unbounded stack class. It is simple:

```
class Stack : public List
{
public:
  void push( int x ) { insert( x ); }
  int pop( int x ) { return remove(); }
};
```

But it is also dangerous. Not only does the Stack class have functions push and pop, but it inherits all the member functions from List. Suppose that the user of the stack class inadvertently calls the advance function. That moves the list cursor, and subsequent calls to push and pop modify the middle of the stack.

The "is-a" test tells us that this inheritance is wrong. A stack isn't a list. You can't insert into the middle of a stack. But it is perfectly reasonable to say that this stack *has* a list and to use a list data member to provide the implementation. That only takes a few more keystrokes:

```
class Stack
{ List l;
public:
  void push( int x ) { l.insert( x ); }
  int pop( int x ) { return l.remove(); }
};
```

Some programmers like to use private inheritance instead (class Stack : private List). That works and still saves keystrokes, but it seems less clear. This book recommends using data members instead of private base classes.

● **Exercise 10.5.1.** Consider the classes Address, Employee, Secretary, Manager, ProgramManager. What "is-a" and "has-a" relationships can you find between these classes? Write class definitions using inheritance and data members.

● **Exercise 10.5.2.** An MS-DOS file name is a kind of string, with a special format (*drive* :*directory*\ ... *directory**name*.*extension*). We could derive Filename from String, adding member functions such as drive() and extension() that parse the string. Does that make sense? Is every filename a string? Is every filename a String? That is, is every String member function appropriate for file names?

● **Exercise 10.5.3.** In Section 10.4, we derive TextBox both from Box and from Text. Which of these derivations pass the "is-a" test?

● **Exercise 10.5.4.** A point is a kind of circle, with radius 0. Would it make sense to derive Point from Circle?

● 10.6. PITFALLS

10.6.1. Using the Base Class Instead of a Pointer

Base classes usually carry no or very little information. Most actual data sits on top of them, in a derived class. It therefore usually makes no sense to pass an actual instance of a base class in or out of a function. For example,

```
void rotate( Shape p, double angle ); // WRONG
```

This function cannot possibly work. A Shape carries *no* information except a virtual function table pointer. If an object is passed into the procedure, only the base portion of it is copied. However,

```
void rotate( Shape& p, double angle ); // OK
```

can work, presumably by virtual function calls through p.

10.6.2. Casting to a Private Base Class

Private base classes are rarely useful. A private base class is as well hidden to the outside world as a private data member. Not even its existence is acknowledged. In particular, it is not possible to cast from a derived class to a private base class. Whenever virtual functions are used, the base class must be made public:

```
class ShapeList // a list of Shape
{ // ...
public:
  void insert( Shape* );
  // ...
};

class Box : Shape // not public
{ // ...
public:
  void plot() const;
}

Box* b = new Box( 10,15,15,20 );
ShapeList l;
l.insert( b ); // ERROR—can't convert Box* → Shape*
```

The remedy is to make Shape a public base class.

10.6.3. Forgetting Defaults for Virtual Functions

Each instance of a virtual function must have a definition, even if it lies in an abstract base class and will never be called. The compiler wants to insert something into the corresponding slot of the virtual function table. Reasonable solutions are as follows:

```
class Shape
{ // no data
public:
  virtual void plot() const {} // do nothing
  virtual void rotate( double )
    { cerr << "This can't happen." }
  virtual int xcenter() { return 0; } // {} would give
                                       // error message
  // ...
};
```

Alternatively, *pure virtual functions* can be declared:

```
class Shape
{
public:
  virtual void plot() const = 0;
  // ...
};
```

The compiler then enforces that Shape is an abstract class, and any attempt to declare an actual Shape will be flagged as an error.

10.6.4. Virtual Destructors

Whenever a derived class has a nontrivial destructor, one must make sure that the destructor actually gets invoked. Consider the following:

```
class Shape
{
public:
  virtual void plot( Grid& g ) const = 0;
  virtual void print() = 0;
};

class Text : public Shape
{ char* text;
  // ...
public:
  Text( int x, int y, const char t[] )
  { text = new char[ strlen( t ) + 1 ];
    // ...
  }
  ~Text() { delete[] text; }
  // ...
};

Shape* figure[ SIZE ];
figure[ 0 ] = new Box( /* ... */ );
figure[ 1 ] = new Text( 10, 10, "Soybean production" );

// ...

for ( int i = 0; i < SIZE; i++ ) delete figure[ i ];
```

The Text destructor is never called, because the argument of delete has the type Shape*. That doesn't mean that insufficient memory is recycled to the heap—the heap knows the size of each object it allocated, independent of the type. But because the Text destructor is not called, the text memory, which is stored outside the Text object, is not deleted, causing a memory leak.

To ensure that the Text destructor is properly called, we must make the destructor *virtual*. A virtual destructor considers the run-time type of the object being destroyed, not the compile-time type of the pointer. This is simple.

```
class Shape
{
public:
  virtual void plot( Grid& g ) const = 0;
  virtual void print() = 0;
  virtual ~Shape() {}
};
```

Nothing special needs to be done to destroy a shape, but the virtual destructor is now in place and can be overridden by a derived class.

10.6.5. Inheritance Is Not Compatible with Arrays

Consider the following simple inheritance hierarchy:

```
class Employee
{ char name[ 30 ];
  double salary;
public:
  void raise( double by_percent );
  // ...
};

class Manager : public Employee
{ char department[ 20 ];
public:
  // ...
};

void make_them_happy( Employee* e, int ne )
{ for ( int i = 0; i < ne; i++ )
    e[ i ].raise_salary( 0.10 );
}

int main()
{ Employee e[ 20 ];
  Manager m[ 5 ];
  m[ 0 ] = Manager( "Joe Bush", "Sales" );
  // ...
  make_them_happy( e, 20 );
  make_them_happy( m + 1, 4 ); // let's skip Joe
  return 0;
}
```

This code compiles without an error, but it cannot possibly work. There is no problem with raising the employee salaries. The manager objects, however, are bigger than the employee objects. In the make_them_happy function, the offset computation e[i] adds only i * sizeof(Employee) bytes to the starting address of the array e. That will not reach the ith manager object in the array. Instead, it will mess up some memory in the middle of a different manager object.

Why does it compile? The type of m + 1 is Manager*. Because of inheritance, a Manager* is convertible to an Employee* base class pointer, and make_them_happy receives an Employee*. Everyone is happy.

There is a moral here: Pointers are overused in C++. Here we see two interpretations of an Employee* e.

1. e points to either an Employee or a derived class object, such as a Manager.
2. e points to either an Employee or a bunch of Employee objects, stacked up in an array.

These two interpretations are incompatible.

Note that the problem does not go away if you declare the array argument of make_them_happy as Employee e[]. That still defines e as an Employee*.

10.6.6. Calling the Base Class

Suppose Manager inherits from Employee. To print a manager, we want to print the standard employee information, but also print the age and department name. The following code does not work.

```
void Manager::print() const
{ print(); // NO
  cout << " " << age(); // i.e., Employee::age()
  cout << " " << department;
}
```

The call to print() is a recursive call to Manager::print(). The base class function must be named explicitly.

```
void Manager::print() const
{ Employee::print();
  cout << " " << age(); // i.e., Employee::age()
  cout << " " << department;
}
```

Now consider the following function, with a typing error—only one : is used.

```
void Manager::print() const
{ Employee:print(); // NO
  cout << " " << age();
  cout << " " << department;
}
```

Surprisingly, it compiles. But when the function is called, the program terminates with a stack fault.

Here, Employee: is a *goto label*. We never use goto, but even a feature that you never use may haunt you if you make a keyboarding error.

MODULES

11.1. FILES AS MODULES

C++ programs are usually broken up into a number of source files, each containing groups of related functions and data. Only one of the files contains main. These source files are compiled separately into object files. Commonly used object files are packed together into a library file. The program is produced by linking object files with modules from custom and standard libraries. The linker takes only the modules that the program needs from the libraries, fixes up data and function addresses, and produces an executable file. The details depend on the operating system.

If one file changes, then that file must be recompiled, and the program must be relinked, but the majority of files are unaffected. This feature is called *separate compilation*. Contrast it with standard Pascal: All functions are nested inside a single **program** statement, all in one file. Any change requires recompilation of the entire code. Of course, many implementations of (nonstandard) Pascal added schemes to support modularity.

Each program module is a collection of global data items and functions. The programmer can control which data and functions are visible to the outside. This is quite similar to the data-hiding capability of classes, although the syntax is rather different. Here are some guidelines for efficient module design:

- *Don't share unless you have to.* Once you share something, other people just might start using it. Then you can't change it without their consent.

- *Keep the interface simple.* If programmers must learn many details to understand your modules, they don't have time to get their own work done.

- *Don't share storage.* In C++ you can't give selective access to global data. *Everyone* can inspect and change global data once you permit access to anyone. Use functions for inspection and controlled modification.

You will note that the same guidelines are applicable for the design of classes.

Let us now consider the details of information hiding in modules. For historical reasons, the syntax has little in common with the syntax for classes. Regrettably, the default is to share all global data and functions in a module.

(However, const and inline objects are private by default.) When prefixed by the word static (!), the item is kept private.

```
static int counter;
static void clearall();
static int lookup( char* word, char* table[], int tsize )
{
  //...
}
```

The choice of static is traditional but unfortunate. The keyword static already has another use, to declare that a local variable retains its value after it is out of scope, as in

```
int random( int s = 0 )
{ static int seed; // static has no connection with data hiding

  if( s != 0 )
  { int oldseed = seed;
    seed = s;
    return oldseed;
  }
  // compute next random number ...
}
```

Of course, seed, being local, is also hidden from other modules (as well as other functions in the same module). There can never be an ambiguity between the two uses of static. When applied to a *local* variable, static means "make it persistent"; when applied to a *global* variable or function, it means "make it private". What's more, static *class* members have a third, unrelated meaning: They are shared among the objects of the class.

The designers of C++ could have offered private as an alternative, letting the C-style use of static sink into obscurity, but they didn't.

You should, as a matter of habit, declare all items static unless they were explicitly promised to the public when the module was designed. Each module makes certain data and functions available to other modules, namely the ones not declared static.

On the other hand, constants default to being private:

```
const Complex j( 0, 1 );
```

is not accessible in other modules. If you want to share a constant, you have to give it "external linkage":

```
extern const Complex j( 0, 1 );
```

If another module needs to access a public variable or function, it must tell the compiler. To use data from another module, give its declaration (but omit any initializer) and prefix it with the keyword extern.

```
extern int linenumber;
extern double scheduleTimes[ NPROCESS ];
extern const Complex j; // no initializer
```

To call a function from another file, the compiler needs to know its name, the types of all of its arguments, argument defaults (if any), and the type of the return value. This information is stated in a *prototype*:

```
int getword( char*, char );
double sqrt( double );
int rand( int = 0 );
```

Variable names and extern are optional.

```
extern int getword( char* buffer, int buflen );
```

It is a good idea to include variable names, because they can remind you of their meanings. Of course, the compiler cares only about type checking and ignores the variable names. It does need argument defaults, in case a function call has less than the maximum number of variables and defaults must be supplied.

For function declarations the extern keyword is optional, because the compiler can tell the difference between a function prototype and a definition. If the (...) are followed by a ;, it is a prototype; if they are followed by { ... }, it is a definition.

Commonly, these prototypes are placed in a header file. See Sections 11.3 and 11.4 for details.

Prototypes can be used to advertise a function that comes later in the same module. In fact, some programmers prefer to list the prototypes of all functions in a module first and then write the function definitions. Others sort functions to have the definition precede their first use; with that style, main comes last in its module. But that arrangement is not always possible. Sometimes there is a circular chain of function calls. For example, in a recursive descent expression parser, expression() calls term(), term() calls factor(), and factor() calls expression(). In that case, use a prototype as a forward declaration for one of the functions to break the deadlock.

When external data and functions are used, the compiler checks for type consistency. Of course, this demands truth in advertising. The compiler sees only the module it is compiling and has no way of comparing the actual definition of a variable with its advertisement in an extern declaration. If a module claims

```
extern double eventDuration( Event );
```

but the defining module actually implements

```
int eventDuration( Event e ) { ... };
```

you are in big trouble. The compiler will generate code that interprets the bit pattern returned by the function as a double. Because floating-point numbers are formatted rather differently from integers, this is a sure recipe for disaster.

Programs change constantly. What was an `int` yesterday may well be a `double` today, and it is easy to have `extern` declarations that reflect yesterday's realities. We will see in Section 11.3 how that can be avoided by placing them into a header file, to be maintained by the designer of the module containing the declarations.

Note that a public variable must be defined in exactly one module, with either a definition (and an optional initializer)

```
int cursor;
```

or an `extern` definition with an explicit initializer

```
extern int cursor = 0; // must be definition because of initializer
```

and declared in all modules that use it:

```
extern int cursor; // no initializer
```

Some compilers are wishy-washy about this requirement, allowing multiple definitions (as long as one has at most one initializer) or none at all (that is, declarations only). Public constants also must have exactly one definition (with `extern` to override the private default)

```
extern const Complex j( 0, 1 );
```

and declarations

```
extern const Complex j; // no initializer
```

in all modules using it.

The `extern` command can take an optional string command to link with non-C++ functions. For example,

```
extern "Pascal" HANDLE winInitialize( USHORT );
extern "C"
{ int strlen( const char* );
  char* strcpy( char*, const char* );
}
extern "C"
{
#include <string.h>
}
```

Such directives tell the translator to use the system-dependent rules for calling functions written in other languages. The compiler may need to generate different code for function calls (such as pushing the arguments in another order) or different linker instructions may need to be generated.

C Note

Some C compilers introduce special keywords such as `pascal` or `cdecl` for mixed-language programming. This is similar to `extern "..."`, except using a string is smarter. It does not introduce new keywords for these machine-dependent constructions.

If a module uses a `struct`, `class`, or `typedef` defined in another module, the entire definition must be made visible to the client module, as must everything it depends on. For example, to use a stack class defined elsewhere:

```
const int STACKSIZE = 20;

class Stack
{ int s[ STACKSIZE ];
  int sptr;
public:
  Stack() { sptr = 0; }
  int push( int );
  int pop();
  int isEmpty() const { return sptr == 0 };
};

Stack numStack;

// ...

if( !numStack.isEmpty() )
  cout << numStack.pop();
```

It may come as a surprise that the *client* module gets so much information about the stack class. It gets to see the stack class definition, including the private portion. Why isn't the private part secret? What stops the client programmer from peeking into it? The second question is easy to answer. Nothing stops the programmer, but of what use is the information? It is impossible to actually access numStack.sptr—the compiler flags it as an error. This entirely conforms to the wish of the stack designer, who might later change from an array to a linked list. But why isn't the private part simply omitted, just as the bodies of external functions are omitted? The client module may define instances of the stack class, and the compiler needs to know how much storage space to allocate for the structure. The compiler also needs to replace inline functions that may contain member accesses. If all classes were represented as pointers to a structure and if inline functions were not supported, the private part could indeed be omitted. Some languages, such as Modula 2, take this route, at the cost of additional pointer indirection and greater function call overhead for trivial functions.

There is no required order for the various declarations in a C++ file. However, professional programming teams usually standardize on some layout. A typical structuring convention is as follows:

- Header comment, including copyright notice and author's name(s)
- Revision list comment

- #include statements
- const definitions
- Class and type definitions
- Global data
- Forward declarations (that is, function prototypes)
- Functions

Such conventions are usually described in a *style guide* document to which each team member is expected to conform. Such style guides can be very detailed, spelling out module layout, comment layout, conventions for naming variables, functions and types, usage of uppercase and lowercase characters, and even the number of spaces per tab stop.

● **Exercise 11.1.1.** Write a small program that is distributed over two source files, one (hello) only containing main:

```
int main() { hello(); return 0; }
```

and the other (message) containing

```
char message[] = "Hello, world\n";
void hello() { cout << message; }
```

Supply static and extern as appropriate. Find out how to compile and link these files on your system. Typical commands are

```
CC hello.C message.C
```

or

```
bcc hello.cpp message.cpp
```

Now change the message string to "Hello, modular world\n" and find out how to rebuild the executable file without recompiling the hello module. Typical commands are

```
CC hello.o message.C
```

or

```
bcc hello.obj message.cpp
```

● **Exercise 11.1.2.** Split up the stack-based calculator program of Section 1.3 into two files, hiding all details of the stack implementation.

● **Exercise 11.1.3.** The previous exercise used a stack *module*, implementing a single stack. Instead, redo the exercise with a stack *class* that potentially can be used to declare several stacks. The stack class should be implemented in a separate source file. The class Stack definition needs to be present in both files.

● **Exercise 11.1.4.** Implement a module that performs *full justification* of text. Fit as many words as possible onto a line. Your module should have the following public functions:

```
void setMargin( int );
  // set the right margin
void addWords( const char* );
  // add more words to the current paragraph
void flush();
  // finish the current paragraph
```

No data and no other functions should be public. Completed lines should be sent to standard output. Use the following code for testing:

```
extern void setMargin( int );
extern void addWords( const char* );
extern void flush();
int main( int argc, char* argv[] )
{ char buffer[ 200 ];
  setMargin( argc > 1 ? atoi( argv[ 1 ]) : 66 );
  while( cin.getline( buffer, sizeof( buffer )))
  { if( strlen( buffer) == 0 ) // blank line
      flush();                 // separates paragraphs
    else
      addWords( buffer );
  }
  flush();
  return 0;
}
```

11.2. THE PREPROCESSOR

We are digressing in this section to introduce the preprocessor tool. The C++ language has no effective built-in mechanism to organize modules, but the preprocessor can be used for that purpose.

Compilation of a C++ program involves several steps. The first step is invariably the *preprocessor*. This is a special program that prepares the source file for the compiler. All lines starting with a # are preprocessor directives.

The #include *<filename>* or #include "*filename*" command directs the preprocessor to open the file and include all of its lines for inspection by the compiler. If the filename is enclosed in <>, only the "standard places" for header files are searched. If the filename is enclosed in "", the preprocessor first looks in the current directory and then in the standard places. The files to be included can contain anything. The preprocessor doesn't understand C++ and just includes the lines for the compiler. Usually they contain class definitions, extern declarations, and function prototypes. Many programmers have a personal header file with their favorite constructs, such as

```
enum Bool { FALSE, TRUE };
inline int max( int x, int y ) { return x > y ? x : y; }
typedef char* PString;
```

They include it at the top of each of their source files.

The #define directive instructs the compiler to perform a "search and replace" on the input text. For example,

```
#define  PRIVATE  static
```

replaces all occurrences of PRIVATE with static, as in

```
PRIVATE void clearall();
```

#undef removes a macro definition.

The preprocessor is heavily used in C programs to define constants and inline functions

```
#define  BUFLEN  20
#define  MAX( x, y ) (( x ) > ( y ) ? ( x ) : ( y ))
```

but the C++ const, enum, and inline facilities do a better job. The MAX macro shows two remarkable features: Macros can do argument substitution, for example,

```
x = MAX( a, 2 );
```

becomes

```
x = (( a ) > ( 2 ) ? ( a ) : ( 2 ));
```

and macros know nothing about the language:

```
x = MAX( a[ i++ ], 2 );
```

becomes

```
x = (( a[ i++ ] ) > ( 2 ) ? ( a[ i++ ]) : ( 2 ));
```

which increments i twice and delivers the wrong result if a[i] is larger than 2. C++ inline functions do not suffer from that problem.

Use of macros frequently points to a deficiency in the language. C programmers use them for constants and inline functions because C does not have the appropriate language constructs. For the same reason, they are used in C++ to implement generic types (Section 12.2). Furthermore, many programmers define their own keywords, such as PRIVATE to replace the ugly static. It is even possible to define

```
#define BEGIN {
#define END }
#define IF if(
#define THEN )
#define WHILE while(
#define DO )
#define REPEAT do {
#define UNTIL( x ) } while( !( x ))
```

and pascalize the language to an amazing degree. Don't do this when working in a team—your fellow C++ programmers will not be happy about having to play preprocessor to be able to read your code.

Code can be conditionally passed to the compiler with the #if directive. The #if line evaluates whether a constant-integer expression (which may not contain any sizeof, enum constants, or casts) is nonzero:

```
#define PROCESSOR 386


    ...

#if PROCESSOR == 386
    ...
#elif PROCESSOR == 68000
    ...
#else
    ...
#endif
```

The expression defined(*name*) is 1 if *name* has been #defined, 0 if not.

```
#if defined( GERMAN ) || defined( FRENCH )
#undef ENGLISH
#endif
```

#ifdef *name* is a shortcut for #if defined(*name*), and #ifndef *name* stands for #if !defined(*name*).

```
#ifdef( GERMAN )
  cout << "Datei " << filename << " nicht gefunden.\n";
#endif
```

To select the German language version, a line

```
#define GERMAN
```

can be placed in the code. GERMAN is then defined to be the empty string, but all that matters for #ifdef is whether or not it is defined. It is also usually possible to pass definitions to the compiler on the command line:

```
bcc  -DGERMAN  wp.cpp
```

Check your compiler manual for details.

● **Exercise 11.2.1.** Take the stack calculator of Section 1.3 and insert debugging code that prints the stack after each push or pop. That code should only be compiled when debugging is in progress. Bracket it with

```
#ifdef DEBUG
    ...
#endif
```

and compile with DEBUG defined as the empty string. Check whether you can define DEBUG in the compiler command line.

More sophisticated debugging can be achieved by setting a debug level (#if DEBUG > 3...).

● **Exercise 11.2.2.** Many source-level debuggers cannot step inside inline functions. Design and test a scheme where the keyword inline is changed to the empty string when DEBUG is defined.

11.3. HEADER FILE MANAGEMENT

Each module makes certain data and functions available to the public, namely, all non-static functions and global variables. Other modules may import them. It would be inconvenient and error-prone if module users had to enter all extern declarations manually. Instead, it is customary that the designer of the module create a special header file, with the same name as the exporting module but extension .h. (Some systems use .hxx or .hpp.) The importing module includes it with an #include directive. You have done this many times, for example, #include <iostream.h>.

This section deals with the design of header files—a boring and unpleasant issue, because C++ offers no language support for it. You may safely skip this section until you feel the need for a header file maintenance strategy.

Header files can contain the following items:

- Prototypes of functions, including default arguments
- Complete definitions of inline functions
- Declarations of variables (without initialization)
- Definitions of numeric constants
- Declaration of const storage (without initialization)
- Class definitions, including the private portion and the inline member functions

Of course, whenever one of these items changes in the defining module, the header file must be updated to reflect the change! For this reason, maintenance of the header file is the responsibility of the module designer. Outdated header files are a major source of trouble. There are several strategies to avoid them. None of them is perfect, but it is important to settle on one of them. Otherwise it is just a matter of time before the source and header files are at odds with each other.

One common strategy is to #include the header file into the defining module as well as the client modules. To a certain extent, C++ cooperates very well. The compiler doesn't mind seeing multiple prototypes of the same function. When it encounters the definition of a function whose prototype it already saw, it will check whether the advertising coincides with the actual definition and issue an error message if not.

For example, suppose we wish to export a function

```
int getRecord( Employee& e ) { ... }
```

A prototype is placed into the header file:

```
int getRecord( Employee& );
```

Because the header file is #included at the top of the source file, the compiler encounters the prototype first and will check the actual function definition against it. If the function definition has been changed to

```
void getRecord( Employee& e ) { ... }
```

but the header file has not yet changed, an error message will be issued. The same protection applies to variables and constants. If a variable

```
extern double scheduleTimes[ 5 ];
```

is advertised in the header file, and the actual definition is

```
int scheduleTimes[ 5 ] = { 1, 1, 2, 3, 5 };
```

the mismatch will be detected. Note that the initializer is only supplied for the actual definition of the variable.

The sharing of struct, class, and typedef is more complicated, because the compiler does *not* like to see them more than once. Rather than checking for consistency, it mindlessly complains about the redefinition. That is unfortunate. The class definitions must then reside in the header file, separate from the code for the member functions.

The situation is even more confusing for constants, because some const are simply inline-replaced by the compiler with their numeric values, such as

```
const int BUFLEN = 30;
```

Others actually occupy storage:

```
extern const char* version = "Version 3.10";
extern const Date bday( 6, 16, 1959 );
```

Inline-replaced constants must be placed in the header file as

```
const int BUFLEN = 30;
```

and *not* duplicated in the source file. The compiler will complain if it sees two declarations of the same inline constant

```
const int BUFLEN = 30;
...
const int BUFLEN = 30; // ERROR
```

rather than quietly checking for consistency. Constants occupying storage should be declared in the header file without the initializer

```
extern const char* version;
extern const Date bday;
```

and defined in the source file, just like variables.

Public inline functions face the same problem as inline constants. The compiler needs to see the definition, not just the declaration, whenever compiling a client module. The definition must therefore reside in the header file. The compiler will not tolerate seeing it twice, and it cannot be replicated in the source file.

Here is a table summarizing the foregoing discussion. All items are global items to be shared with other modules.

Item to Be Shared	In .c File	In .h File
Uninitialized data	`Employee staff[ 100 ];`	`extern Employee staff[];`
Initialized data	`int reportwidth = 80;`	`extern int reportwidth;`
Inline constants		`const int NSTAFF = 100;`
Stored constants	`extern const` ` Complex j( 0, 1 )`	`extern const Complex j;`
Functions	`Complex log(Complex z)` `{ ...}`	`Complex log( Complex );`
Inline functions		`inline int min(int x, int y)` `{ return(x < y ? x : y); }`

Classes, structures, unions	`Date Date::add(int n)`
	`{ ...}`
		`class Date`
		`{ int d, m, y;`
		`public:`
		`  int day() { return d; }`
		`  Date add( int );`
		`  ...`
		`};`

typedef, enum		`typedef void (*FunPtr) ();`

● **Exercise 11.3.1.** Describe the header files for the modules of the programs in Exercises 11.1.2 through 11.1.4.

Sometimes one header file must include another, and it can then happen that the same header file is encountered more than once. Because the compiler cannot tolerate multiple definitions of the same `struct`, `class`, or `typedef`, this can lead to compiler errors. The preprocessor can be used to work around this language deficiency. Surround the declarations with

```
#ifndef symbol
#define symbol
declarations that should be read only once
#endif
```

If this block is encountered for the second time, the *symbol* is defined and the block is skipped. The traditional choice for the symbol is the name of the include file with the period replaced with an underscore, such as `INPUT_H`.

It should be emphasized that C++ does not enforce or support any of the rules that we have laid down here. The responsibility for module management lies with the programmer.

11.4. AUTOMATIC EXTRACTION OF HEADER FILES

This section presents a technique for automatic extraction of header files from source files. It has been my experience that this method is far less error-prone than the manual method described in the previous section. ("The best header files are the ones that are untouched by human hands.") An AWK script is presented that automatically generates the .h files. It can be run whenever the source file changes (see [AKW] for a description of AWK). This section can be safely skipped if you are not interested in automatic header file generation.

The header file maintenance method described in the previous section relies on including each header file in its own source file. This practice is definitely desirable for checking against mismatches between function and variable declarations and definitions, but it has the unpleasant effect of separating logically related items into two files: class declarations and inlines into the header file, other data and functions into the source file, function and variable declarations in both. This section presents a different strategy. The header file is built automatically from the source file but not included into its own source. Conformance between declarations and definitions is guaranteed as long as the header file is rebuilt whenever the source file changes. I have found an AWK script to be reasonably efficient in this regard.

To make it easy on the extraction script, we require that all constructs to be included in the header file be prefixed with the keyword EXPORT. This keyword should be defined in a project header file as the empty string:

```
#define EXPORT
```

Every function or global variable should be preceded by either EXPORT or static. Consider an input module input.c with the following data and functions:

```
#include "project.h"

EXPORT int lineCount = 0;
static int isWhite( char ch )
{ ... }
static char skipWhite()
{ ... }
EXPORT int getline( char* buffer, int buflen )
{ ... }
EXPORT int getword( char* word, int wordlen )
{ ... }
```

The input.h file derived from input.c contains the lines

```
extern int lineCount;
extern int getline( char* buffer, int buflen );
extern int getword( char* word, int wordlen );
```

To include class definitions and inline functions in the header file, precede them by EXPORT as well. Consider the defining module stack.c:

```
#include "project.h"

EXPORT const int STACKSIZE = 20;

EXPORT class Stack
{ int s[ STACKSIZE ];
  int sptr;
public:
  Stack() { sptr = 0; }
  int push( int );
  int pop();
  int isEmpty() const;
};

int Stack::push( int n ) { ... }

int Stack::pop() { ... }

EXPORT inline int Stack::isEmpty() const
{ return sptr == 0; }
```

The extracted header file stack.h is:

```
#ifndef STACK_H
#define STACK_H

const int STACKSIZE = 20;

class Stack
{ int s[ STACKSIZE ];
  int sptr;
public:
  Stack() { sptr = 0; }
  int push( int );
  int pop();
  int isEmpty() const;
};

inline int Stack::isEmpty() const { return sptr == 0; }

#endif
```

The tool has several limitations, imposed by the complicated C++ declaration syntax. Inline constants can be exported by tagging them:

```
EXPORT const int MAXSIZE = 200;
```

This is, of course, the most common case. It is important that the stored constants are correctly declared as EXPORT extern const, for example

```
EXPORT extern const Matrix z;
```

Unfortunately, the script will confuse an exported constant that has constructor arguments, such as

```
EXPORT extern const Complex i( 0, 1 );
```

with a function declaration! Use

```
EXPORT extern const Complex i = Complex( 0, 1 );
```

instead.

Here is the AWK script:

```
function bracecount( s, left, right ) {
  return split( s, lsplit, left ) - split( s, rsplit, right )
}

function strupper(s)
{ for ( _i = 1; _i <= 26; _i++ )
    gsub ( substr( "abcdefghijklmnopqrstuvwxyz", _i, 1 ),
      substr( "ABCDEFGHIJKLMNOPQRSTUVWXYZ", _i, 1 ), s )
  return s
}

BEGIN {
  outfile = ARGV[ 1 ];
  sub( /^[A-Za-z]:/, "", outfile ) # remove directory
  sub( /^.*[\\\/]/, "", outfile ) # remove  subdirectories
  sub( /\..*/, ".H", outfile ) # replace extension with .H
  print "[mdgen.awk]  Copyright (C) Cay S. Horstmann 1995."
  print ARGV[ 1 ] " -> " outfile

  hname = outfile;
  gsub( /[^A-Za-z0-9_]/, "_", hname );
  strupper( outfile );
  print "#ifndef " hname >outfile
  print "#define " hname >outfile
  print "" >outfile

  getline  # copy header comment
  oldStyle = substr( $0, 1, 2 ) == "/*"
  while ( oldStyle || index( $0, "//" )) {
    sub (/\.[cC](xx|pp)?/, ".h")   # change filename to filename.h
    print >outfile
    if ( index( $0, "*/" )) oldStyle = 0
    getline
  }
```

```
   keyword[ "typedef" ] = 1;
   keyword[ "enum" ] = 1;
   keyword[ "class" ] = 1;
   keyword[ "struct" ] = 1;
   keyword[ "union" ] = 1;
   keyword[ "inline" ] = 1;
   keyword[ "const" ] = 1;
   keyword[ "template" ] = 1;
}

$1 == "EXPORT"
   { # tag for items to be included
   print "" >outfile  # separate items by blank line
   print "#line " NR " \"" ARGV[ 1 ] "\"" >outfile
      # print line number for error
   if ( match( $2, "^[a-z]+" )
      && keyword[ substr( $2, 1, RLENGTH )]) {
      # if one of the standard keywords
      b = bracecount($0, "{", "}");  # skip past matching {}
      $1 = ""  # delete  EXPORT
      while ( b != 0 ||
         ( index( $0, ";" ) == 0
         && index( $0, "}" ) == 0))
         print >outfile
         getline
         b += bracecount( $0, "{", "}" )
      }
      print >outfile
   }

   else if ( substr( $2, 1, 2 ) == "/*"
      || substr( $2, 1, 2 ) == "//"
      || $2 == "" ) {
      getline  # test for preprocessor command
      if ( substr( $1, 1, 1 ) == "#") {  # on the next line
         print >outfile # could be #define, #include
         while ( substr( $0, length( $0 )) == "\\" ) {
         getline  # could be multiline #define
         print >outfile
      }
    }
   }

   else {  # function or variable declaration
      if ( $2 == "extern" ) $1 = ""      # extern "C", extern const
      else $1 = "extern"  # replace EXPORT with extern
      b = bracecount( $0, "(", ")" );  # skip past matching ()
```

```
      while ( b ) {
        print >outfile
        getline
        b += bracecount( $0, "(", ")" )
      }
      split( $0, out, "=" )   # split off initialization
      if ( bracecount( out[ 1 ], "(", ")" )
        || index( out[ 1 ], "operator" ))
        print $0 ";" >outfile
        # oops—"=" was for default arg or operator=
      else {
        split( out[ 1 ], out, ";" )   # split off semicolon (if exists)
        print out[ 1 ] ";" >outfile
      }
    }
  }

END {  # print #endif
  print "" >outfile
  print "#endif" >outfile
}
```

The BEGIN portion sets the keyword array, produces the #ifndef FILE_H/ #define FILE_H lines, and copies the first comment of the source file (presumed to contain a copyright notice or the like) into the header file. Any file extension .c, .cxx, or .cpp in the comment is translated into a .h extension.

The main portion checks for the tag EXPORT. If it is present and followed by one of the strings in the keyword array, lines are copied until a matching brace count returns to 0 and (except for inline) a semicolon is found.

If EXPORT is followed by a comment or is alone in the line, the next line is checked for a preprocessor statement (#define or #include). That line is then copied, together with any continuation lines (as for a multiline #define).

Otherwise, the EXPORT is assumed to introduce a function or variable. It is changed to print out as extern. This time, input lines are gathered until a matching parenthesis count returns to 0. An "=" initializer, if present, is stripped off. Note that the generated header file contains #line directives. That way, the compiler will point to the original source location when encountering syntax errors in the automatically generated header file.

If the script is stored in a file mdgen.awk, header files can be produced simply by running

```
awk  -f  mdgen.awk  input.C
```

Naturally, this AWK script is not bulletproof. But it should be easy to adapt it to any reasonable coding style. This flexibility was a major reason for choosing AWK to build the extraction tool.

● **Exercise 11.4.1.** Add EXPORT statements to the modules of the programs in Exercises 11.1.1 through 11.2.4 and test the extraction tool.

● 11.5. PITFALLS

11.5.1. #define and Comments

Never place a //-style comment after a #define. With some preprocessors, it will become part of the substitution text:

```
#define PRIVATE static    // to declare a private
                          // function—WRONG

PRIVATE int count( Widget* w )
```

will be replaced by

```
static      // to declare a private int count ( Widget*  w )
```

and the function header becomes part of the comment! This obviously confuses the compiler to no end and leads to bizarre error messages.

11.5.2. Mismatches between Declarations and Definitions

If header files are maintained manually, it can be very easy to change a definition in the .c file while forgetting to update the .h file. Such errors are typically hard to find. Consider the following examples:

In .c File	In .h File (Forgot to Update)

class Employee
{ int id;
  char name[20];
  int age;
  double salary;
  // ...
};
	class Employee
	{ int id;
	  char name[20];
	  double salary;
	  // ...
	};

double hoursWorked (Employee&);	int hoursWorked(Employee&);

A module including the outdated header file will no longer work. When declaring an employee,

```
Employee* e = new Employee;
```

insufficient storage will be set aside. When calling the changed hoursWorked function,

```
nh = hoursWorked( *e );
```

the return value will be meaningless.

This kind of error is bound to happen unless a *strategy* for header file management is in place. Sections 11.3 and 11.4 discuss two such strategies.

CLASS
LIBRARIES

12.1. CONTAINER CLASSES

Suppose we wish to build a reusable stack class. What kind of objects should be stacked? Pointers are a good choice for a generic stack, as one can always stack the addresses of the objects. (Of course, one must come up with some storage space elsewhere for the actual objects.) But pointers to what? C++ makes available the type void*, a pointer to some unspecified item. It is nothing more than a memory address. It tells us where an item starts in memory, but one cannot tell how many bytes it occupies. For that reason, it is not possible to take the * of a void* (how many bytes should be fetched?) or add a number to it (how many bytes is p + 1 away from p?). The compiler flags any such attempts as errors. Any pointer can be placed into a void* variable without a type mismatch warning. For the opposite conversion, from void*, to any X*, a cast is always necessary. There are only three things we can do with void* pointers: copy them, compare them, or cast them.

The interface of a generic stack class is

```
class Stack
{ // ...
public:
  Stack();
  void* push( void* );
  void* pop();
  void* top() const;
  int isEmpty() const;
};
```

What can we do with a stack of void*? Suppose we actually want to stack Employees. Put their addresses on the stack:

```
Employee staff[ 100 ];
Stack estack;
// ...
```

```
estack.push( &staff[ n ]);
// ...
Employee e = *(Employee*) estack.pop();
   //   the cast is necessary—can't take the * of a void*
```

We are only storing the addresses of the employee structures. If the contents of an address change or the structure is no longer in scope, the pointer on the stack may no longer be valid. It is usually better to make a copy of the information before pushing:

```
Employee* p = new Employee; // get storage space from the
                            // free store
*p = staff[ n ];
estack.push( p );
// ...
p = (Employee*) estack.pop();
Employee e = *p;
delete p; // recycle storage space
```

● **Exercise 12.1.1.** Fill in the details of the "stack of pointers" class. Using the function of Exercise 5.1.2, read in employee records, allocate storage space with new, and push them onto a stack. Then pop them off and print them.

Our next example is a queue. Data can be inserted at one end and removed at the other. The queue contains void* because the size of the objects to be queued can vary. Natural implementations for queues are linked lists and circular arrays.

```
class Queue
{ // ...
public:
  Queue();
  void add( void* );        // add to queue
  void* inspect() const;    // look at next member to be dequeued
  void* remove();           // remove from queue
  int length() const;       // number of currently enqueued objects
};
```

Simulation programs typically contain several queues, one for the cars in front of each traffic light or customers in line at each teller window.

● **Exercise 12.1.2.** Implement the Queue class, using a circular array:

```
class Queue
{ void* q[ MAXENTRIES ];
  int in; // index of next position for insertion
```

```
    int out; // index of next position for removal
public:
    // ...
};
```

● **Exercise 12.1.3.** Implement a simple simulation: Bank customers arrive and enter a queue. An array of tellers serves them. We need a few statistics: The time between two arrivals is well described by the *exponential distribution*. To generate a sequence e_n of random numbers that are exponentially distributed with mean μ, take a sequence of random numbers u_n that are uniformly distributed in the interval $[0, 1]$, and compute

$$e_n = -\mu \cdot \log(u_n)$$

Uniformly distributed random numbers are obtained by a call to rand(), which returns a random integer between 0 and RAND_MAX. (rand and RAND_MAX are declared in stdlib.h, log is declared in math.h.) The time for the next arrival is

```
nextArrival = prevArrival - mu *
    log( rand() / double ( RAND_MAX ));
```

Similarly, assume processing time to be exponentially distributed (with a different mean λ). The purpose of the simulation is to measure the average time each customer spends in the queue, depending on

- The number of tellers
- Arrival rate (average of μ seconds between successive arriving customers)
- Processing rate (average of λ seconds per customer)

Implementation hints: Design a class Customer, which stores the arrival time in the queue, and a class Teller, which stores whether the teller is currently busy and, if so, until when. A loop for(sec = 0; sec < maxsec; sec++) ticks away at the seconds, continually checking whether a teller becomes free or whether a new customer is coming. Use new and delete for obtaining and recycling storage space for customers, as described previously. Try out four tellers, an average of one customer every 30 seconds, and an average transaction length of 120 seconds.

12.2. USING INHERITANCE

Inheritance can be used to provide a type-safe interface to stored void* pointers. Consider a stack stacking void*:

```
class Stack
{ // ...
public:
    Stack();
    void  push( void* );
    void* pop();
    void* top() const;
```

```
    int isEmpty() const;
};
```

Suppose we wish to stack matrices, or rather pointers to them because our stack class can store only pointers. We derive a `MatrixStack`:

```
class MatrixStack : public Stack
{ // no new data
public:
  void push( Matrix* p ) { Stack::push( p ); }
  Matrix* pop() {return (Matrix*) Stack::pop(); }
  Matrix* top() const { return (Matrix*) Stack::top(); }
};
```

No new data has been introduced. Actually, no new functions have been introduced either. The inline functions merely provide a type-safe interface.

```
MatrixStack s;
Matrix* m;
Vector* v;

s.push( m ); // inline replacement: s.Stack::push( m );
v = s.pop(); // WRONG—v cannot receive a
             // (Matrix*) s.Stack::pop()
```

Note that `isEmpty()` is inherited from `Stack` without change.

In the last chapter we saw examples of an abstract base class: a class that had no data members but merely existed to hold together a number of other classes through its virtual functions. The technique introduced in this section is on the other end of the spectrum, where all the work is done in the base class and the derivation merely does type conversion.

● **Exercise 12.2.1.** Implement a type-safe stack of `Employee*` pointers by deriving from a stack of `void*` pointers.

To store small items such as integers or `double`s it just isn't worth allocating additional storage and memory, making the foregoing method unattractive. The next exercise shows how to use derivation to produce generic linked lists that store items directly, without using pointers.

● **Exercise 12.2.2.** Starting with a `List`/`Cell` pair that stores *no information,*

```
class Cell
{ Cell* next;
  friend class List;
};
```

```
class List
{ Cell* head;
  Cell* cur;  // current position
  Cell* pre;  // predecessor of current position
protected:
  Cell* info() const;
  void insert( Cell* );
public:
  List();
  ~ List();
  void remove();  // remove current position
  void advance();
  void reset();
  int atEnd() const;
};
```

derive an `IntList`/`IntCell` type

```
class IntCell : public Cell
{ public:
    int info;  // add info field
  friend class IntList;
};
```

```
class IntList : public List
{ // no additional data
  int info() const;  // info at cursor
  void insert( int n );  // insert integer before cursor
};
```

The `int` field is simply placed above the `next` pointer in each `IntCell`, and no additional pointers are used.

Because reference counting is a fairly mechanical operation, one can use inheritance to supply its behavior to other classes. We have two base classes:

```
class Object
{
protected:
  Storage* stor;

  void copy( const Object& );
  void free();
  void unique();
public:
  Object( Storage* s =0 );
  Object( const Object& b ) { copy(b); }
```

```
    Object& operator=( const Object& b );
    ~Object() { free(); }
};

Object::Object( Storage* s )
{ if( stor = s )
    s->rc++;
}

void Object::copy( const Object& b )
{ if( stor = b.stor )
    stor->rc++;
}

void Object::free()
{ if( stor && !--stor->rc )
    delete stor;
}

void Object::unique()
{ if( stor && stor->rc > 1 )
  { stor->rc--;
    stor = stor->clone();
    stor->rc = 1;
  }
}

class Storage
{ int rc; // reference count
protected:
  Storage() { rc = 0; }
  virtual Storage* clone() const = 0;
  virtual ~Storage() {}
  friend class Object;
}
```

The *virtual destructor* must be replaced by a real destructor in a derived class to perform the necessary cleanup, usually to recycle a block to the free store.

Derived classes must replace the virtual clone function with a function that makes a copy of the storage. The clone function is invoked when an object modifies storage that it shares with other objects.

This class can be used to attach memory management by reference count to any data type. We illustrate the technique first with a Vector class. We separate Vector (a pointer) from VecStor (a structure containing the reference count, a dimension field, and a pointer to an array of doubles). All public access happens through Vector:

```
class Vector : public Object
{ // no additional member data
public:
  Vector( int d ) : Object( new VecStor( d )) {}
  // all actual vector operations go here...
};

class VecStor : public Storage
{ int dim;
  double* co;
  VecStor( int d );
  // sets co to new double[ d ] and clears it
  VecStor( const VecStor& );
  ~VecStor() { delete[] co; }
  // replaces virtual base destructor
  Storage* clone() const { return new VecStor( *this ); }
  friend class Vector;
};
```

It is important that all nonconstant member functions call unique(). This function tests whether the reference count of the storage is larger than 1. In that case, the member function cannot simply modify the shared storage, so unique() calls clone() to obtain a unique copy of the storage data for modification.

The big problem with this technique is the fact that a Vector does not contain a VecStor*. Although not an issue for the class user who simply applies the member functions, it is troublesome for the class designer who has to write them. Consider writing a Vector::length function returning the length ($\sum x_i^2$) of a vector. The stor field points to Storage, not VecStor, and must be cast to access the dim and co fields:

```
double Vector::length() const
{ double r = 0;
  for( int i = 0; i < ( (VecStor*) stor )->dim; i++ )
  { double xi = ( (VecStor*) stor )->co[ i ];
    r += xi*xi;
  }
  return sqrt( r );
}
```

This soon gets tiresome. The solution is to provide a private access function stor():

```
class Vector : public Object
{ // no additional member data
  VecStor* stor() { unique();
    return (VecStor*) Object::stor; }
  const VecStor* stor() const
  { return (const VecStor*) Object::stor; }
```

```
public:
  double length() const;
  // ...
};
```

The length function becomes

```
double Vector::length() const
{ double r = 0;
  for( int i = 0; i < stor()->dim; i++ )
  { double xi = stor()->co[ i ];
    r += xi * xi;
  }
  return sqrt( x );
}
```

which is quite readable and as efficient as the first solution, because the access functions are inline. Note that the nonconstant version of stor() automatically calls unique(). This ensures that shared storage data is not accidentally corrupted.

● **Exercise 12.2.3.** Derive a String class from Object to add memory management to strings.

● **Exercise 12.2.4.** Add reference counting to a List (of integers) class by preceding the entire list with a reference count.

● **Exercise 12.2.5.** Apply the reference count strategy to the List class of Exercise 9.5.4 with a reference count for each cell. That is, List is derived from Object and Cell is derived from Storage.

A Cell contains a List next! Why does Cell not need a copy constructor or destructor?

● **Exercise 12.2.6.** Make a generic list type storing Objects (pointing to storage with reference counts). As in the preceding exercise, each cell should have its own reference counts. Use this to implement a list of strings.

● **Exercise 12.2.7.** Use the generic list type of the preceding exercise to implement a heterogeneous list, containing some strings, some integers, and some lists thereof. Read in lists such as

```
( Joe  12  ( Harry  ( 1 2 3 )  Carl )  -3 )
```

and print them with a print function of Object that calls a virtual print function of Storage.

12.3. TEMPLATES

In the preceding section we saw how to build type-safe generic containers out of containers holding void* pointers. However, to use the generic containers for a specific data type, handcrafted code is required. For example, to make a type-safe stack of matrices, we derive MatrixStack from Stack. To make a type-safe stack of employees, we derive EmployeeStack in exactly the same way. In C++, the *template* programming construct automates this process.

A template is used to specify a family of classes that differ only in a type. All type-safe stacks derived from the Stack class stacking void* pointers are alike, except for the type of the pointers they hold. We specify this by writing a stack template:

```
template<class T>
class PtrStack : public Stack
{
public:
  T* push( T* p ) { return (T*) Stack::push( p ); }
  T* pop() { return (T*) Stack::pop(); }
  T* top() const { return (T*) Stack::top(); }
};
```

This template defines a family of PtrStack classes. For any type T, a specific pointer stack can be obtained by *instantiating* the template. The class PtrStack<Matrix> stores Matrix* pointers, the class PtrStack<Employee> stores Employee* pointers. You can think of a class template as a factory for classes, just as you can think of a class as a factory for objects.

In fact, to get an actual stack of matrices, you still need to declare an object:

```
PtrStack<Matrix> s;
Matrix* m;
s.push( m );
```

Of course, it is possible to construct a template that makes a stack of actual objects, rather than pointers to objects:

```
template<class T, int SIZE>
class Stack
{ T s[ SIZE ];
  int sp;
public:
  Stack() : sp( 0 ) {}
  T push( T t );
  T pop();
  T top();
  int isEmpty() const;
  int isFull() const;
};
```

Here we have taken advantage of the fact that templates can have two kinds of parameters: types (`class T`) and compile time constants (`int SIZE`). To make a stack of up to 20 integers, we must specify both the type and the size:

```
Stack<int, 20> s;
s.push( -10 );
```

In this class template, we do not want to define the member functions inside the stack definition, because they are too big to be replaced inline. Instead, we must write a template for *each* member function:

```
template<class T, int SIZE>
T Stack<T, SIZE>::push( T t )
{ if ( sp < SIZE ) s[ sp++ ] = t;
  return t;
}

template<class T, int SIZE>
T Stack<T, SIZE>::pop( T t )
{ if ( sp > 0 ) return s[ --sp ];
  static T defval;
  return defval;
}

template<class T, int SIZE>
inline int Stack<T, SIZE>::isEmpty() const
{ return sp == 0;
}
```

In the pop function template, we have a problem with error handling. We cannot simply return 0 if an empty stack is popped. If the type T is, say, `Employee`, there is no way to convert the number 0 into an `Employee` object. We therefore return an object of type T that is constructed with the default constructor. That is likely to be the best default value for any type. By making the return value a copy of a `static` object, we do return a 0 if T happens to be `int` or a pointer.

● **Exercise 12.3.1.** Use the `Stack` template to make a stack of `Employee` records.

● **Exercise 12.3.2.** Use the `Stack` template to rewrite the stack-based calculator of Chapter 1.

Class and member function templates must be placed in header files, not in source files, since their code must be accessible to every module that instantiates them.

Once they are instantiated, templates are just like any other classes. For example, you can derive from them. When the object stack template is defined, we can use the `Stack<void*>` instantiation as the base class for the pointer stack template:

```
template<class T>
class PtrStack<T> : public Stack<void*, 20>
{ /* ... */ }
```

Templates are easy to write, and even easier to use, but compilers must work hard to build the necessary code. Suppose you have a linked-list template, along with a template for the list cells:

```
template<class T>
class Cell
{ T info;
  Cell* next;
public:
  Cell( const T& i, Cell* n );
friend class List<T>;
};

template<class T>
class List
{ Cell<T>* head;
public:
  void insert( const T& t );
  // ...
};

template<class T>
void List<T>::insert( const T& t )
{ head = new Cell<T>( t, head );
}
```

When you write the code

```
List<Employee> e;
Employee harry;
e.insert( harry );
```

then the compiler must build

- The List<Employee> class
- The Cell<Employee> class (because List<Employee> has a Cell<Employee> pointer member)
- The List<Employee>::insert member function
- Any functions that List<Employee>::insert calls, such as the Cell<Employee> constructor

The compiler will do all this without programmer intervention.

We have seen templates for classes and member functions. You can also construct families of nonmember functions. A common example is the following function template:

```
template<class T>
inline T min( T a, T b )
{ return a < b ? a : b;
}
```

For example, consider the following calls to min:

```
int m, n;
double x, y;
m = min( m, n );
n = min( x, y );
```

The first call selects the min(int, int) template, the second one the min
(double, double) template. Selection of the right template is a challenge.
There is no <...> to guide the compiler. For example, what should the result
of min(x, 0) be? Should 0 be converted to the double value 0.0, or should
x be converted to an integer? The rules for conversion are complex, have
changed repeatedly in the standardization committee, and are not correctly
implemented by all compilers. As a result, this book cannot recommend this
particular template function.

Here is a more reasonable scenario for a template function. Suppose we
want to define an operator>> that reads a list from a stream. We cannot make it
a member of List<T>, because the first argument is an istream. We define the
following nonmember template function instead.

```
template<class T>
istream& operator>>( istream& is, List<T>& l )
{ char ch;
  is >> ch;
  if ( ch != '(' )
  { is.clear( ios::failbit | is.rdstate() );
    return is;
  }
  List<T> m;
  while ( is )
  { is >> ch;
    if ( ch == ')' ) { l = m; return is; }
    is.putback( ch );
    T t;
    is >> t;
    m.append( t );
  }
  return is;
}
```

● **Exercise 12.3.3.** Write a template Vector<T> that implements vectors of any
data type T. Define operations dim() and [].

● **Exercise 12.3.4.** Continue the previous exercise by building a template
Matrix<T> that inherits from Vector< Vector<T> >.

● **Exercise 12.3.5.** Implement a List<T> template and instantiate a list of integers.

12.4. EXCEPTIONS

In Section 6.6 we recommended that robust classes respond to errors by calling a user-installable error handler. We discussed two possible actions for error handling: You can abort the program with an error message, or return to the caller and report the problem. Of course, aborting the program is an option only during testing. Furthermore, there are quite a few situations in which the immediate caller is powerless to do anything about the error; it too would have to return to its caller with an error report, and its caller may need to do the same, until a part of the program is reached that is competent to handle the problem.

Consider the following nasty problem: Memory is exhausted in the copy constructor of a String object.

```
Bool Map::find( String s ) { /* ... */ }

void Map::add( String a )
{ if ( find( a ) ) // copy constructor exhausts memory
    return;
  // ...
}
```

Who should test that the copy constructor succeeded? The add function can perform the test only after find returns. Let us therefore suppose that find does the test. A copy constructor cannot return an error code, since constructors have no return value. It could set a global error variable or a special error data member in the string object. Either way, find would have to check for the error and return immediately to add, setting another error flag, and add would have to check that flag. It is very likely that the function add has no way of dealing with the problem. If add doesn't have access to the user interface, it cannot ask the user to close down another application to gain more memory. Hence it too must propagate the error. If this is programmed conscientiously, a large fraction of the code concerns itself with the diagnosis of errors that we hope will never happen.

This example shows the problem of propagating an error from its point of detection to a point of competent handling. In C++, an *exception-handling* mechanism offers a solution to this problem. When an error is encountered that cannot be handled where it is detected, an exception can be raised with the command

throw *e*;

This terminates the regular program control flow. In particular, the function throwing the exception *does not return to its caller*. We will see shortly who gains control when an exception is thrown.

An exception can throw any value, such as an integer or string,

```
throw "Stack underflow";
```

but it is far more common to throw objects of special exception classes:

```
throw StackError( "Stack underflow" );
```

Note that

```
throw StackError( "Stack underflow" );
```

is a shortcut for

```
StackError e( "Stack underflow" );
throw  e;
```

Throwing objects of error classes is the right thing to do for two reasons. As we will see shortly, error handlers specify the type of the exception object with which they are willing to deal. We can usefully provide a handler for StackError, but it is unlikely that a handler for ints or strings can do more than report the error and give up. Error objects can conveniently carry an arbitrary amount of information from the locus of detection to the error handler.

● **Exercise 12.4.1.** Implement a StackError class that just stores the error message text. Throw stack error objects upon underflow and overflow of the stack in the stack-based calculator of Chapter 1. What happens when you enter commands that cause a stack error?

Here we show how a stack class template can avoid the problem of coming up with a return value in the case of a stack underflow:

```
template<class T>
T Stack<T>::pop( T t )
{ if ( sp == 0 )
    throw StackError( "Stack underflow" );
  return s[ --sp ];
}
```

If the stack is empty, the pop function throws an exception. The pop function doesn't return to its caller and is not responsible for creating a return value. Contrast this with the pop function in Section 12.3, which needed to return a static default value of type T.

The copy constructor of the String class may throw a different kind of error:

```
String::String( const String& b )
: sp( new char[ strlen( b.sp ) + 1 ])
{ if ( sp == 0 ) // out of memory
    throw MemoryError();
  strcpy( sp, b.sp );
}
```

If memory is exhausted and sp is 0, the copy constructor will throw an error object of type MemoryError (constructed with the default constructor of that class) and leave the function. The line

```
strcpy( sp, b.sp );
```

is not executed, and of course it should not, since it is not legal to perform a string copy into a null pointer. (Note that when this constructor is called, the new operator itself may raise an exception of the type xalloc if memory is exhausted. Here we assume that that behavior has been deactivated by calling set_new_handler(0) in main.)

Now we have learned how to get out of a troublesome situation by throwing an exception, but we do not yet know how to gain control once an error has been detected. This is achieved with the try/catch clause:

```
try
{ one or more lines of code
    that calls functions that perform operations on stacks
}
catch ( StackError s )
{ //  stack is empty, or other stack error
  // s contains error information
  stack error handler code
}
catch ( MemoryError m )
{ //  memory error
  memory error handler code
}
```

When a stack or memory error is thrown in one of the functions called in the try block or by one of the functions they call, control is transferred to the appropriate catch clause.

● **Exercise 12.4.2.** Modify the stack-based calculator of Chapter 1 to throw two kinds of error: A stack error reports stack underflow or overflow, and a math error reports division by zero. When an error happens, print a message indicating the nature of the error and quit the program.

What can the code in the catch clause do? Suppose that the code in question is a parser, reading a file in a known file format that had previously been written by another program that we trust. We then know that a stack error must be the consequence of a corrupted file. In that case, we just want to tell the user that the file is not readable and to abandon the reading process. If we run out of memory, we ask the user to close another application, or ask for permission to abandon some information on the "undo" stack.

This example illustrates why it is important to design special classes for exception reporting. The type of exception thrown is used to locate the appropriate handler.

● **Exercise 12.4.3.** Modify the stack-based calculator of Chapter 1 to abort the program when a stack error is thrown but to continue accepting commands when a math error occurs.

An important aspect of exception handling is the process of *unwinding the run-time stack*. When an exception is thrown, all function calls between the try block and the throw point are terminated. As part of that termination, all class-type variables on the run-time stack are properly destroyed.

Suppose, for example, that a terminated function had local variables of type String. Since the String class has a destructor, all those variables are destroyed and their heap memory is recycled to the free store.

```
void f( char name[] )
{ String s( name ); // destroyed if f terminated
  g( s );
}
```

However, the same process does not work if the function uses variables of type char*:

```
void f( char name[] )
{ char* s = new char[ strlen( name ) + 1 ];
  strcpy( s, name );
  g( s );
  delete[] s; // not executed if f terminated
}
```

In this situation the variable s is not of class type, and it has no destructor. Suppose g throws an exception. Then the delete statement is not executed, and heap memory is irretrievably lost.

The process of destroying constructed objects in exception processing is particularly useful to handle errors in constructors. Consider a constructor

```
Employee::Employee( char n[], int d, int m, int y )
: name( n ), // name of the type string
  hiredate( d, m, y )
{}
```

If the Date constructor throws an exception because an illegal date was specified, then the name field is automatically destroyed as well, and no heap memory is lost. It would be very difficult to implement that recovery without the exception mechanism.

While exception handling is excellent for transferring control over long distances, it is not a good idea to use it as a substitute for normal error checking:

```
Stack s;
// ...
// not sure if s is empty
try
{ x = s.pop(); // what the heck
}
```

```
catch ( StackError e )
{ // oh well, it was empty
  x = 0;
}
```

This is much slower than a straightforward check:

```
Stack s;
// ...
// not sure if s is empty
if ( s.isEmpty() ) x = 0;
else x = s.pop();
```

Exceptions are also undeniably dangerous. When an exception is thrown, and there is no matching catch clause for that kind of error, then the program is terminated. In theory, you can guard against rogue exceptions with the "catch all" clause.

```
try
{ // ...
}
catch ( ... )
{ // get here when ANY exception occurred in the try block
    // now what?
}
```

But what can you do? You have now left the try block and cannot simply resume where the computation was interrupted by the throw statement.

Because exceptions have the danger of terminating a program, we recommend that the user of a class be given the choice. When an error occurs, the class user should be able to choose whether the class throws an exception or switches to a robust failure mode, bringing all objects into a well-defined state and returning to the caller. This is best done by a user-installable error function.

It is convenient to have all error-reporting objects derive from a common base class, say Error.

```
class Error
{ enum { MSGSIZE = 256 };
  char msg[ MSGSIZE ];
public:
  Error( const char[] );
  operator const char*() const { return msg; }
};

class StackError : public Error { /* ... */ };
class MemoryError : public Error { /* ... */ };
```

Note that the error class purposefully uses a fixed-size array to store the message string. We do not want to have the possibility of running out of memory when an error object is copied. If a second exception occurs while the first exception is processed, for example in the copy constructor of the error object, the program terminates. For that reason, error-reporting objects tend to be small and simple.

Using the technique of Section 6.6, we can then have the user install an error function of type

```
typedef void (*ErrorFun)( Error& )
```

Then the user can install one of the following functions:

```
void ignore( Error& ) {}
void raise( Error& e ) { throw( e ); }
void abort ( Error& e ) { cerr << e; exit( 1 ); }
```

Of course, since the error function may continue, a robust failure mode must be programmed whenever an error is reported:

```
template<class T>
T Stack<T>::pop( T t )
{ if ( sp == 0 )
    { StackError e( "Stack underflow" )
      (*stackError)( e );
      static T defval;
      return T:
    }
    return s[ --sp ];
}
```

Now the class user really has the best of all worlds—simple error reporting during debugging, and the choice between robust failure and exception handling in production code.

● **Exercise 12.4.4.** Implement a user-installable error handler for the stack template. Install a handler that throws the error object.

● **Exercise 12.4.5.** Add an error handler to the String class of Exercise 9.5.3. There are two kinds of error: memory exhaustion, and an invalid argument to the [] operator. Install a handler that throws the error object. Overload String::operator new to fail after a certain number of attempts. Read strings from a file. When memory is exhausted, inform the user that the file was too big to read, and ask for another file to read.

● 12.5. PITFALLS

12.5.1. Template Syntax

Occasionally, the < and > delimiters used for templates can conflict with other tokens. Here is the most common case:

```
Vector<Vector<double>> m;
```

Because tokens are scanned before the meaning of an expression is determined, the >> is interpreted as a shift operator, not as two > tokens. Some compilers are fiendishly clever about breaking up the >> token again when parsing templates, but others aren't. The language standard doesn't require this heroic effort, and you should always insert a space

```
Vector< Vector<double> > m;
```

to ensure portability of the code.

12.5.2. Exceptions Can Cause Resource Loss

Exceptions have a dramatic impact on writing correct code. Consider this function:

```
int read_stuff( const char filename[] )
{ FILE* fp = fopen( filename, "r" );
  do_reading( fp );
  fclose( fp ); // NO
}
```

Why is that an "exception pitfall"? There aren't any exceptions in the code!

There is no guarantee that we ever reach the fclose(fp) command. Suppose that do_reading throws an exception. Then that function does not return to read_stuff. Instead, suppose the exception is caught in an outer block and the program keeps running. The file fp is never closed. If this happens often enough, the application may run out of file handles.

There are two remedies. The first one is popular but foolish:

```
int read_stuff( const char filename[] )
{ FILE* fp = fopen( filename, "r" );
  try
    do_reading( fp );
  catch( ... )
  { fclose( fp );
    throw;
  }
  fclose( fp );
}
```

This strategy clutters up the code with endless checks against exceptions that we expect to be very rare. There is a better way:

```
int read_stuff( const char filename[] )
{ ifstream fp( filename, ios::in );
  do_reading( fp );
}
```

Even if do_reading throws an exception, fp is closed by the ifstream destructor. By using a class ifstream instead of a pointer FILE*, we are assured that cleanup happens whether or not an exception occurs.

C H A P T E R   13

EXAMPLES OF OBJECT-ORIENTED DESIGN

13.1. SIMULATION

One of the origins of C++is the Simula simulation language, and indeed C++ is well suited to event-simulation programs. In a simulation, objects such as cars or customers are moved around an environment. Typically objects have varying characteristics (speed, fuel level, number of items to purchase) and varying behavior under certain situations (will not enter a queue if it is longer than 10 people, will accelerate if the traffic light turns yellow and is less than 100 meters away).

A base class is prepared for each kind of object that holds the values describing state, properties, and default behaviors. Alternative behaviors are modeled with virtual functions. An event queue contains events, with time stamps, that are executed by a scheduler.

13.1.1. The Factory Layout

Consider the example of a factory automation simulation. Certain machines produce objects that are to be picked up by mobile robots and brought to other machines consuming them. Here is a typical layout:

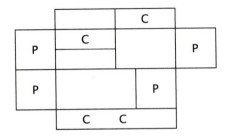

P Producer

C Consumer

———— Tracks for the robots

The robot vehicles move on the tracks and perform the following actions:

- A moving robot moves one unit ahead in its current direction every 15 seconds.
- An empty robot passing a widget piled up by a producer stops and picks up the widget. This takes 45 seconds.
- A full robot passing an empty consumer stops, unloads the widget, and passes it to the consumer. This takes 45 seconds.

The producers produce goods at a certain rate (whose maximum the simulation is supposed to determine) and pile them around them into the first free position, clockwise starting from the right. The consumers consume the goods and need 90 seconds to digest each one.

The layout of the factory is read in from a text file containing the corridors marked with blank spaces and the robots with 1, 2, 3, 4 .... The . around the producers are storage pads for the widgets.

```
xxxxxxxxxxxxxxxxxxxxxxxx
xxxxx                xxxxx
xxxxx xxxxx xxCxx xxxxx
x                        x
x ... xxCxx xxxxx ... x
x .P.          xxxxx .P. x
x ... xxxxx xxxxx ... x
x                        x
x ... xxxxxxx ... xxxxx
x .P. xxxxxxx .P. xxxxx
x ... xxxxxxx ... xxxxx
x                    xxxxx
xxxxx xxCxxCxxxxx xxxxx
xxxxx                xxxxx
xxxxxxxxxxxxxxxxxxxxxxxx
```

To describe the geometry of the situation, we introduce data types `Point` and `Direction`:

```
enum Direction { NORTH, NE, EAST, SE, SOUTH, SW, WEST, NW };

class Point
{ int _x, _y;
public:
  Point( int x = 0, int y = 0 ) { _x = x; _y = y; }
  int x() const { return _x; }
  int y() const { return _y; }
  int operator==( const Point& ) const;
};

int Point::operator==( const Point& b ) const
{ return _x == b._x && _y == b._y;
}
```

```
Point operator+( Point p, Direction d )
{ static int xDir[] = { 0, 1, 1, 1, 0, -1, -1, -1 };
  static int yDir[] = { -1, -1, 0, 1, 1, 1, 0, -1 };

  return Point( p.x() + xDir[ d ], p.y() + yDir[ d ]);
}
```

The following function computes the rotated directions:

```
Direction turn( Direction d, int deg )
{ while( deg < 0 ) deg += 360;
  return Direction( ( d + deg / 45 ) % 8 );
}
```

Recall that the values in an enum are assigned to the integers 0, 1, 2,...unless explicitly set otherwise.

To further move around in our factory world, we will define a Layout class that holds the factory layout (simply by storing the character pattern).

```
class Layout
{ enum { XSIZE = 79, YSIZE = 24 };
  char g[ YSIZE ][ XSIZE+1 ];
  int yrows; // the actual number of rows
public:
  void read();
  char& operator[]( Point );
  void advance( Point& ); // iterator
  int atEnd( Point ); // for iterator
  void show() const;
};
```

The following function reads a pattern from standard input:

```
void Layout::read()
{ yrows = 0;
  char buffer[ XSIZE + 1 ];
  char nl;

  while( cin && yrows < YSIZE )
  { cin.getline( buffer, sizeof( buffer ));
    if ( !cin || buffer[ 0 ] == 0 ) return;
    int i = 0;
    do
      g[ yrows ][ i ] = buffer[ i ];
    while ( buffer[ i++ ] != 0 );
    yrows++;
  }
}
```

We define an operator[] taking a Point argument:

```
char& Layout::operator[]( Point p )
{ return g[ p.y() ][ p.x() ];
}
```

For example,

```
Layout l;
Point c( 2, 3 );
if( l[ c ] == ' ' ) l[ c + NW ] = '@';
```

Finally, we supply a way of walking a Point variable through the layout, advancing it to the right until the end and then wrapping to first position of the next line.

```
void Layout::advance( Point& p )
{ if( (*this) [ p ] != '\0' ) p = p + EAST;
  else if ( p.y() < yrows ) { p = Point( 0, p.y() + 1 ); }
}


int Layout::atEnd( Point p )
{ return p.y() == yrows;
}
```

These functions implement an iterator mechanism:

```
for( Point c( 0, 0 ); !l.atEnd( c ); l.advance( c ))
  // do something with l[ c ]
```

13.1.2. Event Scheduling

Let us define the basic objects of the simulation: robots, producers, and consumers.

```
class Robot
{ Point pos;
  Direction dir;
  int full;        // 1 if carrying a widget, 0 if not
  char id;         // '1', '2', ...
  void step();
public:
  Robot( Point, char );
  void pickup( Point );
  void feed( Point );
  void move();
};
```

```
class Producer
{ int rate; // widget production rate
  Point pos;
public:
  Producer( Point, int );
  void produce();
};


class Consumer
{ Point pos;
  int full; // 1 if currently eating, 0 otherwise
public:
  Consumer( Point );
  void consume();
  void done() { full = 0; }
friend void Robot::feed( Point );
};
```

The main activity throughout the simulation is the transaction of *events*. For example, when a consumer receives a widget, it tells the scheduler, "Remind me in 90 seconds that consumption is completed." All events are held in an event queue that is continually traversed by the scheduler. When the simulated system time has reached the time stamp of an event, it is removed from the queue and executed. This is a perfect setup for derived classes and virtual functions. A base class Event holds the time stamp and a virtual process function. Derived DoneEating, Move, and Produce events supply actual process functions describing how to process the events.

```
typedef long Time;
class Event
{
protected:
  Time time;
  Event( Time t ) { time = t; }
public:
  virtual void process() {};
friend class EventQueue;
};


class Move : public Event
{ Robot* r;
public:
  Move( Robot* rp, Time t ) : Event( t ) { r = rp; }
  void process() { r->move(); }
};
```

```
class DoneEating : public Event
{ Consumer* c;
public:
  DoneEating( Consumer* cp, Time t ) : Event( t ) { c = cp; }
  void process() { c->done(); }
};

class Produce : public Event
{ Producer* p;
public:
  Produce( Producer* pp, Time t ) : Event( t ) { p = pp; }
  void process() { p->produce(); }
};
```

The events are kept on a queue that is implemented as a linked list. An EventQueue contains a List<Event*>. The list is kept sorted by increasing time stamps. Event processing simply consists of removing events from the head of the list, as long as their time stamps are no later than the system time, and executing their process functions:

```
class EventQueue
{ List<Event*> q;
public:
  void enqueue( Event* e );
  int dequeue( Time t );
};

void EventQueue::enqueue( Event* e )
{ q.reset();
  while ( !q.atEnd() && ( (Event*) q.info() )->time < e->time )
    q.advance();
  q.insert(e);
}

int EventQueue::dequeue( Time t )
// removes head of queue if its time stamp is < t and signals event
// returns 1 if event with time stamp < t found, 0 otherwise
{ q.reset();
  if( q.atEnd() ) return 0;
  Event* e = (Event*) q.info();
  if ( e->time > t ) return 0;
  q.remove();
  e->process();
  delete e;
  return 1;
}
```

It is assumed that all events are placed on the queue with a call like enqueue (new Move(...)), with storage for the event data allocated on the free store. The dequeue function hands the event storage to the deallocator after execution.

13.1.3. The Main Program

Here is the main program. It supports three command line options:

-R*n*   Production rate. Produce a widget every *n* seconds.
-T*n*   Total simulation time. Run simulation for *n* minutes.
-S*n*   Show intervals. Display status every *n* seconds.

The program processes the command line options, reads in the layout, and scans it for the locations of robots, consumers, and producers. Those are inserted into linked lists. Then the robot and producer lists are traversed, and for each element a "move" or "produce" event is scheduled. The main loop removes events from the queue, checks whether the new status should be displayed, and advances the simulated clock.

We use terminal escape sequences to clear the screen and to move the cursor to the home position before each display. This causes the display to overwrite itself continually, creating a visual sensation of robots moving through the corridors. Under DOS you must install ANSI.SYS to enable interpretation of the escape sequences. If you have a non-ANSI terminal, you may substitute the appropriate commands for clearing the screen and moving the cursor, or you can just remove the print statements for a sequential display.

```
class Terminal
{
public:
  void clearScreen();
  void cursorHome();
};

void Terminal::clearScreen()
{ cout << "\x1B[2J"; // clear  screen
  cout.flush();
}

void Terminal::cursorHome()
{ cout << "\x1B[H";   // move cursor to home position
  cout.flush();
}

Time now = 0;

List<Consumer*> consList;
List<Robot*> robotList;
List<Producer*> prodList;
```

```
Layout factory;
EventQueue schedule;
Terminal term;

void main( int argc, char *argv[] )
{ int prodRate = 360;
  int totalTime = 180;
  int showTime = 180;
  int nextShowTime = 0;

  for ( int i = 1; i < argc; i++ )
    if (argv[ i ][ 0 ] == '-')
      switch ( toupper( argv[ i ][ 1 ]))
      { case 'R':
          prodRate = atoi( argv[ i ] + 2 );
          break;
        case 'T':
          totalTime = atoi( argv[ i ] + 2 ) * 60;
          break;
        case 'S':
          showTime = atoi( argv[ i ] + 2 );
          break;
      }
  factory.read();

  char ch;
  for ( Point p( 0, 0 );
      !factory.atEnd( p );
      factory.advance( p ))
    switch ( ch = factory[ p ] )
    { case 'P':
        prodList.insert( new Producer( p, prodRate ));
        break;
      case 'C':
        consList.insert( new Consumer( p ));
        break;
      default:
        if ('0' <= ch && ch <= '9')
          robotList.insert( new Robot( p, ch ));
        break;
    }

  for ( robotList.reset();
      !robotList.atEnd();
      robotList.advance() )
    schedule.enqueue( new Move( robotList.info(), 15L ));
```

```
Time n = 0; // to start production at time 15, 30, ...

for ( prodList.reset();
     !prodList.atEnd();
     prodList.advance() )
  schedule.enqueue( new Producer(
    prodList.info(), n += 15 ));

term.clearScreen();
while ( now <= totalTime )
{ while ( schedule.dequeue( now ))
    ;
  if ( now >= nextShowTime )
  { term.cursorHome();
    cout << now << "\n\n";
    factory.show();
    nextShowTime += showTime;
  }
  now+=15;
  }
}
```

13.1.4. The Behavior of the Objects

Finally, we must specify how our simulated objects behave. Consumers are easiest. They just need a constructor and they need to signal a 90-second delay when starting to eat a widget:

```
Consumer::Consumer( Point p )
{ pos = p;
  full = 0;
}

void Consumer::consume()
{ full = 1;
  schedule.enqueue( new DoneEating( this, now + 90 ));
}
```

Producers pile up widgets in the area surrounding them, until it becomes full. Then they enter the next production event, with a delay depending on their production rate.

```
Producer::Producer( Point c, int r )
{ pos = c;
  rate = r;
}
```

```
void Producer::produce()
{ int found = 0;
  Direction d = EAST;

  do
  { if( factory[ pos + d ] == '.' )
    { factory[ pos + d ] = '@';
      found = 1;
    }
    else
    d = ( d + 1 ) % 8;
  }
  while( !found && d != EAST );
  schedule.enqueue( new Producer( this, now + rate ));
}
```

Robots are necessarily more sophisticated. They must be able to pick up a widget and feed it to a consumer. After a move, they must look around if there is a widget available for pickup or a consumer to feed. The move function is very simple-minded. When the robot encounters a barrier, it merely rotates 90 degrees and tries again next time.

```
Robot::Robot( Point c, char ch )
{ pos = c;
  dir = EAST;
  full = 0;
  id = ch;
}

void Robot::pickup( Point pos )
{ factory[ pos ] = '.';
  full = 1;
  schedule.enqueue( new Move( this, now + 45 ));
}

void Robot::feed( Point p )
{ Consumer* c;

  for( consList.reset();
    !(( c = consList.info() )->pos == p );
    consList.advance() )
    ; // find the consumer with those
      // coords in the list
  if( !c->full )
  { c->consume();
    full = 0;
  }
  schedule.enqueue( new Move( this, now + 45 ));
}
```

```
void Robot::step()
{ if( factory[ pos + dir ] == ' ' )
  { Point p;

    factory[ pos ] = ' ';
    pos = pos + dir; // += not defined
    factory[ pos ] = id;
      // look around and see whether there is
      // anything interesting on the wayside
    for( int i = 0; i < 4; i++ )
      switch( factory[ p = pos + turn( dir, i * 90 )])
      { case '@':
          if( !full ) { pickup( p ); return; }
          break;
        case 'C':
          if( full ) { feed( p ); return; }
          break;

      }
  }
  schedule.enqueue( new Move( this, now + 15 ));
}

void Robot::move()
{ if( factory[ pos + dir ] != ' ' )
    dir = turn( dir, 90 );
  step();
}
```

● **Exercise 13.1.1.** Put all pieces together and compile the program into an executable file with name sim. To start the program, the layout must be populated with robots,

```
xxxxxxxxxxxxxxxxxxxxxxxx
xxxxx   1            xxxxx
xxxxx xxxxx xxCxx xxxxx
x               2       x
x ... xxCxx xxxxx ... x
x .P.           xxxxx ... x
x ... xxxxx xxxxx ... x
x                       x
x ... xxxxxxx ... xxxxx
x .P. xxxxxxx .P. xxxxx
x ... xxxxxxx ... xxxxx
x       3            xxxxx
xxxxx xxCxxCxxxxx xxxxx
xxxxx               xxxxx
xxxxxxxxxxxxxxxxxxxxxxxx
```

Place these lines in a file named layout and start the program with

```
sim < layout -S15 -T30
```

This displays the state of the factory every 15 seconds, for a total of 30 minutes. Experiment to get a better traffic flow. Place more robots to achieve full production, with empty space on each producer's launch pad. You can erect or knock down some factory walls as well. To get a view of the long-term behavior, try running sim < layout -S3600 -T1440 (one day with outputs every hour).

● **Exercise 13.1.2.** When the simulation runs, a flaw of the Robot::move function becomes apparent: When two robots collide, both change direction. Design a "Mark II" model that has a more reasonable behavior. Derive a class Mark2 from Robot and make move a virtual function. Make all even-numbered robots Mark IIs. Note that the change is very straightforward, illustrating the C++promise of easy code maintenance.

● **Exercise 13.1.3.** Improve the bank teller simulation of Exercise 12.1.3 by adding an event queue. Events are new customer arrival and teller work completion.

● **Exercise 13.1.4.** Design a traffic-light simulation. Model an intersection of four roads with a traffic light. Cars enter all four ends with a certain arrival rate (see Exercise 12.1.3). Let the cars enter with average speed v_0 and no acceleration. When a car gets faster than v_0, comes too close to the one in front of it or a red traffic light, it decelerates. When a car is slower than v_0 and there is no other car or red light too close, it accelerates. A typical compact car accelerates from 0 to 30 miles/hour in about 4 seconds, from 0 to 60 miles/hour in about 13 seconds. To come to a complete stop from 60 miles/hour takes about 150 feet. Make your life easier by using the metric system: distance in meter, speed in meter/second, and acceleration in meter/second^2. Then determine reasonable values for acceleration and deceleration.

Each second, adjust speed and position of the car: Remember from calculus or physics that $\Delta v = a \cdot \Delta t$ and $\Delta s = v \cdot \Delta t + \frac{1}{2} a \cdot (\Delta t)^2$. Make each stretch of road 500 meters long. Choose reasonable values for initial speed and traffic-light phases. Display the moving cars on a grid.

13.2. A HOME ACCOUNTING SYSTEM

In this section, we will build a rudimentary accounting system for balancing checking accounts and gathering information for income tax filing.

13.2.1. Basic Accounting Concepts

We have a collection of *accounts,* including actual checking and savings accounts as well as accounts for rent, food, medical expenses, and charitable contributions. Each account has a parent account. For example, the accounts RENT, FOOD, MEDICAL have the parent account EXPENSES. The account SALARY has the parent account INCOME. If you receive salary from more than one source, each source may be arranged as a child account of SALARY. We make the account graph into a tree with the node TOP. TOP has four children: ASSETS, LIABILITIES, INCOME, and EXPENSES. Checking and savings accounts as well as cash are assets; bank loans are liabilities. The accounting system processes *transactions*, such as

> Pay $700 rent out of my checking account on February 5th.

This transaction reduces the CHECKING account balance by $700 and increases the RENT account balance by the same amount. We will enter this transaction as

```
T CHECKING  RENT  700  5
```

ignoring the month. The plan is to enter a batch consisting of all transactions in a given month and reconcile them with the checking account statement. We need the day to compute the checking account interest, which depends on the daily balance.

In general, a transaction

> T *a b amount date*

is processed by telling account *a* to reduce itself by the given amount and posting a corresponding increase to account *b*. When an amount is posted to an account, it recomputes its balance and passes the posted amount on to its parent account. Because both *a* and *b* are updated simultaneously, this is double-entry bookkeeping in its most basic form. The accounts balance if

$$\text{ASSETS} - \text{LIABILITIES} = \text{INCOME} - \text{EXPENSES}$$

For example, the foregoing transaction reduces ASSETS by $700 and increases EXPENSES by the same amount. If the equation held before the transaction, it continues to hold afterward.

Some transactions are different. For example, when you deposit your paycheck on the second of the month,

```
T  SALARY  CHECKING  2435.10  2
```

it appears that both SALARY and CHECKING should go up. If you pay back an installment of a loan,

```
T  CHECKING  BANKLOAN  500  30
```

the surpluses of both CHECKING and BANKLOAN should be reduced. This seeming anomaly can be explained by looking at the balance equation,

$$\text{ASSETS} - \text{LIABILITIES} - \text{INCOME} + \text{EXPENSES} = 0$$

Surpluses in accounts with ancestor LIABILITIES and INCOME (with minus signs in the equation) should be kept as negative values, in ASSETS and EXPENSES (with plus signs in the equation) as positive values. Accountants call the first kind of accounts *debit accounts*, the second kind *credit accounts*. (These names are unrelated to the terms "crediting" and "debiting" of an account.) When printing the balance of a debit account, the sign should be reversed. The TOP account should always have balance 0.

Undoubtedly, any certified public accountant will shudder when confronted with this exposition of double-entry bookkeeping, but it will serve well enough for our purpose.

13.2.2. The Account Classes

We could build a class hierarchy with a base class for the TOP account and a derived class for each actual account. The class hierarchy would then parallel the account tree. But this would be very inflexible. To add another account (say BRIBES), another class would have to be designed and the program would have to be recompiled. Marketing such a program can hardly be expected to do wonders to our ROYALTIES account.

Instead, we will classify accounts by their behavior. We already saw that credit accounts act differently from debit accounts—the latter reverse the sign when reporting their balance. CHECKING is an example of an interest-bearing account. Interest is computed on the daily balance and compounded monthly. Finally, we will implement an account type for recurring payments. For example, the amount for the rent stays constant at $700 every month. To pay rent, the RENT account can be established as an "autopay" account with a payment amount of $700. A transaction

    P RENT   5

pays out rent on the fifth of the month.

We have discovered four classes of accounts: debit, credit, interest-bearing, and autopay. We will model them with the following inheritance hierarchy:

(Arrows point to base class)

Here are the class definitions.

```
const int CODELEN = 10;

class Account
{
protected:
  char code[ CODELEN ];
  int level;
  double bal;
  Account* parent;
public:
  Account( const char[], Account* = 0 );
  virtual double balance() const { return 0; }
  virtual void post( double, int );
  virtual void print( ostream& ) const;
  virtual void pay( int ) {};
friend class AccountChart;
};

class Debit : public Account
{
public:
  Debit( const char[], Account* = 0 );
  double balance() const { return -bal; }
};

class Credit : public Account
{
public:
  Credit( const char[], Account* = 0 );
  double balance() const { return bal; }
};

class Interest : public Credit
{ double rate;
  int lastday;
  double accumInt;
  Account* payto;
public:
  Interest( const char[], double, Account*, Account* );
  void pay( int );
  void post( double, int );
};

class Autopay : public Credit
{ double amount;
  Account* payto;
```

```
public:
  Autopay( const char[], double, Account*, Account* );
  void pay( int );
};
```

The level field in Account indicates the level, that is, the distance from the root TOP. It is used when printing the account. The post virtual function posts a balance change to the account. For an Interest account, it also compounds the interest accumulated between the day of the last transaction and the day of the current transaction. These data are stored in the lastday and accumInt fields. The pay virtual function generates an autopay action when applied to an Autopay account, and it pays out the interest on an Interest account. (It should then be called with the last day of the month as argument.)

Here are the class constructors:

```
Account::Account( const char c[], Account* p )
{ strcpy( code, c );
  parent = p;
  level = parent ? parent->level + 1 : 0;
  bal = 0;
}

Debit::Debit( const char c[], Account* p )
: Account( c, p ) {}

Credit::Credit( const char c[], Account* p )
: Account( c, p ) {}

Autopay::Autopay(
  const char c[], double a, Account* p, Account* t )
: Credit( c, p )
{ amount = a;
  payto = t;
}

Interest::Interest(
  const char c[], double r, Account* p, Account* t )
: Credit( c, p )
{ rate    = r;
  accumInt = 0;
  lastday = 0;
  payto = t;
}
```

We will read the accounts from standard input in the format

A *type code parent* [*pay-to*] [*amt*]

where *type* is C, D, A, or I for a credit, debit, autopay, or interest-bearing account. The last two also carry *pay-to* and *amt* fields, for the name of the account for payment or interest deposit, and the autopay amount or the interest rate. Sample inputs are

```
A  I  CHECKING  ASSETS  INTEREST 5.5
A  D  INCOME  TOP
```

The accounts are kept in an account chart:

```
class AccountChart
{ enum { NACCOUNT = 100 };
  int na;
  Account* accts[ NACCOUNT ];
public:
  AccountChart();
  int readAccount( istream& );
  Account* find( const char n[] ) const;
  void print( ostream&, Account* parent = 0 ) const;
};

AccountChart::AccountChart()
{ accts[ 0 ] = new Credit( "TOP" );
  na = 1;
}
```

The following function locates an account, given its code:

```
Account* AccountChart::find( const char n[] ) const
{ for ( int i = 0; i < na; i++ )
    if ( strcmp( n, accts[ i ]->code ) == 0 )
      return accts[ i ];
  return 0;
}
```

An account is read in with the readAccount function, which is called after the initial A has been read from the input stream.

```
int AccountChart::readAccount( istream& is )
{ char cmd;
  double a;
  char acode[ CODELEN ], pcode[ CODELEN ], tcode[ CODELEN ];

  is >> cmd;
  is >> acode >> pcode;

  Account* p = find( pcode );
  if ( p == 0 ) return 0;
```

```
    Account* n = 0;
    switch ( cmd )
    { case 'C':
        n = new Credit( acode, p ); break;
      case 'D':
        n = new Debit( acode, p ); break;
      case 'I':
        is >> tcode >> a;
        n = new Interest( acode, a, p, find( tcode ));
        break;
      case 'A':
        is >> tcode >> a;
        n = new Autopay( acode, a, p, find( tcode ));
        break;
    }
    if ( n && na < NACCOUNT ) accts[ na++ ] = n;

    return 1;
}
```

We discovered two kinds of commands: transactions and payments. We supply classes for each of them.

```
class Transaction
{ Account* from;
  Account* to;
  double amt;
  int day;
public:
  void read( istream&, AccountChart& );
  void execute();
};

void Transaction::read( istream& is, AccountChart& ac )
{ char cmd;
  char acode[ CODELEN ], bcode[ CODELEN ];
  is >> acode >> bcode >> amt >> day;
  from = ac.find( acode );
  to = ac.find( bcode );
}

void Transaction::execute()
{ if ( from && to )
  {  from->post( -amt, day );
     to->post( amt, day );
  }
}
```

```
class Payment
{ Account* a;
  int day;
public:
  void read( istream&, AccountChart& );
  void execute();
};

void Payment::read( istream& is, AccountChart& ac )
{ char acode[ CODELEN ];
  is >> acode >> day;
  a = ac.find( acode );
}

void Payment::execute()
{ if ( a ) a->pay( day );
}
```

13.2.3. Putting It Together

The main function reads in all A, T, and P commands from standard input, creates all accounts defined with A commands, posts all transactions from the T commands, and handles all pays from the P commands. At the end of the input file, all accounts are printed.

```
int main()
{ AccountChart accounts;
  Transaction t;
  Payment p;
  char cmd;

  while ( cin >> cmd )
  { switch ( cmd )
    { case 'A':
        accounts.readAccount( cin );
        break;
      case 'T':
        t.read( cin, accounts );
        t.execute();
        break;
      case 'P':
        p.read( cin, accounts );
        p.execute();
        break;
    }
  }
  accounts.print( cout );
  return 0;
}
```

An account is printed with the `print` member function. `print` calls `balance` to get the correct value for a debit account. The account chart is recursively printed as a tree:

```
void Account::print( ostream& os ) const
{ for ( int i = 0; i < 4 * level; i++ ) os << " ";
    os << code;
    for ( i = 4 * level + strlen( code ); i < 40; i++ ) os << ".";
    os.width( 10 );
    os.precision( 2 );
    os.setf( ios::fixed, ios::floatfield );
    os.setf( ios::showpoint );
    os << balance();
    os << "\n";
}

void AccountChart::print
  ( ostream& os, Account* parent ) const
{ for ( int i = 0; i < na; i++ )
  { if ( accts[ i ]->parent == parent )
    { accts[ i ]->print( os );
      print( os, accts[ i ]);
    }
  }
}
```

The basic `post` message simply updates the balance and posts the amount to the parent. The date is ignored:

```
void Account::post( double amt, int day )
{ bal += amt;
  if( parent )
    parent->post( amt, day );
}
```

When an amount is posted to an interest-bearing account, the interest accumulated since the last posting is computed. (It is assumed that postings occur in chronological order.) Then the amount is posted.

```
void Interest::post( double amt, int day )
{ if( day > lastday )
  { accumInt += ( day - lastday ) * bal * rate / 100 / 365;
    lastday = day;
  }
  Account::post( amt, day );
}
```

The `pay` action for an autopay account involves posting a transaction to the account from which the payment is made, making the payment and the current account, recording the payment.

```
void Autopay::pay( int day )
{ if( payto )
  { payto->post( -amount, day );
    this->post( amount, day );
  }
}
```

The pay action for an interest-bearing account receives as day argument the last day of the month, computes the remaining interest, and pays it out to the interest accumulation account.

```
void Interest::pay( int day )
{ if( payto )
  { this->post( 0, day );
    payto->post( -accumInt, day );
    this->post( accumInt, day );
    accumInt = 0;
    lastday = 0;
  }
}
```

Here is a typical input. We first list all accounts and then the transactions, in chronological order. The starting balances for the checking and savings accounts are obtained by transferring them out of the liability account ADJUST. This is a "generally accepted accounting practice", which keeps the accounts balanced from the outset. The last two transactions force the computation of the interest.

```
A C ASSETS      TOP
A D LIABILIT    TOP
A D INCOME      TOP
A D INTEREST    INCOME
A I CHECKING    ASSETS        INTEREST    4.0
A I SAVING      ASSETS        INTEREST    5.25
A D ADJUST      LIABILIT
A D SALARY      INCOME
A C EXPENSES    TOP
A A RENT        EXPENSES      CHECKING  700
A C FOOD        EXPENSES
A C MEDICAL     EXPENSES
A C UTILITIES   EXPENSES
A C ELECTRIC    UTILITIES
A C PHONE       UTILITIES
A C MISC        EXPENSES
T   ADJUST      CHECKING       814.43      1
T   ADJUST      SAVING        4312.50      1
P   RENT                                   1
```

T	SALARY	CHECKING	2415.12	2
T	CHECKING	SAVING	1000.00	5
T	CHECKING	ELECTRIC	23.37	8
T	CHECKING	FOOD	14.05	12
T	CHECKING	PHONE	104.93	14
T	CHECKING	FOOD	39.12	18
T	CHECKING	MISC	100.00	20
T	CHECKING	FOOD	84.50	25
P	CHECKING			31
P	SAVING			31

The program output is the following account chart.

```
-------------------------
TOP..................0.00
  ASSETS..........6504.01
    CHECKING......1168.39
    SAVING........5335.61
  LIABILIT........5126.93
    ADJUST........5126.93
  INCOME..........2443.05
    INTEREST........27.04
    SALARY........2415.12
  EXPENSES........1065.97
    RENT............700.00
    FOOD............137.67
    MEDICAL..........0.00
    UTILITIES......128.30
      ELECTRIC......23.37
      PHONE........104.93
    MISC............100.00
-------------------------
```

The TOP account is 0, as it should be. The CHECKING, SAVING, and INTEREST fields can be checked against the bank statement.

● **Exercise 13.2.1.** Find out how your bank account accumulates interest. (This can be surprisingly difficult. Some banks apparently believe that these details should be of no concern to mere mortals. If you tell your bank that you want to check the calculations by computer, they may really clam up. In that case, be persistent.) If necessary, modify the Interest class to reflect your bank's method. Run one month's worth of actual transactions. Check whether the account chart agrees with your bank statement.

● **Exercise 13.2.2.** Change the day field to a Date field to accommodate bank statements that start in the middle of the month.

● **Exercise 13.2.3.** Make the system more user-friendly. The accounts should be kept in a file separate from the transactions. That file should list the initial balances of all accounts. The new transactions should be read in from another file. The names of the files are given on the command line. After entering all transactions, show the account chart, with the balances updated to reflect the transactions. Accountants call this a *trial balance*. When the trial balance is OK, the program should be run again with three file names on the command line. The third file is a file containing old transactions.

13.3. A MATRIX CALCULATOR

We will end this book the way we began: with a calculator. However, our new calculator will be quite sophisticated. It handles vectors and matrices in addition to regular numbers.

13.3.1. Overview of the Design

Vectors will be entered as

    (1 0 -2)

and matrices as sequences of row vectors. For example,

    [(1 0 -2) (0 2 4) (0 0 1)]

stands for

$$\begin{pmatrix} 1 & 0 & -2 \\ 0 & 2 & 4 \\ 0 & 0 & 1 \end{pmatrix}.$$

For simplicity, we restrict ourselves to 3-vectors and 3×3 matrices. Operations are again stack-based (reverse Polish notation):

    (1 1 1) (1 0 -2) *

computes the scalar product (-1), and

    (1 1 1) [(1 0 -2) (0 2 4) (0 0 1)] *

the product "vector · matrix", resulting in the vector (1 2 3). We will support +, -, *, but no division. We want the main program to be substantially like the one in Section 1.2. Let us review a number of design constraints:

- Numbers, vectors, and matrices should be derived from a common class. For example, printing the result should be achieved simply by cout << pop(), with an overloaded printing function.

- Numbers, vectors, and matrices have different sizes and cannot be stacked. The stack must therefore contain pointers.

- Because the object information is not stored on the stack, storage space must be obtained through new.

- The type and size of the result of an arithmetic function depends on the arguments supplied at run time. For example, vector · vector = number, vector · number = vector.
- Storage space for return value information must be obtained through new as well, and the function must return a pointer, because at compile time it cannot be determined how much information to copy.
- The space obtained from the free store should be automatically deallocated.

The following design achieves these goals: A class Value contains a pointer to a class ValStor from which Number, Vector, and Matrix are derived. Value has the usual complement of storage management functions (constructor, destructor, copy-initializer, and operator=). ValStor has virtual print and arithmetic functions.

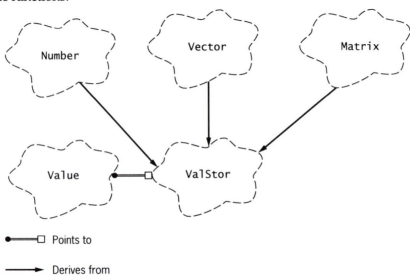

●━━━▢ Points to

━━━▶ Derives from

13.3.2. The Main Program

The code for the main program is almost identical to the code in Section 1.2, with all int replaced by Value. Division has been removed and multiplication made order-dependent. (Matrix multiplication is not commutative!)

```
const int STACKSIZE = 20;

Value stack[ STACKSIZE ];
int stackPointer = 0; // points to the next free stack entry

void push( Value n )
{ if( stackPointer <= STACKSIZE - 1 )
  { stack[ stackPointer ] = n;
    stackPointer++;
  }
}
```

```
Value pop()
{ if( stackPointer > 0 )
    stackPointer++;
  return stack[ stackPointer ];
}

int main()
{ char ch;
  Value num, second;
  cin >> ch;
  while( ch != '=' )
  {
    if( '0' <= ch && ch <= '9' ||
        ch == '(' || ch == '[' )
    {  cin.putback( ch );
       cin >> num;
       push( num );
    }
    else
      switch( ch )
      { case '+':
          push( pop() + pop() ); break;
        case '*':
          second = pop();
          push( pop() * second ); break;
        case '-':
          second = pop();
          push( pop() - second ); break;
        default:
          cout << "Input error."; return 1;
      }
    cin >> ch;
  }
  cout << pop() << "\n";
  return 0;
}
```

This is ideal for the class user. The objects can be used naturally, without any further knowledge of implementation details. As we will see, the implementation of this comfort poses considerable problems.

13.3.3. Mathematical Objects

Let us begin with the requirements for the Value class:

```
class Value
{ ValStor* stor; // actually points to number, vector, or matrix
```

```
   void copy( const Value& );
   void free();
public:
   Value(); // initialize to number 0
   Value( ValStor* );
   Value( const Value& );
   ~Value();
   Value& operator=( const Value& );

friend Value operator+( Value, Value );
friend Value operator-( Value );
friend Value operator*( Value, Value );
friend istream& operator>>( istream&, Value& );
friend ostream& operator<<( ostream&, Value );
};
```

The output is straightforward:

```
ostream& operator<<( ostream& s, Value o )
{ o.stor->print( s );
  return s;
}
```

where print is a virtual member function of ValStor, which is replaced by actual print functions in each derived class Number, Vector, and Matrix.

```
class ValStor
{ // ...
public:
   virtual void print( ostream& ) const;
};

class Number : public ValStor
{ int val;
public:
   void print( ostream& s ) const { s << val; }
   // ...
};

class Vector : public ValStor
{ int val[ 3 ];
public:
   void print( ostream& s ) const
   { s << "(" << val[ 0 ] << " " << val[ 1 ] << " "
      << val[ 2 ] << ")"; }
   // ...
};
```

```
class Matrix : public ValStor
{ int val[ 3 ][ 3 ];
public:
  void print( ostream& s ) const;
  // ...
};

void Matrix::print( ostream& s ) const
{ s << "[";
  row( 0 ).print( s ); s << "\n";
  row( 1 ).print( s ); s << "\n";
  row( 2 ).print( s );
  s << "]";
}
```

For input, we must allocate storage for the new result.

```
istream& operator>>( istream& s, Value& o )
{ char ch;
  ValStor* p;

  cin >> ch;
  switch( ch )
  { case '(':
      p = new Vector; break;
    case '[':
      p = new Matrix; break;
    default:
      p = new Number; break;
  }
  s.putback( ch );
  p->read( s );
  o = Value( p );
  return s;
}
```

read is a virtual function of MathBase, and actual versions are

```
void Number::read( istream& s )
{ s >> val;
}

void Vector::read( istream& s )
{ char ch;

  s >> ch;
  if( ch != '(' ) error( "( expected" );
  s >> val[ 0 ] >> val[ 1 ] >> val[ 2 ] >> ch;
  if( ch != ')' ) error( ") expected" );
}
```

```
void Matrix::read( istream& s )
{ char ch;

  s >> ch; if( ch != '[' ) error( "[ expected" );
  for( int i = 0; i < 3; i++ )
  { Vector v;
    v.read( s );
    for( int j = 0; j < 3; j++ )
      val[ i ][ j ] = v.val[ j ];
  }
  s >> ch; if( ch != ']' ) error( "] expected" );
}
```

13.3.4. Vector and Matrix Operations

Next, we need to overload the arithmetic operations. Let us start with the multiplication operator. The following combinations occur:

```
Number * Number : Number
Number * Vector : Vector
Number * Matrix : Matrix
Vector * Number : Vector
Vector * Vector : Number (scalar product)
Vector * Matrix : Vector
Matrix * Number : Matrix
Matrix * Vector : error (vectors are row vectors)
Matrix * Matrix : Matrix
```

We want to define a multiplication function mul that selects the correct multiplication at run time. It must be a virtual function of ValStor. Its return value must be a ValStor* because its actual realizations can return various objects of different sizes. For the same reason, its second argument must be a ValStor*. The first argument is implicit: Virtual functions must be member functions. The prototype therefore is

```
virtual ValStor* ValStor::mul( const ValStor* ) const
```

This forces the prototypes of the three actual mul functions in the derived classes, because instantiations of virtual functions *must* agree with the virtual prototype:

```
ValStor* Number::mul( const ValStor* ) const
ValStor* Vector::mul( const ValStor* ) const
ValStor* Matrix::mul( const ValStor* ) const
```

The class user is interested in Values, and mul is really a service function for

```
Value operator*( Value a, Value b )
{ return Value( a.stor->mul( b.stor ));
}
```

Consider `Number::mul`. We know that the first (implicit) argument is a `Number`. The second argument still could be a pointer to any type. A second run-time selection is necessary. To that end, we define a virtual function

```
virtual ValStor* ValStor::mulNum( const Number* ) const
```

`mulNum` is a multiplication with an argument known to be a number. Each derived class has its own definition of `mulNum`:

```
ValStor* Number::mulNum( const Number* p ) const
{ return new Number( val * p->val );
}
```

```
ValStor* Vector::mulNum( const Number* n ) const
{ Vector* r = new Vector;
  for ( int i = 0; i < 3; i++ )
    r->val[ i ] = n->val * val[ i ];
  return r;
}
```

```
ValStor* Matrix::mulNum( const Number* n ) const
{ Matrix* r = new Matrix;
  for ( int i = 0; i < 3; i++ )
    for ( int j = 0; j < 3; j++ )
      r->val[ i ][ j ] = n->val * val[ i ][ j ];
  return r;
}
```

The return value must still be a `ValStor*`, although we know its precise return types in each of the three cases. However, it must agree with the declaration of the virtual function in the base class.

`Number::mul` simply makes a virtual function call on its second argument:

```
ValStor* Number::mul( const ValStor* q ) const
{ return q->mulNum( this );
}
```

Similarly, there are virtual functions `mulVec` and `mulMat`. A total of nine functions

$$
\left. \begin{array}{l} \text{Number} \\ \text{Vector} \\ \text{Matrix} \end{array} \right\} \text{::mul} \left\{ \begin{array}{l} \text{Num} \\ \text{Vec} \\ \text{Mat} \end{array} \right. \text{(const ValStor* q) const}
$$

implement the nine combinations from the table. Note that because of the argument flip, these functions must return the product of `*q` and `*this`. For example,

```
ValStor* Matrix::mulVec( const Vector* v ) const
{ Vector* r = new Vector;
  for ( int i = 0; i < 3; i++ )
  { r->val[ i ] = 0;
    for ( int j = 0; j < 3; j++ )
      r->val[ i ] += v->val[ j ] * val[ j ][ i ];
  }
  return r;
}
```

● **Exercise 13.3.1.** Write the five remaining multiplication functions.

If p and q are ValStor*, the call

```
p->mul( q )
```

first causes selection of the appropriate version of mul, depending on the actual type of the object to which p points. That mul function is simply of the form

$$\text{return } q\text{->mul} \left\{ \begin{array}{l} \text{Num} \\ \text{Vec} \\ \text{Mat} \end{array} \right. (\text{ this });$$

and the type of q selects the correct function. This double virtual function call is necessary because we need run-time overloading of both arguments of the multiplication.

The operator+ must similarly be resolved through functions   add, addNum, addVec, addMat. Because adding is only permitted for objects of the same type, six of the nine ... :: add ... functions simply exit with an error message. For subtraction, it is easiest to define a unary minus function and code

```
Value operator-( Value a, Value b )
{ return a + ( -b );
}
```

● **Exercise 13.3.2.** Program the addition and subtraction functions.

13.3.5. Memory Management

As always, there is the issue of memory management. All values obtained from the read routines and all results of arithmetic operations are allocated on the free store. They should be recycled at the proper moment. Because the program user merely handles Values that point to ValStor, a reference count can be placed in ValStor. The reference count keeps track of the number of Value objects pointing to it. When a ValStor is created, it starts with 0. The constructor Value(ValStor*) increments it:

```
Value::Value( ValStor* p )
{ stor = p;
  p->rc++;
}
```

The copy constructor Value(const Value&), the destructor ~Value, and operator= manipulate the reference count in the usual way.

● **Exercise 13.3.3.** Trace the reference counts of all objects (the two inputs and the result) during the processing of the input

    (1 -3 2) (1 1 2) * =

Pay attention to unnamed temporaries and function arguments. Verify that all reference counts drop to zero at the end of the program.

● **Exercise 13.3.4.** Complete the matrix calculator and test it.

● **Exercise 13.3.5.** Change the calculator to handle vectors and matrices with Complex entries.

● **Exercise 13.3.6.** Change the calculator to handle vectors and square matrices of arbitrary size.

● **Exercise 13.3.7.** Add operations to compute the determinant and matrix inverse.

● **Exercise 13.3.8.** Add polynomials (of arbitrary degree) to the calculator. Implement the operation of inserting a matrix into a polynomial (for example, if $p(x) = 1 + 2x + x^3$ and $\mathbf{A}$ is a square matrix, then $p(\mathbf{A}) = 1 + 2\mathbf{A} + \mathbf{A} \cdot \mathbf{A} \cdot \mathbf{A}$). Extend matrix operations to matrices with polynomial entries and compute the *characteristic polynomial*, $\det(\mathbf{A} - x\mathbf{I})$ of a matrix, where $\mathbf{I}$ is the identity matrix, whose diagonal entries equal 1 and other entries equal 0. Verify with a few examples that inserting a matrix into its characteristic polynomial results in the 0 matrix (the Cayley-Hamilton theorem).

13.4. SUGGESTIONS FOR PROJECTS

This section suggests a number of programming projects that would be suitable for individuals or small teams. Here we just give the ideas for projects that are successful applications of object-oriented techniques, in particular the use of polymorphism. Teams are encouraged to add requirements, such as support for scrollable views and printing, to make the resulting programs more useful.

● **Project 13.4.1.** Write a *graphics editor* program to create and manipulate graphical images. The program should have a toolbar of shapes. Implement operations to place a shape onto the screen, to select a shape, to move, resize, and delete the selected shapes, to select multiple shapes and perform cut and paste, to save the image to disk, and to reload it from disk.

● **Project 13.4.2.** Write a simple graphics editor program with *multiple undo and redo* for all commands. The key observation is that each command has an inverse: the inverse of "add a shape" is "remove a shape", the inverse of "grow" is "shrink", and so on. As described in Exercise 10.2.4, derive specific commands from a base class Command. Keep a list of commands and their inverses. Undo and redo call the virtual process function on the stored commands.

● **Project 13.4.3.** Write a *flowchart editor* program to draw flowcharts. As with the general graphics editor, supply a toolbar of shapes and operations to place shapes on the screen and to reposition them. Unlike a general graphical editor, connecting shapes should be simple. Connections should automatically snap to suitable points on the shape, and it should be possible to draw an arrow connecting two shapes with a simple operation. Shapes should grow to accommodate the text inside them.

● **Project 13.4.4.** Programs for drawing certain kinds of diagrams have much underlying logic in common. Consider a program to draw flowcharts, a program to draw diagrams of logic gates, and a program to draw chemical structures. Each of them has a similar underlying logic. There are nodes (flowchart shapes, gates, atoms) and joins (arrows, connections, or bonds). There is a user interface for placing nodes and for joining them. Write a *framework* for this type of application, that is, a set of abstract classes that handles those tasks that are common to all diagram editors. Then validate the framework by creating two specific applications, for example a simple flowchart editor and a simple logic circuit editor. The specific applications should tell the generic framework only what kinds of nodes and joins are available. The behavior of the specific nodes and joins should be controlled by virtual functions.

● **Project 13.4.5.** A set of data points can be visualized in numerous ways. Write a *chart package* that shows a one-dimensional sequence of data points, either as a pie chart or a bar chart. Support multiple views to show the data in tabular form, as a pie chart, and as a bar chart. Each of these views should be editable. Editing a table value causes redraw of the two charts. Dragging a bar or pie segment with the mouse should cause the numbers in the table as well as the pie chart to change.

● **Project 13.4.6.** Write a simple *project scheduling* application. A project is composed of *tasks* and *dependencies*. A task has a description and a duration, such as "Write user manual—2 weeks", and may depend on other tasks. For example, "Write user manual" may depend on the completion of "Design user interface". The first job of the program is to compute an *optimal schedule*, that is, a sequence of the tasks that respects all dependencies and finishes the project as early as possible. See for example [Smith], p. 352, for an algorithm.

Your package should support multiple views of the project data, in particular a so-called Gantt chart, which shows a time line and a horizontal bar for each task, and a so-called PERT chart, which shows a box for each task and arrows that link tasks with the tasks on which they depend. Program users should be able to drag the ends of the task bars on the Gantt chart to change task duration, add or remove arrows in the PERT chart to change the dependencies, and add or remove tasks in either view.

Use the *model-view* architecture to manage the simultaneous update of both views. The project data are stored in a *model,* and the two graphical representations are *views* of that model. A view can process mouse and keyboard events but cannot do any computation. Instead, it notifies the model of the change, and the model carries out the computation and in turn notifies all attached views of the need to update themselves. Derive GanttView and PertView from View.

● **Project 13.4.7.** Write an *appointment book* program. Handle simple appointments and different kinds of recurring appointments (daily, weekly, monthly, yearly, the first Monday of every month, and so forth). When a recurring appointment is moved or deleted, offer to move or delete just that one date or the entire set of dates. Have a base class Appointment and derive other classes from it.

● **Project 13.4.8.** Certain simple grammars can be parsed with a recursive-descent parser with one token lookahead. For example, here is the standard example, a grammar describing arithmetic expressions:

expression ::= *term* (+ *term*)*
term ::= *factor* (∗ *factor*)*
factor ::= number | (*expression*)

Here number is a decimal number, which is tokenized by the lexer. Traditionally, such a parser has one function per nonterminal variable:

```
void expression( Lexer& l )
{ term();
  while ( strcmp( l.peek(), "+" ) == 0 )
  { l.get();
    term();
  }
}

void term( Lexer& l )
{ factor();
  while ( strcmp( l.peek(), "*" ) == 0 )
  { l.get();
    factor();
  }
}

void factor( Lexer& l )
{ if ( strcmp( l.peek(), "(" ) == 0 )
  { l.get();
    expression(); // here is the recursion
    l.get(); // get ')'
  }
  else l.get(); // get the number
}
```

But this is not very useful. The functions do nothing. One easy modification is to have each function return an `int`, namely the value of the subexpression. But that isn't helpful if we want to translate an expression into machine instructions. A more helpful way is an object-oriented approach: make a *class* for each nonterminal variable. That is, have classes `Expression`, `Term`, `Factor`, `Number`, that all derive from a common base class, `Value`. A factor contains a collection c of terms of type `Value*`, say as a linked list. Each class has a function parse. For example, here is

```
void Factor::parse( Lexer& l )
{ if ( strcmp( l.peek(), "(" ) == 0 )
   { l.get();
     Expression* e = new Expression;
     e->parse( l );
     c.append( e );
     l.get(); // get ')'
   }
   else
     c.append( new Number( l.get() ));
}
```

Now parsing builds a *typed parse tree*, and we can write virtual functions `process` that do something useful, such as generate code.

Put this design to work on the following situation. Design a clean Pascal-like syntax for a simple subset of C++, removing the syntactic ugliness that you hate most. Then write a program that translates your language into C++.

● **Project 13.4.9.** Write a library of *container class templates*. Implement lists, queues, priority queues, and sorted trees. Provide *iterators* for all containers. Provide base classes `Container` and `Iterator` that permit the writing of generic algorithms such as

```
template<class T> void print( const Container<T>& c )
{ ConstIterator<T> it( c );
  while ( it.more() ) { cout << it.info(); it.advance(); }
}
```

Provide two kinds of iterators. Constant iterators can only traverse containers, not modify them. Nonconstant iterators can modify the containers through `insert` and `remove` member functions. Your focus should lie on safety. For example, if two iterators are attached to a container, and they both point to the same element that is then removed by the first iterator, then the second iterator should be moved. If an iterator is past the end of a container, then `info` should throw an exception.

● **Project 13.4.10.** Implement a *traffic simulation* that is based on Exercise 13.1.4. Let the user specify an arbitrary pattern of intersections and straight roads by dragging tiles with various patterns onto the grid. Provide for zoom in and zoom out. Provide a mechanism for synchronizing traffic lights.

● **Project 13.4.11.** Implement an arbitrary-precision arithmetic package. Objects of type Integer have a sign and a sequence of digits, stored as a dynamic array on the heap. Overload + - * / %. (Of these, division is the most challenging. Do not implement division by repeated subtraction—this gives unacceptable performance for large numbers. [Knuth], p. 255, has a good algorithm.) Write a program that generates random large integers and tests them for primality (see for example [Knuth], p. 379) and prints the first 10 prime numbers it finds.

BIBLIOGRAPHY

[**AKW**]   Alfred Aho, Brian Kernighan, and Peter Weinberger. *The AWK Programming Language,* Addison-Wesley, 1988.

Describes the AWK programming languages. We use AWK for a header file extraction tool (Section 11.4).

[**Hansen**]   Tony L. Hansen. *The C++ Answer Book.* Addison-Wesley, 1989.

Advertised as providing solutions to all exercises in [Stroustrup] (1986 edition), this book delivers much more. It contains many annotated examples of excellent C++ code.

[**Kernighan & Ritchie**] Brian Kernighan and Dennis Ritchie. *The C Programming Language,* 2nd ed. Prentice-Hall, 1988.

[**Knuth**] Donald E. Knuth. *The Art of Computer Programming, Vol. 2: Seminumerical Algorithms,* Addison-Wesley, 1981.

[**Koenig**]   Andrew Koenig. *C Traps and Pitfalls,* Addison-Wesley, 1988.

A delightful book, full of advice for the C programmer. Much of it is of interest to the C++ programmer as well.

[**Lippman**]   Stan Lippman. *C++ Primer,* Addison-Wesley, 1992.

A thorough reference for all the murky details of C++.

[**Meyer**]   Bertrand Meyer. *Object-Oriented Software Construction,* Prentice-Hall, 1988.

This book lucidly explains techniques of object-oriented programming. Contains an introduction into Eiffel, a language designed by B. Meyer. Several chapters are devoted to explaining why no other language quite measures up. This is a great book, even if you don't care about Eiffel.

[**Pokorny & Gerard**]   C. Pokorny and C. Gerard. *Computer Graphics: The Principles Behind the Art and Science,* Franklin, Beedle, 1989.

A very usable reference for computer graphics. Contains the usual 2D and 3D lines and curve algorithms, color models, and a nice introduction to fractals.

[**Smith**]   Harry F. Smith. *Data Structures: Form and Function,* Harcourt Brace Jovanovich, 1987.

[**Stroustrup**]   B. Stroustrup. *The C++ Programming Language,* Addison-Wesley, 1992.

A complete description of C++, by the designer of the language.

[**Teale**]   Steve Teale. *The Iostreams Handbook,* Addison-Wesley, 1993.

INDEX